READING POWER

Reading for Pleasure • Comprehension Skills
Thinking Skills • Reading Faster

THIRD EDITION

Beatrice S. Mikulecky
Linda Jeffries

longman.com

Reading Power:
Reading for Pleasure, Comprehension Skills, Thinking Skills, Reading Faster
Third Edition

Pearson Education, 10 Bank Street, White Plains, NY 10606

Executive editor: Laura Le Dréan
Acquisitions editor: Lucille M. Kennedy
Development editor: Mykan White
Associate development editor: Dana Klinek
Production editor: Michael Mone
Senior manufacturing buyer: Nancy Flaggman
Cover design: Ann France
Text design: Wendy Wolf
Text composition: Laserwords

Library of Congress Cataloging-in-Publication Data

Mikulecky, Beatrice S.
     Reading power: reading for pleasure, comprehension skills, thinking skills,
reading faster / Beatrice S. Mikulecky, Linda Jeffries.—3rd ed.
        p. cm.
     ISBN 0-13-130548-4 (pbk. : alk. paper)
     1. English language—Textbooks for foreign speakers. 2. Reading
comprehension—Problems, exercises, etc. I. Jeffries, Linda. II. Title.

2002030160

Printed in the United States of America
     5   6   7   8   9   10—BAH—08   07   06

Contents

Introduction

To the Teacher

Reading Power is unlike most other reading textbooks.
- First, the focus is different. This book directs the students' attention to their own reading processes, while most other books focus primarily on the content.
- Second, Reading Power is organized to be used in a unique way. It contains *four separate sections* that correspond to four important aspects of proficient reading, and therefore it is like four books in one. *Teachers should assign work on all four parts of the book concurrently.*

In this, the third edition of *Reading Power*, the approach remains the same. New features have been added and original exercises updated. The changes in this new edition include:

A format that is more user friendly.
- Part 1: Pleasure Reading—a new introduction and an expanded list of suggested books.
- Part 2: Comprehension Skills—Updated exercises and additional writing exercises.
- Part 3: Thinking Skills—Updated exercises.
- Part 4: Faster Reading—Three units: Fiction, Biography, and Non-fiction.
- Separate Answer Key (not at the back of the student text).

The purpose of *Reading Power* is to develop your students' awareness of the reading process so that they will be able to read in ways that are expected in school, college, or business. In order to allow the students to focus on the process of reading, the lexical and syntactic content of the materials has been controlled.

Many students have a concept of reading that can interfere with their ability to read well in English. *Reading Power* aims to help students acquire an accurate understanding of what it means to read in English. To accomplish this, the book addresses the reading process in a direct manner, and the various reading skills involved are presented as part of that process.

Student awareness of reading and thinking processes is further encouraged in many parts of the book by exercises that require students to work in pairs or small groups. In discussions with others, students formulate and articulate their ideas more precisely, and so they also acquire new ways of talking and thinking about a text. Students are asked to write and then to read each other's work so they can experience the connections between reading and writing.

The teacher is the most important element in a successful reading class. In your class, you can boost the value of *Reading Power* by providing:
- an anxiety-free environment in which students feel comfortable taking risks and trying new ways of reading.
- enough practice so the students can master new strategies.
- friendly pressure in the form of persuasion and timing.
- positive examples of how to approach a text.

- a model for the kind of thinking that good reading requires.
- an inspiring example of an enthusiastic reader.

Specific suggestions for using *Reading Power* are located in the Teacher's Guide (pages 271–287).

(For a more complete explanation of the theory and methodology found in *Reading Power*, see *A Short Course in Teaching Reading Skills* by Beatrice S. Mikulecky (Addison-Wesley, 1990).

A note about the Answer Key: In this third edition of Reading Power, the Answer Key is provided as a separate booklet. It is <u>not</u> included at the back of the student book.

To the Student

Reading is one way to improve your English language skills. When you read in English

- You learn to think in English.
- You build your English vocabulary.
- You learn to write better in English.
- You practice English, even if you live in a non-English-speaking country.
- You get ready to study in an English-speaking country.
- You can find out about new ideas, facts, and experiences.

How to use *Reading Power* to become a better reader

This book is different from other reading books. *Reading Power* has **four parts**. In each part you'll work on reading in a different way. You should **work on all four parts of the book every week.**

Part 1: Reading for Pleasure. The best way to become a better reader is to read a lot. Reading for pleasure helps you do that. You'll read books that you choose—books that are interesting to you. The more you read, the better you will read.

Part 2: Reading Comprehension Skills. Reading comprehension means reading with understanding. The skills in this part of *Reading Power* will help you understand and remember what you read.

Part 3: Thinking Skills. Reading is more than understanding words and grammar. It is not just translation. Reading is thinking. In order to read well, you must learn to think in English. In this part, you'll practice careful reading for understanding English sentences. You'll learn how to get the meaning of what you read. You'll find out how ideas follow each other in English.

Part 4: Reading Faster. In this part you'll learn to read faster. It may surprise you, but you can understand much more if you read faster!

Acknowledgments

We thank teachers and students all around the world for their feedback regarding *Reading Power*. We have made every effort to respond to their concerns in this third edition. Special thanks to Mykan White, development editor *par excellence*.

About the Authors

Bea Mikulecky holds a master's degree in TESOL and a doctorate in Applied Psycholinguistics from Boston University. In addition to teaching reading, writing, and ESL, she has worked as a teacher-trainer in the Harvard University Summer ESL Program, in the Simmons College MATESL Program, and in Moscow, Russia. Bea Mikulecky is the author of *A Short Course in Teaching Reading Skills* and co-author of the Reading Power series.

Linda Jeffries holds a master's degree in TESOL from Boston University. She has taught reading, writing, and ESL/EFL at Boston College, Boston University, in the Harvard University Summer ESL Program, and at the University of Opole, in Poland. She currently resides in Italy, where she has taught EFL and academic writing at the University of Bologna and the University of Modena. Linda Jeffries is co-author of the Reading Power series.

PART 1
Reading for
Pleasure

Introduction to Reading for Pleasure

Reading for pleasure is the easiest way to become a better reader in English. It's also the most important way. That's why it is the first part of *Reading Power*.

Some students say they don't want to read for pleasure. They prefer to work on grammar lessons and vocabulary drills. They say that pleasure reading is too easy.

However, pleasure reading is very important for learning English. Dr. Stephen Krashen is a famous expert on learning language. He says that pleasure reading helps you learn many important things about English. Students learn more grammar and vocabulary when they read for pleasure. They also learn more about good writing.

Professor Krashen explains that pleasure reading helps each student in a different way. Each student needs to learn something different. Pleasure reading makes it possible for each student to learn what he or she needs.

Reading for pleasure is not the same as studying. When you read for pleasure, you choose your own books, and you don't have to remember everything. There are no tests on your pleasure reading books.

Remember

Reading for pleasure is very important for learning English. It will help you:

- learn how English speakers use English
- read faster in English
- find examples of good writing in English
- learn new words
- learn about the cultures of English speakers

Talking about Your Reading

You can understand what you read better if you talk about it. On the following pages there are two stories to read and talk about. "The Lost City of Pompeii" is a true story (nonfiction); "A Day's Wait" is not a true story (fiction). You will read these stories and practice new ways of reading and talking about your reading.

Example a: Nonfiction

Follow these steps:

1. The title of this story is "The Lost City of Pompeii." It's a report of events that really happened in the past. Before you read, talk with another student. What do you think the story is about? Have your ever heard about Pompeii before? What do you know about it?

2. Read the story, beginning on page 4, all the way to the end. Don't stop for new words. (You'll have another chance to read the story.)

3. Talk about the story with another student. Ask each other:

   - Where does the story take place?

   - When does it take place?

   - What happens in the story?

   - Was any part of the story hard to understand?

4. Read the story again. Mark with a pencil the new words that you want to learn.

5. Talk to another student about the new words. Guess the meanings. Write them here.

   ____

   ____

   ____

   ____

   ____

   ____

   ____

6. Work with a group of three or four students. Retell the story from beginning to end. Then ask one another these questions:

   - Was this story interesting to you? Why?

   - Why is Pompeii important to scientists?

   - Do you know about any other volcanoes or natural disasters?

The Lost City of Pompeii

In 79 C.E., Pompeii was a busy Roman city in southern Italy. On one side of the city was the sea. Pompeii was on a wide bay that was good for boats and for fishing. On the other side was a tall mountain, Mt. Vesuvius. In many ways, this was a good place for a city. The land near it was good for growing things. The weather was also good for farming most of the year. Vesuvius was a volcano, but it was quiet. It had been quiet for 800 years.

On the morning of August 25, the marketplace in Pompeii was busy. The weather was hot and many people were out early. Farmers came in from the countryside. They brought fruits and vegetables to sell in the market. The shops opened, selling food, pots, cloth, and many other things. Bakeries had piles of bread to sell. The cafés had snacks and drinks. The streets were soon crowded. There was noise, and music, too, as traveling musicians entertained in the marketplace. Children ran around everywhere, and dogs barked.

By late morning, there were many people in the center of the city. In the cafés, they were talking about the games in the stadium. That afternoon, gladiators (Roman fighters) were going to have a battle. The gladiators were already practicing in the stadium. At the city meeting place, some of the important men of Pompeii were talking about their city. They were talking about problems, laws, and buildings. Other men were at the bathhouse. They were sitting in the steam room or in the hot pools and talking with their friends.

Suddenly, the ground began to shake. All the houses in Pompeii moved a little. People looked around, and they looked at each other. Was this another earthquake? Earthquakes were common in the area. Suddenly there was a terrible, loud sound—boom! The top of Mt. Vesuvius blew off. Fire came shooting out of the mountain. A huge black cloud of ash and smoke rose into the sky.

The ground shook again, and this time people went running outside. They looked at the mountain and were afraid. Women held onto their children. Husbands looked for their wives. Children cried, and dogs barked.

In a short time, the sun was hidden by the ash and smoke from the mountain. It was as dark as night in Pompeii. Ash and rocks began to fall from the sky. Some of the rocks were very small, but some were the size of tennis balls. People ran screaming through the streets. In the marketplace, bakers forgot about their bread. Farmers forgot about their vegetables. Even the gladiators in the stadium dropped their weapons and ran.

Everyone was terrified. Rich people ran to get their jewelry and gold. Religious people called to the gods for help. As the people ran, hot ash fell on them. It stuck in people's throats and got in their eyes. Their clothes were soon covered with ash. The rocks fell on their heads. Some people tied cushions to their heads to protect themselves.

The air became so thick with ash and smoke that people couldn't breathe. The ash soon filled the streets and piled up on roofs. The weight of the ash and rocks caused houses to fall in. The town was quickly disappearing under a blanket of gray ash. Some people ran to the seaside and tried to get into boats. The sea was wild. Huge waves crashed onto the beach. Still, some families were able to escape that way. Other people ran into the countryside, away from the mountain.

In the end, most of the people—about 20,000—got away from Pompeii in time. But about 2,000 people didn't get away. They were buried under the ashes. In less than two days, the whole city was buried under about 15–20 feet (4.5–6 meters) of ashes. Then it rained, and the ashes became hard as rock.

Across the bay from Pompeii was another small city. The people who lived there saw everything. They saw the mountain explode and a black cloud cover Pompeii. They saw people trying to escape by water or by land. They talked to the people who arrived by boat. A boy named Pliny was there. He watched and listened to everything. When he grew up, he became a writer and he wrote about what happened to Pompeii.

Many years later, new houses were built on top of the old ones in Pompeii. People forgot what had happened to the old Roman city. For the next 1,800 years, it lay underground. Then, in the 19th century, scientists discovered some of Pliny's writing. They read his story about Pompeii and they wondered where it was. One day, some workers were digging a tunnel for water. They found pieces of an old wall underground. Some years later, other people found more walls and buildings. Then they found a stone with writing on it. On the stone was the name of the city—Pompeii.

In 1860, the king of Italy told scientists to uncover Pompeii. They dug away many layers of rock and dirt. They found the city just as it was when the volcano exploded. There was money on a table in a café. There were pots and pans in a fireplace. There was a bowl of unbroken eggs in a kitchen.

At first, the scientists found only a few human bones. But then they made an important discovery. The bodies of most of the people had disappeared. In their place, there were holes in the rocks. From these holes, the scientists could make models of the bodies. These models showed how people looked when they died. Some people were holding on to each other. Other people were holding on to their jewels. There was even a dog on a chain.

Today, Pompeii is an open-air museum. People come from all over the world to see it. Scientists continue to study the Roman city. They learn new things about the way people lived in those days.

Other scientists study Mt. Vesuvius. They wonder when it will explode again. Now, there are many people living near the mountain. If it explodes, hundreds of thousands of people will be in danger. The scientists tell this to the Italian government. The government says it has a plan to save all the people. But will it work? Few people know about the plan. However, few people think about the volcano. They worry about the problems in their town. They worry about their family or their job. They can't imagine that there could be another Pompeii disaster.

Follow these steps:

1. The title of this story is "A Day's Wait." The author is Ernest Hemingway. Before you read, talk with another student. What do you think the story is about? How can you tell? Write your guess here.

   ____

2. Read the story all the way to the end. Don't stop for new words. (You'll have another chance to read the story.)

3. Talk about the story with another student. Ask each other:
   - Where does the story take place?
   - Who are the people in the story?
   - What happens in the story?
   - Was any part of the story hard to understand?

4. Read the story again. Mark with a pencil the new words that you want to learn.

5. Talk to another student about the new words. Guess the meanings. Write them here.

   ____

   ____

   ____

   ____

   ____

   ____

   ____

6. Work with a group of three or four students. Retell the story from beginning to end. Then ask each other these questions:
   - Did you like the story? Why?
   - Did you like the ending? Why?
   - Can you think of a different ending?
   - Have you ever had trouble with different ways of measuring things?

A Day's Wait

by Ernest Hemingway

He came into the room to shut the windows while we were still in bed and I saw he looked ill. He was shivering, his face was white, and he walked slowly as though it ached to move.

"What's the matter, Schatz?"

"I've got a headache."

"You better go back to bed."

"No. I'm all right."

"You go to bed. I'll see you when I'm dressed."

But when I came downstairs he was dressed, sitting by the fire, looking a very sick and miserable boy of nine years. When I put my hand on his forehead I knew he had a fever.

"You go up to bed," I said, "you're sick."

"I'm all right," he said.

When the doctor came he took the boy's temperature.

"What is it?" I asked him.

"One hundred and two."

Downstairs, the doctor left three different medicines in different colored capsules with instructions for giving them. One was to bring down the fever, another a purgative, the third to overcome an acid condition. The germs of influenza can only exist in an acid condition, he explained. He seemed to know all about influenza and said there was nothing to worry about if the fever did not go above one hundred and four degrees. This was a light epidemic of flu and there was no danger if you avoided pneumonia.

Back in the room I wrote the boy's temperature down and made a note of the time to give the various capsules.

"Do you want me to read to you?"

"All right. If you want to," said the boy. His face was very white and there were dark areas under his eyes. He lay still in the bed and seemed very detached from what was going on.

I read aloud from Howard Pyle's *Book of Pirates*; but I could see he was not following what I was reading.

"How do you feel, Schatz?" I asked him.

"Just the same, so far," he said.

I sat at the foot of the bed and read to myself while I waited for it to be time to give another capsule. It would have been natural for him to go to sleep, but when I looked up he was looking at the foot of the bed, looking very strangely.

"Why don't you try to go to sleep? I'll wake you up for the medicine."

"I'd rather stay awake."

After a while he said to me, "You don't have to stay in here with me, Papa, if it bothers you."

"It doesn't bother me."

"No, I mean you don't have to stay if it's going to bother you."

I thought perhaps he was a little lightheaded and after giving him the prescribed capsules at eleven o'clock I went out for a while.

It was a bright, cold day, the ground covered with a sleet that had frozen so that it seemed as if all the bare trees, the bushes, the cut brush and all the grass and the bare ground had been varnished with ice. I took the young Irish setter for a little walk up the road and along a frozen creek, but it was difficult to stand or walk on the glassy surface

and the red dog slipped and slithered and I fell twice, hard, once dropping my gun and having it slide away over the ice.

We flushed a covey of quail under a high clay bank with overhanging brush and I killed two as they went out of sight over the top of the bank. Some of the covey lit in trees, but most of them scattered into brush piles and it was necessary to jump on the ice-coated mounds of brush several times before they would flush. Coming out while you were poised unsteadily on the icy, springy brush they made difficult shooting and I killed two, missed five, and started back pleased to have found a covey close to the house and happy there were so many left to find another day.

At the house they said the boy had refused to let anyone come into the room.

"You can't come in," he said. "You mustn't get what I have."

I went up to him and found him in exactly the position I had left him, white-faced, but with the tops of his cheeks flushed by the fever, staring still, as he stared, at the foot of the bed.

I took his temperature.

"What is it?"

"Something like a hundred," I said. It was one hundred and two and four tenths.

"It was a hundred and two," he said.

"Who said so?"

"The doctor."

"Your temperature is all right," I said. "It's nothing to worry about."

"I don't worry," he said, "but I can't keep from thinking."

"Don't think," I said. "Just take it easy."

"I'm taking it easy," he said and looked straight ahead. He was evidently holding tight onto himself about something.

"Take this with water."

"Do you think it will do any good?"

"Of course it will."

I sat down and opened the Pirate book and commenced to read, but I could see he was not following, so I stopped.

"About what time do you think I'm going to die?" he asked.

"What?"

"About how long will it be before I die?"

"You aren't going to die. What's the matter with you?"

"Oh, yes, I am. I heard him say a hundred and two."

"People don't die with a fever of one hundred and two. That's a silly way to talk."

"I know they do. At school in France the boys told me you can't live with forty-four degrees. I've got a hundred and two."

He had been waiting to die all day, ever since nine o'clock in the morning.

"You poor Schatz," I said. "Poor old Schatz. It's like miles and kilometers. You aren't going to die. That's a different thermometer. On that thermometer thirty-seven is normal. On this kind it's ninety-eight."

"Are you sure?"

"Absolutely," I said. "It's like miles and kilometers. You know, like how many kilometers we make when we do seventy miles in the car?"

"Oh," he said.

But his gaze at the foot of the bed relaxed slowly. The hold over himself relaxed too, finally, and the next day it was very slack and he cried very easily at little things that were of no importance.

Choosing a Pleasure Reading Book

Finding good books

Now you will choose a book of your own to read. You can find a good book from the book list on pages 10–14. The books on this list are not difficult to read, and they are popular with English speakers. You can find them in many libraries and bookstores.

The books on the list are just suggestions. You don't have to read one of these books. However, if you want to read a book that is not on the list, check with your teacher. If the book is too easy or too difficult, you won't enjoy it. You can find many other good and not-too-difficult books in the Young Adult section of bookstores or libraries.

You can also find books written for English learners. These are called *graded readers*. They are often easier to read, especially if you are not used to reading in English. However, they may also be less interesting than books for English speakers. You should look at them carefully before choosing one. You may find some of these books in your classroom or in the school library. If you want to read a graded reader, start with level 2 or 3.

Previewing a book

When you find a book that interests you, preview it. This means you should look at it carefully, following these steps:

1. Read the front cover and back cover of the book. Does it seem interesting?

2. How long it is? A short book is better to start with.

3. Are there any pictures? In a nonfiction book, pictures can help you understand.

4. Check to make sure that the book is not too difficult or too easy. Read one page. If you know all the words on the page, the book may be too easy. If you find more than ten new words, the book may be too difficult for you.

5. Remember: **The book should be interesting to you.** It should not be something you think you *should* read. It should be something you *want* to read!

Getting the most from pleasure reading

- Read your book every day. On a separate page in your notebook, keep a record of the number of pages you read each day. Try to read your book quickly.

- You may find some new words in your book. Don't use a dictionary for every new word. Try to guess the meaning or skip over the word. If you use a dictionary often, you won't be able to follow the story.

- After you finish the book, tell your teacher. She may talk to you about it. She may ask you to tell the class or write about your book.

- If you liked your book, tell a friend about it, too.

- Keep a record of the books you read. See page 22.

Book list

This list has two main sections: **Fiction** and **Nonfiction**. Fiction books are not true stories. The stories are made up by the authors. Nonfiction books are written to give facts and information. They are about every kind of topic: biography, history, travel, adventure, nature, science, and many others.

Fiction

A Lantern in Her Hand, by Bess Streeter Aldrich. The story of Abby MacKenzie Deal, who lived in the American West during the Civil War. (251 pages)

Under the Domim Tree, by Gila Almagor. Three teenage girls learn to become women in 1953 in Israel. (164 pages)

Sometimes I Think I Hear My Name, by Avi. The story of a thirteen-year-old boy who tries to understand his parents. Humorous. (139 pages)

If Beale Street Could Talk, by James Baldwin. The story of a young black American family. A man is in jail, but he did not do anything wrong. A sad love story. (197 pages)

The Squared Circle, by James Bennett. Sonny Youngblood is a star basketball player. But who is he, really? (247 pages)

Forever, by Judy Blume. The famous story of teenage love. The question is, can you love two people at the same time? A best-seller. (220 pages)

Paper Moon, by Joe David Brown. The story of an eleven-year-old girl in the American South during the 1930 Depression years. (308 pages)

SOS Titanic, by Eve Bunting. A young man tries to rescue his friends as the ship *Titanic* sinks into the cold sea. (246 pages)

The Incredible Journey, by Sheila Burnford. Two dogs and a cat travel many miles to return to their home. (146 pages)

The White Mountains, by John Christopher. One hundred years from now, Switzerland is the only free country. This is science fiction and a thriller. (214 pages)

The House on Mango Street, by Sandra Cisneros. Esperánza is a young girl growing up in the Hispanic section of Chicago. She learns to make a happy life in the middle of broken-down buildings and personal difficulties. (110 pages)

Me, Too, by Vera and Bill Cleaver. A twelve-year-old girl tries to help her twin sister. (158 pages)

Where the Lilies Bloom, by Vera and Bill Cleaver. A young girl keeps her brothers and sisters together after both of their parents die. Set in the Great Smoky Mountains in the American South. (175 pages)

The Chocolate War, by Robert Cormier. A student fights a secret society of other students and becomes a hero in the school. (191 pages)

Children of the River, by Linda Crew. Sundara has fled Cambodia and is now living in Oregon, trying to be a "good Cambodian girl" in America. (213 pages)

I Know What You Did Last Summer, by Lois Duncan. A horror story about a secret. (198 pages)

Ransom, by Lois Duncan. Five students take a strange and scary bus ride. (172 pages)

The Slave Dancer, by Paula Fox. A boy finds himself on a slave ship, a place of horrible violence and cruelty. (152 pages)

The Autobiography of Miss Jane Pittman, by Ernest J. Gaines. The story of an American black woman born during the days of slavery. Later in her life, she saw black people get freedom. (245 pages)

Julie of the Wolves, by Jean Craighead George. Julie, an Eskimo girl, is to be married at the age of thirteen. She runs away, makes friends with a wolf pack, and survives. (170 pages)

The Miracle Worker, by William Gibson. A play about Annie Sullivan and how she helped a blind girl named Helen Keller. (122 pages)

Morning Is a Long Time Coming, by Bette Greene. A young American finds adventure and love in Paris after World War II. (261 pages)

Summer of My German Soldier, by Bette Greene. A friendship between a young Jewish girl and a German prisoner in America. (199 pages)

The Drowning of Stephan Jones, by Bette Greene. Stephan and his friends hate gay couples, especially two men who live nearby. His girlfriend, Carla, doesn't know what to think. Then Stephan drowns himself. (217 pages)

The Friends, by Rosa Guy. A family moves to the United States from the West Indies. This story tells about the love and friendship they find. (185 pages)

Ruby, by Rosa Guy. The problems of an eighteen-year-old girl as she tries to become a woman. (186 pages)

Zed, by Rosemary Harris. A young boy tells the story of his experience as a hostage of political terrorists. (185 pages)

The Old Man and the Sea, by Ernest Hemingway. A lonely, old fisherman struggles to catch a big fish. Then he has to fight off the sharks who want to eat it. A young boy is with him. (140 pages)

Jazz Country, by Nat Hentoff. Life in New York City is tough for a young musician. (146 pages)

This School Is Driving Me Crazy, by Nat Hentoff. More about life in New York City. (154 pages)

Letters from Rifka, by Karen Hesse. Rifka and her family have to leave Russia in 1919, and then her family has to leave her. (147 pages)

Rumblefish, by S. E. Hinton. Rusty wants to be tough, like his older brother, but he gets into trouble. (122 pages)

That Was Then, This Is Now, by S. E. Hinton. Sixteen-year-olds Mark and Bryon were like brothers. But now they begin to grow apart. (159 pages)

Gentlehands, by M. E. Kerr. A policeman's son falls in love with a rich girl and then they discover an ex-Nazi in the family. (135 pages)

Night Shift, by Stephen King. Twenty horror stories to make you afraid of the dark. A best-seller! (326 pages)

I Want to Keep My Baby, by Joanna Lee. A fifteen-year-old girl is going to have a baby. (166 pages)

Very Far Away from Anywhere Else, by Ursula K. LeGuin. A young man wants to become a scientist, but his parents want him to be like everyone else. (87 pages)

The Lion, the Witch, and the Wardrobe, by C. S. Lewis. Three children climb into a wardrobe and find a strange new world when they go through the back of it. For readers who like fantasy. (154 pages)

The Contender, by Robert Lipsyte. Alfred, a high-school dropout, wants to be a champion boxer. Then he learns a very important lesson. (167 pages)

A Summer to Die, by Lois Lowry. The story of a young girl whose sister dies of leukemia. (120 pages)

Anne of Green Gables, by Lucy Maud Montgomery. The beloved classic story of a red-haired, lively orphan girl who is loved by everyone she meets. (310 pages)

The Dog Who Wouldn't Be, by Farley Mowat. A funny story about an unusual dog. (195 pages)

The Boat Who Wouldn't Float, by Farley Mowat. Another funny story by a very amusing writer. (241 pages)

No Turning Back, by Beverly Naidoo. A boy in South Africa runs away to the city and lives on the streets. (189 pages)

Edgar Allen, by John Neufeld. A white American family adopts a black child. (128 pages)

Lisa, Bright and Dark, by John Neufeld. A sixteen-year-old girl knows she is losing control of her thoughts and feelings. But no one believes her except her three good friends, who help her. (143 pages)

The Black Pearl, by Scott O'Dell. Ramon wants to find the "Pearl of Heaven" in order to show how good a diver he is. Ramon finds the pearl, but he learns an important lesson. (140 pages)

Animal Farm, by George Orwell. The animals are not happy on the farm. They send away the humans and run the farm themselves. Is their life any better? Read and find out! (132 pages)

The Light in the Forest, by Conrad Richter. A white boy is raised by American Indians in Pennsylvania. This book tells about early life in the United States. (117 pages)

Harry Potter and the Sorcerer's Stone (Harry Potter and the Philosopher's Stone), by J. K. Rowling. The adventures of a boy who discovers that he is a wizard. Very entertaining and exciting. (312 pages)

Shane, by Jack Schaefer. A stranger helps a family in the American West. He teaches a young boy courage and self-respect. (119 pages)

My Name Is Davy—I'm an Alcoholic, by Anne Snyder. A lonely high-school student drinks too much. (128 pages)

The Pearl, by John Steinbeck. A poor fisherman finds a big pearl and hopes to get rich by selling it. Can a pearl bring happiness to his family? (118 pages)

Sons from Afar, by Cynthia Voigt. Two brothers are very different from each other, but both wish they could find their father. (263 pages)

Wrestling Sturbridge, by Rick Wallace. A young wrestler in a small town wants to be the champion. (134 pages)

A Boat to Nowhere, by Maureen Crane Wartski. Kien is a young Vietnamese boy who is trying to escape from the government. This is his story. (191 pages)

My Brother, My Sister, and I, by Yoko Kawashima Watkins. A family struggles in poverty in war-torn Japan. Then the brother is accused of murder! (233 pages)

Charlotte's Web, by E. B. White. Written for children, this book is popular with all ages. It tells a story of love and loyalty that everyone can understand. (184 pages)

Nonfiction

Go Ask Alice, by Anonymous. The true story of a fifteen-year-old girl who became addicted to drugs. She tells how and why it happened. (188 pages)

New Burlington: The Life and Death of an American Village, by John Baskin. A village is moved to make way for a new lake. The people from the village tell their own stories. (259 pages)

Sacajawea, by Joseph Bruchai. This is the story of a young American Indian woman. She helped the explorers Lewis and Clark find a way to the Pacific Ocean. (199 pages)

There Comes a Time: The Struggle for Civil Rights, by Milton Meltzer. This is an easy-to-read book about the civil rights movement in the 1960s in the United States. (180 pages)

J. R. R. Tolkien: The Man Who Created the Lord of the Rings, by Michael Coren. Tolkien's life was not easy. He was an orphan and a soldier. Later, he was a professor. He used his life experiences to write his books. (125 pages)

Boy, by Roald Dahl. This famous writer tells about his childhood and his unhappy experiences in school in England. (176 pages)

The Double Life of Pocahontas, by Jean Fritz. Pocahontas was an American Indian girl who grew up in a white family. Then she went back to live with her own people. (85 pages)

Homesick, by Jean Fritz. The true story of her early life in China and how her family had to leave suddenly because of the war. (163 pages)

Red Scarf Girl, by Ji-Li Jiang. Ji-Li remembers when she was a girl during the Cultural Revolution in China. (285 pages)

Rosa Parks: My Story, by Rosa Parks with Jim Haskins. On December 1, 1953, Mrs. Parks was on a bus in the U.S. South. She refused to give up her seat to a white man. As a result, the U.S. civil rights movement began. (188 pages)

The Upstairs Room, by Johanna Reiss. How two Jewish sisters lived with a Christian family during World War II in Holland. (196 pages)

J. K. Rowling: The Wizard Behind Harry Potter, by Marc Shapiro. This is the life story of one of the most successful writers of our time. (163 pages)

Almost Lost, by Beatrice Sparks. The true story of an anonymous teenager's life on the streets of a big city. (239 pages)

It Happened to Nancy, by Beatrice Sparks. A true story from Nancy's diary. She thought she had found love, but instead she found AIDS. (238 pages)

Helen Keller: From Tragedy to Triumph, by Katherine E. Wilkie. Helen became deaf and blind when she was a small child. This is the story of her success as a student, a writer, and a lecturer. (192 pages)

Writing about Your Pleasure Reading Book

Write a letter

Write a letter to a friend about your book. Below you'll find an outline for a letter.
Use the outline to help you write your letter on a separate piece of paper.

____
(date)

Dear _________________,

    I just finished reading a book called _________________________________
____________________________. It was written by _______________________
____________________________. It is _________ pages long.

    This book is about ____
____
____
____.

    The book is ___________________________________ to read. The best
part is ____
____.

    I think you would _______________ this book because ___________
____
____.

                                     Sincerely,

                                  ____

Some words to use in writing about the book:

like/not like	sad/happy	action
interesting/not interesting	difficult/easy	fiction/nonfiction
exciting/boring	people	imaginary/real life
long/short		

Write a pleasure reading report

*Copy this form on a separate piece of paper. Then fill it in and give it to your teacher.
Other students can read your report and decide if they want to read the book.*

Pleasure Reading Report

Title of book: ____

Author: ____

Number of pages: _______________   Date published: _______________

Fiction or nonfiction? _______________________________________

What is this book about? ______________________________________

____

____

____

What is the best part? ____

____

____

____

Would you tell a friend to read this book? Why? ________________

____

____

____

Fill in this information about yourself:

Name: _______________________   Date: _______________

Native language: _______________   Age: _______________

Gender: _______________   Profession: _______________

This book is _______ easy _______ just right _______ difficult

Using Your Pleasure Reading Book to Practice Reading Faster

Here are two ways to use your pleasure reading book to work on reading faster.

Finding your reading rate in your pleasure reading book

Before you use your pleasure reading book to practice reading faster, you must find out how fast you read now. Follow these directions to find your reading rate.

Read this sample page from a book called Murder in the Language Lab. **Before you start to read, write the starting time: _____ min. _____ sec.**

Murder in the Language Lab

1   Against one wall there was a large machine. The sides of the machine were made of black metal. The bottom half of it looked like a large typewriter. The top part of the machine was like a television set.

5   The man walked over to the tree. He looked up at the hole in the roof.

The man called out, "Sally! Come down, Sally!"

After a short time, a face appeared in the opening. The face had small, bright eyes. The mouth was very wide, and

10   the nose was flat. There were very big ears. The face was covered with short brown hair. It was the face of a chimpanzee.

The animal's lips opened, showing yellow teeth. It looked like a smile. The chimpanzee made a happy sound.

15   "Come down here, Sally," the man said again.

Sally climbed down the tree very quickly. With her long arms, it was easy for her to climb up or down very fast. Sally looked at the man and smiled again.

"Do you want a banana, Sally?" the man asked.

20   Sally made another happy sound. She ran across the room to the machine. She stood in front of the machine. It looked like she was thinking very hard. She was studying the part that was like a typewriter. There were many more keys than are usually found on a typewriter. Also,

25   instead of letters there were little pictures or symbols on the keys. There were circles and squares in different colors, and many other symbols as well.

Sally looked at the keys with their symbols. She put out her finger and pressed several keys. When she pressed

30   a key, that symbol appeared on the television part of the machine. At the same time, words in English appeared above the symbols. Sally finished pressing the keys. She looked at the symbols on the television.

Write the time you finished reading: _____ min. _____ sec.

Look at the next page and read the directions carefully.

To figure out your reading rate:

1. Count the number of words in the first three lines. There are 30 words in the first three lines on the sample page from *Murder in the Language Lab*.

2. Divide the number of words by three (the number of lines). Then you will know the average number of words in one line.

    30 ÷ 3 =   10
  (words)   (lines)   (words in one line)

3. Count the lines on the page. On the sample page from *Murder in the Language Lab*, there are 33 lines.

4. Find out how many words there are on the page. Multiply the number of words in a line by the number of lines on the page.

    10 ×   33   =   330
  (words)   (lines on the page)   (words on the page)

Now that you know there are about 330 words on the page, you can find out how many words you can read in one minute.

5. How many minutes did you take to read the page of *Murder in the Language Lab?* (finishing time minus starting time equals reading time) _______ minutes

To find your reading rate, divide the number of words on the page by the number of minutes it took you to read the page.

    330 words on a page ÷ _________ minutes = _________ words per minute.

For example, if you read the page in 5 minutes,

    330 words on a page ÷ 5 minutes = 66 words per minute.

Next, you will learn how to figure out your reading rate for your own book.

Figure out your reading rate for your own book

You can use your own book to learn to read faster. About once a week, check your pleasure reading rate. Just remember to time yourself when you read.

———— Pleasure Reading Rate Finder ————

Book Title: ____

1. Find a full page in your book. Count the number of words in three lines: _______ words.

2. Divide that number by three to get the average number of words in one line: _______ words.

3. Count the lines on one page: _______ lines.

4. Find out how many words there are on the page. Multiply the average number of words in one line by the number of lines on the page.

    _______________ × _______________ = _______________
      (words in one line)   (lines on one page)   (words on one page)

    Now that you know how many words there are on one page in your book, you can figure out your reading rate (words per minute).

5. Open your book and mark the page you are on.

    Before you start to read, write the starting time: _______ min. _______ sec.

    When you stop reading, write the finishing time: _______ min. _______ sec.

6. How many minutes did you read? Finishing time minus starting time equals reading time: _______ min. _______ sec.

7. How many pages did you read? _______

8. How many words did you read?

    _______________ × _______________ = _______________
        (pages)   (words on one page)   (number of words you read)

9. To find your reading rate, divide the number of words you read by the number of minutes.

    _______ words ÷ _______ minutes = _______ words per minute.

Turn to page 21 and write the title and author of your book, today's date, and your reading rate on the Pleasure Reading Progress Charts.

Reading Sprints

Reading quickly is important in reading for pleasure. When you read too slowly, you can't follow the story. You can become bored and want to stop reading.

You can improve your reading speed by doing reading sprints. Runners often use sprints (short runs at fast speeds) to learn to run faster. They can help you read your book faster. Then you will enjoy it more.

Use your pleasure reading book for reading sprints.

Reading Sprints

Title of book: ____

1. Find out how many pages you can read normally in five minutes. Write the number of pages here: _______ (If you read only part of a page, include that amount.)

2. From where you just finished reading, count ahead that number of pages. (For example, if you read one and a half pages in five minutes, count ahead one and a half pages.) Mark the place in the margin with a pencil.

3. Try to read those next pages in only *four* minutes. If you cannot do it the first time, try again. (Use new pages.) Make your eyes move faster across the page. You may need to try several times.

4. Now try to read that same number of pages in *three* minutes. Count the number of pages again, and mark the place. Again, try until you can do it.

5. Finally, try to read the same number of pages in *two* minutes. You may feel that you do not understand very much. In fact, you may be able to read only some of the words on the page. This doesn't matter. You aren't reading for comprehension in this exercise; you are learning to move your eyes more quickly. It's enough to understand *something* from the text.

6. Now you are ready to read "normally" again. Read for five minutes. Don't push yourself, but don't relax too much either!

   How many pages did you read? _______

   Compare that with your first reading. Is it the same?

Repeat these reading sprints regularly. They will help you read your pleasure reading books quickly. And you will build up speed in all of your other reading, too. Reading faster will become easier, and your comprehension will improve.

Pleasure Reading Progress Charts

Use these charts to keep track of your pleasure reading rate.

Book Title _________________________   Book Title _________________________

Author _________________________   Author _________________________

RATE (words per minute—WPM)

| 480 |
| 460 |
| 440 |
| 420 |
| 400 |
| 380 |
| 360 |
| 340 |
| 320 |
| 300 |
| 280 |
| 260 |
| 240 |
| 220 |
| 200 |
| 180 |
| 160 |
| 140 |
| 120 |
| 100 |
| 80 |
| 60 |
| 40 |
| 20 |

Date

Record of Books Read

Title	Author	Date begun	Date finished	Number of pages

PART 2

Comprehension Skills

Introduction to Comprehension Skills

In Part 2, you'll work on many important reading skills:

Unit 1 Previewing and Making Predictions

Unit 2 Scanning

Unit 3 Making Inferences

Unit 4 Building a Powerful Vocabulary

Unit 5 Learning to Look for the Topic

Unit 6 Understanding Paragraphs

Unit 7 Finding the Pattern of Organization

Unit 8 Skimming

The first few exercises in each unit may be easy. Then the exercises become more difficult. Do the exercises in order. Don't skip any exercises.

Read the directions for each exercise before you start. In some of the exercises, you should work with another student. This will help you improve your English.

Previewing and Making Predictions

Before you start on a road trip, you usually look at a map. Then you have a better idea of the roads and the places. You can plan your trip better and have fewer problems.

You can do this before you start reading, too. Some parts of a passage are like a map. If you look at these parts, you can get a lot of information before you read a passage. Then you can make guesses about the passage.

When you look for information before you read, this is called **previewing**. When you make guesses about the passage, this is called **making predictions**.

Previewing and making predictions help you read faster and understand better. The reason for this is simple: You know a little more about what you will read. You should *always* preview and make predictions before you read!

Example:

Practice previewing and making predictions with these three envelopes. Look at the writing and the return addresses. Look at the stamps and the dates in the postmarks. Then answer the questions that follow.

A.

University of New Mexico
12 College Avenue
Albuquerque, NM 76543

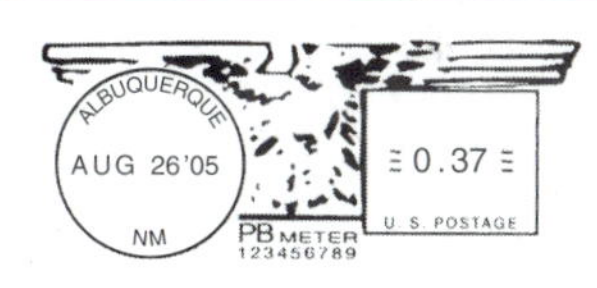

Mr. Eduardo Duran
5407 S. California St.
Apartment 36
Chicago, IL 21212

1. Is this a personal letter or a business letter?

2. Who is it from?

3. Where is it from?

4. Do you think it will be an interesting letter? Why or why not?

5. Make a prediction about what may be in this letter.

B.

Chicago Electric Company
42 High Street
North Newton, IL 21203

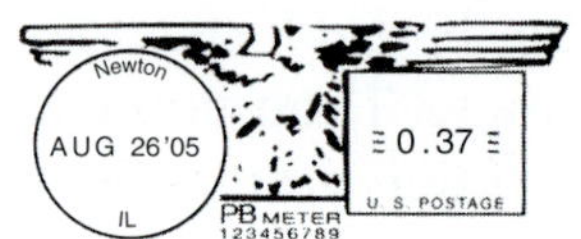

Mr. Eduardo Duran
5407 S. California St.
Apartment 36
Chicago, IL 21212

1. Is this a personal letter or a business letter?

2. Who is it from?

3. Where is it from?

4. Do you think it will be an interesting letter? Why or why not?

5. Make a prediction about what may be in this letter.

c.

1. Is this a personal letter or a business letter?

2. Who is it from?

3. Where is it from?

4. Do you think it will be an interesting letter? Why or why not?

5. Make a prediction about what may be in this letter.

Here is a picture of the place you have decided to go on your vacation. Preview the picture and make predictions about your vacation.

1. What will you do during the day?

2. What will you do in the evening?

3. What will you eat?

4. What will you wear?

5. What will you buy?

6. How will you feel when you come home?

Talk to another student about your answers. Are they the same?

Here is a picture of the place where your friend is going on vacation. Preview the picture and make predictions about your friend's vacation.

1. What will she do during the day?

2. What will she do in the evening?

3. What will she wear?

4. What will she eat?

5. What will she buy?

6. How will she feel when she comes home?

Talk to another student about your answers. Are they the same?

Each picture below is part of a magazine article. Make predictions. Match the pictures with the titles of the stories.

| **Picture** | **Title of story** |

1. _____    a. Women in Science

2. _____    b. How Americans Shop for Food

3. _____    c. How Animals Build Their Homes

4. _____ 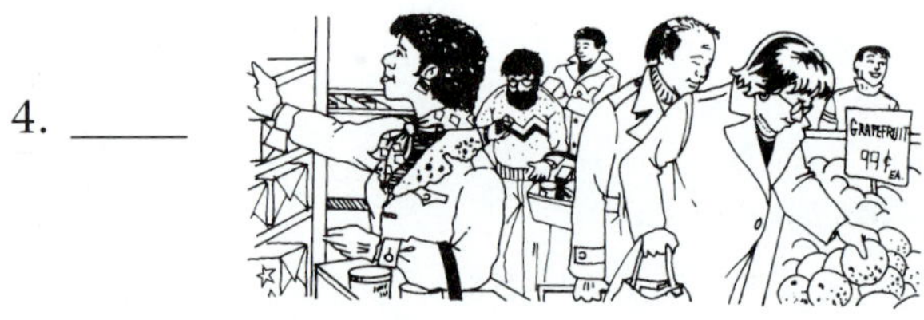   d. When Your Child Goes to the Dentist

5. _____    e. The Violin in the Symphony Orchestra

Talk to another student about your answers. Are they the same?

Could you find these ideas in a magazine article with this title? Check (✓) Yes or No.

BOSTON: A GOOD PLACE TO LIVE

	Yes	No
1. Boston has many wonderful museums.	_____	_____
2. The sports teams in Boston are exciting to watch.	_____	_____
3. There are many poor people in Boston.	_____	_____
4. The Boston Symphony Orchestra is one of the best.	_____	_____
5. People are not very friendly in Boston.	_____	_____
6. There are many famous old buildings in Boston.	_____	_____
7. Apartments are expensive and hard to find.	_____	_____
8. Jobs are hard to find in the Boston area.	_____	_____
9. People like to walk and jog in the city parks.	_____	_____
10. Winters in Boston are cold and snowy.	_____	_____

Talk to another student about your answers. Are they the same?

EXERCISE 5

Could you find these ideas in a magazine article with this title? Check (✓) Yes or No.

Modern Dentists

How They Help You

	Yes	No
1. Dentists hurt your teeth.	_____	_____
2. Dentists use many up-to-date machines.	_____	_____
3. Some dentists play the radio for their patients.	_____	_____
4. Some dentists will pull out all your teeth.	_____	_____
5. You can get your teeth cleaned at the dentist's office.	_____	_____
6. The dentist may x-ray your teeth.	_____	_____
7. A visit to the dentist is very expensive.	_____	_____
8. The dentist tells you how to take care of your teeth.	_____	_____
9. Some dentists become very rich.	_____	_____
10. Modern dentists must study for many years.	_____	_____

Talk to another student about your answers. Are they the same?

Make predictions about what will come next. Circle the letter of the sentence that could come next.

Example:

Yesterday, there was a big snowstorm in Detroit. Many schools were closed, and people had to stay home from work.

    a. It was a warm, sunny day and the beaches were crowded.
    b. It was very cold, but the snow on the trees looked beautiful.
    c. Only one inch of snow fell in the downtown area.

The correct choice is *b*. Choice *a* is not correct. People don't go to beaches when there is snow! Choice *c* is not correct. In a big snowstorm, many inches of snow fall.

1. There were many good shows on TV last night. The Smith family stayed home.
    a. They turned off the TV and went to bed early.
    b. The only interesting show was about traveling by bicycle.
    c. They saw a play, a music show, and the news.

2. John and Alice Babson are not happy with the school in their town.
    a. Their children love to go to school.
    b. The classrooms are too crowded.
    c. It is a beautiful building.

3. Many young people move to New York City after college.
    a. New York is a dangerous city.
    b. It's difficult to find jobs in New York.
    c. There are lots of interesting things to do in New York.

4. Fly Happy Time Airlines! Take an exciting trip to Holiday Island!
    a. This trip is very expensive.
    b. Holiday Island has warm, sunny weather.
    c. Happy Time Airlines is never on time.

5. Alex had trouble falling asleep last night. He was awake until 3:00 A.M.
    a. This morning, he feels tired.
    b. This morning, he feels rested and ready to work.
    c. This morning, he is hungry.

6. The roads were covered with ice and were dangerous today.
    a. Sam drove home quickly.
    b. Sam took a long time to drive home.
    c. Sam enjoyed driving home.

Talk to another student about your answers. Are they the same?

Make predictions about what will come next. Circle the letter of the sentence that could come next.

1. Tomiko got a cat last week. It's a pretty little cat, and it follows her everywhere.
   a. Tomiko can never find the cat.
   b. It even goes out for walks with her in the park.
   c. Tomiko's father doesn't like cats.

2. Sergio likes to listen to classical music in the evenings.
   a. Sometimes he falls asleep while he is listening.
   b. He works hard all morning and afternoon.
   c. His favorite kinds of music are pop and country.

3. Miriam and her brother, Peter, both go to dance classes.
   a. Peter likes to be different from his sister.
   b. Peter doesn't like dancing.
   c. Peter likes to do the same things as his sister.

4. My clock doesn't work very well. It's always a little slow.
   a. I'm often late for work.
   b. It's black with white numbers.
   c. It helps me get to work on time.

5. Rudy went to China last month. He didn't know how to speak Chinese.
   a. He didn't know any Japanese or Korean.
   b. Some Chinese people visited Rudy in Dallas, Texas.
   c. But a lot of Chinese people spoke English.

6. The weatherman on TV predicted cold weather on Saturday.
   a. I like to watch the weather report on TV.
   b. You don't have to bring any warm clothes this weekend.
   c. You should bring some warm clothes this weekend.

7. On Sundays, Gina's grandmother often cooks a big meal.
   a. Gina doesn't like cooking very much.
   b. She invites Gina and all her cousins for dinner.
   c. Gina doesn't see her grandmother very often.

8. Daren wants to go to Europe next summer.
   a. He says he is not interested in European history.
   b. In college, he is studying African history.
   c. He is saving money to pay for the plane ticket.

Talk to another student about your answers. Are they the same?

EXERCISE 8

Previewing: *In the passage on page 35, you can see the parts to preview. Read these parts. Then make predictions about the parts you cannot see.*

A Mexican Artist in New York

The artist Maria Arroyo-Diamond is back in New York. She was born in Oaxaca, Mexico, and she first studied art in Mexico City. Then she came to New York to study with several famous

Maria loves to paint large, colorful paintings. She is a small, quiet person, but her

Last month, Maria moved back to New York with her husband. He now has a job with the

She thinks that New York is a good place for an artist.

Making predictions:

1. What is in the rest of the first paragraph?

2. What is paragraph 2 about?

3. What is paragraph 3 about?

Turn the page and read the whole passage. Check your predictions.

A Mexican Artist in New York

The artist Maria Arroyo-Diamond is back in New York. She was born in Oaxaca, Mexico, and she first studied art in Mexico City. Then she came to New York to study with several famous artists. She met Ted Diamond, a newspaper reporter, at an art show. They married, and soon after that, her husband's job took them to Brazil. She won several important awards in Brazil, where her work became very popular. She also showed her work in Mexico and other countries.

Maria loves to paint large, colorful paintings. She is a small, quiet person, but her paintings are full of color and large shapes. She says that she uses Mexican colors. In Mexico, the sky and the sea are usually very bright blue. The houses are often bright colors, too. The large shapes in Maria's paintings do not show real things. They show her feelings about things. With these colors and shapes, Maria's paintings seem alive and exciting.

Last month, Maria moved back to New York with her husband. He now has a job with the *New York Times*. She is working in a studio with some other artists. She hopes to show some of her new work soon. Maria says that she is happy to be back in this city. She thinks that New York is a good place for an artist.

Did you make good predictions? Talk to another student. Did he or she make good predictions?

EXERCISE 9

Previewing: *In this exercise, you should read only the <u>underlined</u> parts. Follow the Guidelines on page 34. Work very fast!*

Thomas and the Gorillas

It was a hot summer day in Chicago. The Kemper family decided it was a good day to go to the Brookfield Zoo. Janet and Kevin Kemper had two children: Thomas, 3, and Sally, 6 months. Thomas loved going to the zoo. He liked watching all the animals, but he especially loved the gorillas.

The Kempers went straight to the gorilla exhibit. There were six adult gorillas and a three-month-old baby gorilla. In the Brookfield Zoo, the animals are not in cages. They are in large areas dug out of the ground. These areas have fences around them so the animals cannot get out and people cannot fall in.

But, three-year-old boys are good climbers. While the Kempers were watching the gorillas, little Sally started to cry. Kevin took her from Janet, and Janet looked in her bag for a bottle of juice. In those few seconds, Thomas climbed up the fence.

A woman saw him and shouted, "Stop him!" A tall man reached up to get him, but it was too late. Thomas fell down the other side of the fence. He fell eighteen feet onto the hard concrete floor. He lay very still, with blood on his head. Janet and Kevin shouted for help. People crowded around the fence, and someone ran to get a zoo worker.

But before the zoo worker arrived, a gorilla went over to Thomas. It was Binti Jua, an eight-year-old mother gorilla. She had her baby gorilla on her back. With one arm she picked up the little boy. She carried him carefully over to a door, walking on three legs. There she put Thomas down so a zoo worker could get him.

Janet and Kevin ran to the door, too. Thomas was badly hurt and had to go to the hospital, but after a few days he was better. The story was on the evening news in Chicago. Some people cheered and others cried when they heard it. But many of them thought about that mother gorilla and asked themselves, "What is she doing in a zoo? What is the difference between a gorilla and me?"

Making predictions: *Don't look back at the passage. Close your book and talk about the passage with another student. Make predictions about the rest of the passage.*

Then read the whole passage. Did you make good predictions?

Previewing: *In this passage, you have to decide which parts to preview. Follow the Guidelines on page 34. Read only those parts. Don't read the whole passage. Work very fast!*

Do Pigeons Take the Train?

Pigeons are smart birds. They are good at finding places. They can find their way home from many miles away. Scientists are not sure how pigeons know their way, but they do. They almost never get lost.

Can pigeons find their way under the ground? Some Underground passengers in London say that they see pigeons on the Underground trains. Rachel Robson says she saw a pigeon at Paddington Station. It got on the train and then got off again at the next stop.

Some train lines are especially popular with pigeons. They are often seen on the Northern and Picadilly lines. Lorna Read also sees pigeons at the Paddington Station. Once, a passenger tried to get a pigeon off the train. The pigeon flew back in just before the doors closed. It seemed all upset—like a person who doesn't want to miss the train.

Why do pigeons get on the trains? Some people say that the pigeons are not looking for food. They say the pigeons want to save time. London is a big city. The pigeons get tired of flying and they do what people do. They take the train. What do the scientists think of this? They say they must have some more information—but anything is possible with pigeons!

Making predictions: *Don't look back at the passage. Close your book and talk about the passage with another student. Make predictions about the rest of the passage.*

Then read the whole passage. Did you make good predictions?

UNIT 2 — Scanning

What Is Scanning?

Scanning is very fast reading. When you scan, you look for information as quickly as you can.

Scanning can help you improve your reading. Many students try to read every word in a passage, so they read very slowly. When you scan, you can't read every word. You have to skip many words. Practice with scanning helps you learn how to skip over words. You can learn to read faster and understand better.

You may already scan many things in English or in another language.

You can scan:	**You usually don't scan:**
a table of contents in a magazine or a book	a mystery story
an index in a textbook	a textbook for an important course
a timetable	important papers from a lawyer
the ads in a newspaper	a map for finding your way home
a list of movies in the newspaper	a question on a test
a telephone book	a poem
the pages of a dictionary	

Example:

Your friend made a list of things you need to buy for school. Did he remember to include a *dictionary*?

pen	paper
notebook	dictionary
eraser	pencil sharpener
pencils	glue
pencil case	assignment book

How many words did you read? You didn't need to read all the words to find *dictionary*. The other words were not important to you.

In this unit, you will practice scanning. Don't try to read every word. Scan to find the answers to the questions. Work fast.

Scanning a Table of Contents

The table of contents is always at the front of a magazine or a book. It tells you what you can find in each chapter or part. On the next page is the table of contents for *Sanctuary* magazine.

EXERCISE 1

Read each question and then scan the table of contents to find the answers. Work fast!

1. How many features are there in the magazine?

2. Who is the author of the article about canaries?

3. What kind of paper is this magazine printed on?

4. How many departments are there in the magazine?

5. Does this magazine have information about beavers?

6. On what page can you read about a swamp?

7. Does this magazine have an editor? What is his or her name?

8. On what page is the Habitat Department?

9. What is the title of the article by Wendall Waters?

10. Who is the designer of the magazine?

Write two more questions about this table of contents.

1.

2.

Ask other students to scan the table of contents for the answers to your questions.

SANCTUARY

SPRING
Volume 42 Number 3

STAFF

Editor:
John H. Mitchell

Associate Editor:
Ann Prince Hecker

Managing Editor:
Rose M. Murphy

Field Editor:
Thomas Conuel

Poetry Editor:
Gene Zeiger

Designer:
Valerie Bessette

Cover: Spring Freshet, Tributary of the Swift River, Petersham, Massachusetts © *1998 by Paul Rezendes*

Printed on recycled paper with soy-based ink.

FEATURES

DEPARTMENTS

Sanctuary is a quarterly journal dealing with natural history and the environment and is open to diverse points of view. Opinions expressed herein are those of the authors and not necessarily those of the Massachusetts Audubon Society. To respond to stories in this issue, e-mail us at sancmag@massaudubon.org.

Sanctuary (ISSN 0272-8966), South Great Rd., Lincoln, MA 01773. Published quarterly. Memberships are $50 (family); $40 (individual); $20 (student) of which $7.50 is applied toward a subscription to *Sanctuary*. Postmaster: send address changes to *Sanctuary*, Massachusetts Audubon Society, Lincoln, MA 01773, 781-259-9500. Periodicals postage paid at Lincoln, MA, and at additional offices. Reprints of this issue are available. Write or call the publications office at Massachusetts Audubon, Lincoln, MA 01773, 781-259-2167. Printed in the U.S.A.

Scanning an Index

An index is usually at the back of a book. It lists all the topics in the book in alphabetical order. You can use an index to find information quickly. The index on the next page is from a book titled *The Theater Arts and the Teaching of Second Languages*.

Scan the index to find the page numbers for the topics below. (If many page numbers are listed, write down the first two or three page numbers and then write "and many more.") Work fast!

Topic	Page(s)
1. TOEFL	_________________________
2. taste	_________________________
3. vocabulary	_________________________
4. writing	_________________________
5. sound	_________________________
6. stereotype	_________________________
7. *Time* magazine	_________________________
8. University of Illinois	_________________________
9. Andrew Wright	_________________________
10. Garry Trudeau	_________________________

Write three more topics from this index.

1.

2.

3.

Ask other students to scan the index for the topics you wrote.

Scanning a List

A traveler can find lots of important information on the Internet. On the next page is a list of useful websites for someone visiting Canada.

EXERCISE 3

Read each question and then scan the list to find the answer. Work fast!

1. What is the name of a Canadian newspaper (paper)?

2. Where can you find out about sports?

3. Does the Greyhound Bus site give ticket prices?

4. Where can you find out about camping?

5. If you want to read some stories about Canada, where can you look?

6. If you need a map of Toronto, where can you find it?

7. Which sites give you information about air travel?

8. What can you find on the site of the Royal Canadian Mounted Police?

9. If you want information about bicycling in Quebec, where can you look?

10. Where can you look for tickets to a rock concert (gig) in Vancouver?

Write three more questions about this list of websites.

1.

2.

3.

Ask other students to scan the list for the answers to your questions.

CANADA ON THE INTERNET

Air Canada
www.aircanada.com
Details of flight times, fares, and reservations.

Bed and Breakfasts
www.bbcanada.com
An extensive online source, with over 1,900 color listings of B&Bs across the country.

Canada's Most Wanted
www.rcmp-grc.gc.ca/html/wanted/wanted_e.htm
A few people to avoid on your trip. A site reserved by the Royal Canadian Mounted Police for their favorite villains.

Canada Airlines
www.canadaairlines.ca
Schedule, fares, and reservations.

Canadian Parks
www.parkscanada.ca
A good site by Canadian Heritage detailing opening times, camping facilities, and how to get to all major Canadian parks.

Canadian Tourism Commission
www.travelcanada.com
Excellent site answering almost any query you care to think of concerning travel within Canada.

The Globe and Mail
www.theglobeandmail.com
Canada's premier paper online.

Greyhound Buses
www.greyhound.ca
Provides schedules and prices for a ream of destinations.

Infospace
www.infospace.com/canada/index_ylw_ca.htm
Exhaustive Yellow-Pages-like listings. If you want to find a vet in Labrador or a body piercer in Toronto, this will have it.

MacLean's
www.macleans.ca
Top stories and the editors' picks from past issues of Canada's premier news magazine.

Maps on the Net
www.mapquest.com
Maps from all over the world, including all major Canadian cities and towns.

Skiing
www.skinetcanada.com
Latest ski conditions, weather, prices, facts, and figures from Canada's ski resorts.

Tickets
www.ticketmaster.ca
Ticket booking service for shows, gigs, and sporting events across Canada.

Slam! Sport
www.canoe.ca/slam
A very thorough Canadian site on all matters of sporting.

Trains
www.viarail.ca
VIA Rail's page with times and tickets for Canada's train services.

Yahoo! Canada
www.yahoo.ca
The Canuck section of the useful Web directory provides good avenues of investigation.

Scanning Classified Ads

Newspapers usually have a part called "classified ads." In this part of the newspaper, people can find things to buy, sell, or rent. The ads on the next page are for apartments (apts.) in towns near Boston. The names of the towns are in alphabetical order.

EXERCISE 4

Read each question and then scan the ads for the answer. Work fast! Try to answer all of the questions in three minutes.

1. How many apartments are for rent in Malden?

2. How much is the cheapest apartment in Brockton?

3. Whom would you call about an apartment in Canton?

4. Is there an apartment in Brighton that is near transportation?

5. Can you have a cat at the Lakeside Village apartment in Easton?

6. What is the phone number for the apartment in Lynn with parking?

7. If you want a three-bedroom (3 bdrm.) apartment, where could you find one? (Name at least three towns.)

8. What is the phone number for the Essex Realty Company?

9. Where is the apartment with the highest rent?

10. Where is the apartment with the lowest rent?

11. What is the rent for a one-bedroom (1 bdrm.) apartment in Charlestown?

12. What is the rent for a one-bedroom (1 bdrm.) apartment near Boston University?

Write three more questions about these ads.

1.

2.

3.

Ask other students to scan the ads for the answers to your questions.

CLASSIFIED ADS

BRIGHTON, 2 bdrm., full kitchen, dining area, $1,260. Call 876-5522.

BRIGHTON, Sunny studio, fresh paint, laundry. $850. Downtown Real Estate Company. 521-0021.

BRIGHTON, Near Boston Univ. Studio. $925; Move in 9/1. 341-8003.

BRIGHTON, Near transportation. Extra large studio. Clean. Good owner. $890 with heat. Call 741-8800.

BRIGHTON, New, 1 bdrm. in house, dishwasher, garden. $950. Real Estate Company. 452-0667.

BRIGHTON, Cozy 1 bdrm. with new kitchen & bath. Laundry. Parking. Near Boston Univ. $965. Call 962-5431.

BRIGHTON, 3 bdrm. in house, new kitchen, tile bath, lg BR's. $1,395, no heat. Real Estate Company. 286-3152.

BROCKTON, Oak Park. Many large new apts. w/ dishwasher, heat, carpeting, balcony, walk-in closet, pool, sauna, clubhouse, tennis court. Convenient to public transpt. & shop'g. 1 bdrm. $775, 2 bdrms. $835–$980. Equal Housing Opportunity. ESSEX REALTY COMPANY 598-8440.

BROCKTON, Oak Green Apts. near Stoughton. New apts. w/ dishwasher, carpeting, parking & pool. Studio $710, 1 bdrm. $770, 2 bdrms. $860. Rent includes heat. Equal Housing Opportunity. ESSEX REALTY 598-8440.

BROOKLINE. 6 rooms, 3 bdrm., new kitchen and bath. Porch, parking. $1,599, no heat. Collins Real Estate Company. 776-1461.

BROOKLINE VILLAGE, 2 bdrm. in 3-family house. New kitchen. $825, no heat. Village Real Estate Company. 542-3200.

BURLINGTON, Ideal locale, neighboring mall and major routes, large 1 & 2 bdrm. apts. Tennis, pool & more. Model open Mon.–Fri. 9–5, Sat. & Sun. 10–4. SIR WINDSOR APTS. 756-6422.

CAMBRIDGE, 2 bdrm. luxury apt. in new brick building, w/ carpeting, tile bath, all-electric kit., balcony, & assigned prkg. $1,125, with heat. Call Bonnie 355-4400 or 626-8181.

CAMBRIDGE, Shepard St., large 4 rms.-1 bdrm., large closets, porch. With heat, prkg., no fee. $1,084. 5/1. 341-8003.

CANTON, 2 bdrm., eat-in kitchen, sunny, garden, near shops & transportation. $875. May 1. Call Susan 792-5670 or Mrs. Young 265-4147.

CHARLESTOWN, Bunker Hill St. near city pool, 1 bdrm. with heat. $925. 256-8622, after 5pm.

CHELMSFORD, Lowell line, nr. Rtes 3 & 128. Large 2 bdrm. $570 incl. heat, air conditioning. 745-5420.

CHELSEA, Luxury 1 & 2 bdrm. apts. near subway, deck, with heat. $590–$750. 465-2881.

CONCORD, 3 bdrm. apt., pool, tennis, near river. $1,450 with heat. 532-4591, after 7 pm.

DORCHESTER, At Ashmont. Studios $310. 1 bdrm. $435–$600, with heat $700. 983-4257.

DORCHESTER, So. Boston. New 1 & 2 bdrm. apts. $460–$475. 983-7330.

EASTON. Lakeside Village. Unique 1 & 2 bdrm. spacious townhouses. Just 30 minutes from Boston, convenient bus service available. Spectacular sports complex, private backyard. Small pets allowed & owner managed. Reasonable. 832-1186.

EASTON, 1 & 2 bdrm. condos avail. Pool & tennis courts. Some with garages. Starting at $675 mo. Some include utilities. KINGSLEY PROPERTIES. 832-9501.

EAST BOSTON, 2 bdrm. condo, deck, overlooking harbor & skyline, all new, with laundry, carpeting, and dishwasher. $800 mo. Call Ed 754-0432.

EAST BOSTON, 6 modern rooms, 2nd floor. Call 755-6016.

LYNN, Newly painted studio & 2 bdrm. apts. ocean views. Rents from $750 with heat, hot water, and new kitchens & baths. 654-9876.

LYNN, Nahant line, steps to ocean, studio. $475, with parking. NSP R.E. 954-4121.

LYNN, Ultra-modern ocean front 1 bdrm. apt., including new kitchen & bathrm., carpets, many extras. $775. 955-8653.

LYNN, Steps from beach. Completely new 1 bdrm. apt. $600. Studios $495, with heat. HALL R.E. 954-2025.

MALDEN, Huxley Estates. Beautiful 1-1/2 bdrm., new kitchen, air-conditioned, heated, with parking, pool, walk to subway. No pets please. Avail. 6/1. 644-2281. M–F 9–5, Sun 1–5.

MALDEN, Very clean 4 rooms, 1 bdrm. $545, no heat. Baldwin R.E. 644-7562.

MATTAPAN, Modern 2 bdrm., a/c, $575 no heat. 288-5001.

NEEDHAM, Modern apts. 1 & 2 bdrm. Rents $795 to $1,125 + heat. Call 453-2986. Mon–Fri 9-5.

NEWTON, Luxury 1 bdrm., $850 with pool, tennis, parking, heat, near subway. No pets. Rental fee - $200. For Info, 256-5488.

NEWTON, Large, sunny 2 rm. apt, new kitchen & bath. Air conditioned. $425. R.E. 256-9753.

Scanning a Newspaper Ad

Scan the ad below to find the answers to these questions. Work fast!

1. Which notebook computer has the lowest price?

2. What is the price of the computer that comes with a 16" flat-panel monitor?

3. What is the name of the computer store?

4. How many different courses can you take at this computer store?

5. Which computers come with printers?

6. What is the price of the OPUS-WORKS package?

Write two more questions about this ad.

1. ____

2. ____

Ask other students to scan the ad for the answers to your questions.

New! BITOSHI Plus Notebook Computer
Only $1,949 with 60GB HD

- 2.4 GHz Processor
- 512MB DDR memory
- DVD-RW/DVD-R/CD-RW combo drive
- 15.4" XGA display

Super Noteworks Notebook Computer
Special price—$1,349

- 2.8 GHz Processor
- 64MB Integrated video memory
- 40GB Ultra DMA HD

BITOSHI desktop package
This month only! $749

- 512MB DDR memory
- CD-RW drive
- 16" viewable flat-panel monitor
- TEXA color printer

OPUS-WORKS desktop package
Save $250! Pay only $1,479

- 512MB DDR memory
- High-speed MX440 graphics card
- DVD-RW/CD-RW combo drive
- TEXA color printer

COMPUTER TRAINING—Courses in:

* Networking   * Website development   * Power Point   * Troubleshooting

dsi **data systems international**
150 West 17th St., San Diego, CA 95661
M–F 9–5, Sat. & Sun. 10–6 or www.dsi.com

Scanning Newspaper Stories

Scan the news article to find the answers to these questions. Work fast!

1. How many stores were damaged in the fire?

2. In which store did the fire (blaze) start?

3. What time did the fire start?

4. Where is the shopping center?

Write two more questions about this news article.

1. ____

2. ____

Ask other students to scan the article for the answers to your questions.

THE NEW YORK TIMES

14 Yonkers Stores Damaged by Fire

Special to *The New York Times*

YONKERS, Nov. 12—A four-alarm fire damaged 14 stores today in the Cross County Shopping Center, the largest shopping center in Westchester County.

Fire investigators said the blaze apparently started in a pile of cardboard cartons at the rear of a shoe store and spread through a utilities duct above the 13 other stores. The fire started at 4:40 P.M. and was declared under control at 6:14 P.M. The center is on the Cross County Parkway at the Gov. Thomas E. Dewey Thruway.

Two firefighters were treated at the scene for minor cuts. Lieut. John Carey of the Yonkers Arson Squad said the cause of the fire was under investigation.

Scan the two news articles on page 51 to answer these questions. Work fast!

1. How many passengers and crew members were on the train?

2. What time did the accident happen?

3. Where was the train when it derailed (went off the track)?

4. Where was the train going?

5. Did anyone have to stay in the hospital overnight?

6. What is the name of the senator who visited the crash site?

7. Where has train travel stopped because of the accident?

8. What bridge was the train going across?

Write three more questions about these articles.

1.

2.

3.

Ask other students to scan the articles for the answers to your questions.

THE BOSTON TIMES

Boston-Bound Train Derails, 34 Hurt

by Madelyn Burton

New York, Nov. 23—An Amtrak train headed for Boston derailed just south of New York City yesterday, falling into a muddy marsh and injuring thirty-four people, none of them seriously. The train was a passenger and mail train en route from Washington, D.C., to Boston.

Railroad officials described the wreck as one of the worst in recent memory in this part of the country, called the Northeast Corridor. The accident stopped all train travel between New York and Newark. The tracks to and from New York to Boston, however, were still open and in use.

According to Amtrak officials, fifteen crew members and seventeen passengers suffered only minor injuries. Most were treated and released from hospitals in the area. Two crew members, however, stayed in the hospital overnight.

THE NEW YORK GLOBE

Amtrak Derailment Near Secaucus Injures 35

by Richard L. O'Brien

NEW YORK, Nov. 23—An Amtrak fast-mail train carrying 108 passengers and crew members derailed as it was nearing New York at 6:33 A.M. on Saturday. The train was speeding across the Hackensack River Bridge when it left the track, almost hit a train headed in the opposite direction, and then fell thirty feet down an embankment into a marsh.

Amtrak announced that no one was killed. But thirty-five persons were injured, including two who were injured seriously. Dozens of other passengers were badly shaken up in the crash. The two train locomotives were hurled nose down into the muddy marsh of an empty New Jersey meadow.

The Hackensack River Bridge is a swing bridge. It is the type that opens to allow tall boats to pass through. Senator Frank Lautenberg, a member of the Transportation Appropriations Subcommittee in the Senate, went to the accident scene and talked to railroad officials. He was informed that a boat had

Several cars of a derailed train headed to Boston lie in the remote marshes of Secaucus, N.J., yesterday.

passed through the bridge just two hours earlier. It was speculated that the bridge may not have closed completely after the boat went through, and a gap in the track may have caused the crash.

Scan the news article below to find the answers to these questions. Work fast!

1. How many people died in the typhoon (storm)?

2. On what day did the typhoon begin?

3. How many people lost their homes (were homeless)?

4. What is the name of the island that was hit the worst?

5. What is the name of the typhoon?

6. How many people are missing?

Write two more questions about this news article.

1. ____

2. ____

Ask other students to scan the article for the answers to your questions.

THE NEW YORK TIMES

Philippines Sends Aid for Typhoon Damage

MANILA, Nov. 10 (AP)—The Philippine Air Force ferried medical teams and relief supplies today to provinces ravaged by Typhoon Agnes. The authorities said 515 people had died in the typhoon and more than 400 were missing.

An Air Force spokesman said more than 163 tons of food, medicine, and clothing had been sent to the Visayan region, 300 miles south of Manila, and more aid was on the way.

The typhoon hit the region Monday. The spokesman said helicopters were rescuing people stranded by floods that remained chest-deep today in some areas of Panay Island, which appeared to have been hit the worst. Most of the fatalities and missing were on the island, where 445,000 people were homeless.

The Philippine National Red Cross reported that 90 percent of the 86,000 houses in Capiz Province on Panay were destroyed. Many of the dead were children who drowned as thirty-foot waves smashed into coastal villages.

Making Inferences

Writers in English often do not explain everything to the reader. For example, in stories, the writer may not tell the reader the time or place. Often the reader has to guess these things. This is called **making inferences.**

Making inferences is sometimes called "reading between the lines." This means you use the information in the text to guess other things about the text. It is often necessary to make inferences when you read. Sometimes you need to guess about information the writer has not put there. Other times you may need to guess about meaning when you do not know all the words. Good readers make inferences all the time as they read.

Making Inferences from Conversations

In the following example, you will find part of a conversation. Read through it and make some inferences about the people who are talking.

Example:

Read the conversation and answer the questions. Work with another student.

A: Look at the long line! Do you think we'll get in?

B: I think so. Some of these people already have tickets.

A: How much are the tickets?

B: Only nine dollars for the first show. I'll pay.

A: Thanks. I'll buy some popcorn.

1. Where are these people? *in front of a movie theater*

2. What are they talking about? *going to a movie*

3. Which words helped you guess the topic? *line, get in, tickets, show, popcorn*

Read the conversation and answer the questions. Work with another student.

A: When did this happen?

B: Yesterday. I was playing soccer and I fell down.

A: Can you move it at all?

B: Only a little.

A: Can you walk on it?

B: No. It hurts too much.

A: I think we'll have to take an X-ray.

B: Will I be able to play in the game tomorrow?

A: I'm afraid not.

1. Where are these people?

2. Who are they?

3. What are the people talking about?

Read the conversation and answer the questions. Work with another student.

A: Do you think Mom and Dad will be late?

B: No. Swiss Air is usually on time.

A: But it's raining so hard, and there's a lot of wind.

B: There's no message on the announcement board, and they didn't say anything to us at the airline counter. They always make an announcement if the flight is late.

A: Well, I hope you're right. I hate waiting around!

1. Where are these people?

2. What are they talking about?

Read the conversation and answer the questions. Work with another student.

A: Well, what do you think?

B: The color is perfect on you.

A: What about the style?

B: It's a very popular style.

A: How does it look on me?

B: It looks great on you. It looks great on everybody.

A: You don't think I look funny in it?

B: Not at all. You look very nice.

1. Where are these people?

2. What are they talking about?

EXERCISE 4

Read the conversation and answer the questions. Work with another student.

A: Do you want to hear something interesting?

B: Sure. Tell me.

A: Yesterday I had to stay late to finish that report. Well, I was here at my desk, just typing away. Then, who should come along, but Sheila.

B: Sheila? You mean Sheila Gifford, in marketing?

A: That's right. She went right into his office with a briefcase. She stayed in there for about ten minutes.

B: You're kidding!

A: No, I'm serious. Then she came out, looked around, and walked quickly to the elevator.

1. Where are these people?

2. What are they talking about?

Read the conversation and answer the questions. Work with another student.

A: Don't I know you from somewhere?

B: I don't think so.

A: Yes, I'm sure. You were at Joe's party last week.

B: No, I wasn't.

A: No?

B: No.

A: Then you were at Pete's party the week before.

B: No, really. I don't know you.

A: Well, my name's Larry. What's your name?

B: Listen, Larry . . .

A: You live around here?

B: Excuse me. . . . Oh, Jim! There you are! I've been looking for you!

1. Where are these people?

2. What is happening in this conversation?

EXERCISE 6

Read the conversation and answer the questions. Work with another student.

A: Where to?

B: The airport.

A: Okay. How much time do you have?

B: About an hour.

A: I don't know . . . there's a lot of traffic now.

B: I can't miss this flight!

A: Well, I'll do my best.

B: Oh! Look out!

A: Listen, lady. Do you want to catch your flight?

B: I sure do.

A: Then close your eyes and keep quiet. And I'll get you there on time.

1. Where are these people?

2. What is happening in this conversation?

Read the conversation and answer the questions. Work with another student.

A: This is one of the reasons I hate working in a big city.

B: I know. Every day, it's the same thing.

A: This is terrible! We may be here all night! I hope we don't run out of gas.

B: No, I think there's enough.

A: Let's turn on the radio. Maybe there's some good music.

B: Sorry, the radio's not working.

A: I think I'll take the train tomorrow!

1. Where are these people?

2. What are they talking about?

3. What do you think will happen next?

EXERCISE 8

Read the conversation and answer the questions. Work with another student.

A: Excuse me. Do you have the time?

B: Nine o'clock.

A: Already! Are you sure?

B: Of course.

A: Then where's the Number 13?

B: The Number 13? It's probably downtown by now.

A: What do you mean?

B: It came twenty minutes ago. It always comes at twenty minutes before the hour.

A: So the next one comes at nine forty?

B: No. There is no next one!

A: That was the last one?

B: Yeah. After nine o'clock there aren't any more.

A: Then what are you doing here?

B: I'm waiting for a taxi.

1. Where are these people?

2. What are they talking about?

3. What do you think will happen next?

Making Inferences from Stories

Now you'll practice making inferences from parts of stories. Read each passage quickly and answer the questions. Don't stop for a new word. Try to guess the meaning. If you can't guess, skip the word and continue reading.

Read this passage from Girl Against the Jungle, by Monica Vincent. Try to infer the answers to the questions below. Underline the words or phrases that helped you. Work with another student.

Girl Against the Jungle

I woke up very late the next morning. The sun was high in the sky, so I got up quickly and started to walk along the bank of the stream. I still followed the rules carefully. First I poked my stick into the undergrowth. Then I took a step or two. I watched for snakes and spiders. I listened for the sounds of danger. I listened to the
5   birds. My mother knew all about birds.

"The birds can tell you about the jungle," she told me. "Listen to them."

She taught me a lot about birds, so I recognized the terrible cries in the sky. I recognised the big, black wings and the ugly, bare heads. I knew those sharp, hungry beaks. King vultures! The biggest vultures in the world. They don't kill.
10   They only watch and wait. They fly over the jungle and look for dead bodies. The sky was black with their wings. They flew down between the trees. There was food on the ground—dead flesh. It was the passengers from the plane. I didn't see the bodies, but I knew. The vultures told me.

I didn't feel sad. I didn't feel afraid. I still didn't feel any pain. I walked through
15   the jungle, but I walked slowly. Very slowly.

I passed some pieces of the plane. I saw the number clearly on one piece of metal: OBR 941. I saw other passengers' cases. I could smell dead bodies. I could hear the hungry vultures. But I couldn't hear people's voices. I couldn't see any people. I was afraid. "Are all the other passengers dead?" I thought. "Am I alone
20   in the jungle?"

1. Where is the girl in the story?

2. What happened before this passage in the story?

3. Why is she walking slowly?

4. Why is she alone?

5. What do you think will happen after this?

Read this passage from Project Omega, *a story by Elaine O'Reilly. Try to infer the answers to the questions below. Underline the words or phrases that helped you. Work with another student.*

Project Omega

"My name's Julia Baker. You saved my life."

"Oh, I do that kind of thing when I get the chance," laughed the young man. "I'm Edward West."

"Well, how can I thank you, Edward? Why don't you come in and have some
5   coffee? I think I need a cup too, after that."

They went into the apartment. Clara brought them two cups of coffee—very good Italian coffee.

"The elevator," Julia said. "It wasn't there."

"I know."

10   "But you were there. Was that by chance?"

Edward looked at her. She saw that he was thinking.

"Yes," he said slowly. "I think it was."

"I think they broke the elevator door."

"Yes. That's clear."

15   "You don't think it was an accident?"

"No, I don't think so."

Julia drank the hot, sweet, black coffee. When she put the cup down, she began to cry. For the first time in her eighteen years of life, she knew she needed a friend. She knew it because she was with this young man—this young man
20   with the clear, friendly eyes.

"It's all right," he said. "You're safe now."

"No, I'm not," Julia answered. "I'm in terrible danger." And she told him the story—every part of it, from her father's disappearance to Miss Harper's telephone call. She told him about Project Omega.

1. Where are these people?

2. What happened before this passage in the story?

3. Why does Julia start to cry?

4. What do you think Project Omega is?

Read this passage from Sarah, Plain and Tall, **by Patricia MacLachlan. Try to infer the answers to the questions below. Underline the words or phrases that helped you. Work with another student.**

Sarah, Plain and Tall

"You don't sing anymore," he said. He said it harshly. Not because he meant to, but because he had been thinking of it for so long. "Why?" he asked more gently.

Slowly, Papa straightened up. There was a long silence, and the dogs looked up, wondering at it.

"I've forgotten the old songs," said Papa quietly. He sat down. "But maybe there's a way to remember them." He looked at us.

"How?" asked Caleb eagerly.

Papa leaned back in the chair. "I've placed an advertisement in the newspapers. For help."

"You mean a housekeeper?" I asked, surprised.

Caleb and I looked at each other and burst out laughing, remembering Hilly, our housekeeper. She was round and slow and shuffling. She snored in a high whistle at night, like a teakettle, and let the fire go out.

"No," said Papa slowly. "Not a housekeeper." He paused. "A wife."

Caleb stared at Papa. "A wife? You mean a mother?"

Nick slid his face onto Papa's lap and Papa stroked his ears.

"That, too," said Papa. "Like Maggie."

Matthew, our neighbor to the south, had written to ask for a wife and mother for his children. And Maggie had come from Tennessee. Her hair was the color of turnips and she laughed.

Papa reached into his pocket and unfolded a letter written on white paper. "And I have received an answer."

1. Who are the people in the passage?

2. What happened before this in the story?

3. Why doesn't Papa remember the old songs?

4. What is in Papa's letter?

5. What do you think will happen after this?

In this exercise, you will read two passages from Gentlehands, a story by M. E. Kerr. Try to infer the answers to each set of questions on page 62. Underline the words or phrases that helped you. Work with another student.

Gentlehands

Passage 1

I tried to convince Skye to let me drive to Beauregard with her that night, and hitch a ride back to my house, but she wouldn't hear of it. She dropped me and took off like a rocket. I saw my father standing in our driveway by his Toyota, smoking a cigarette, watching me. He was in uniform because

5 he was working nights that week.

"That was a Jensen she was driving," I said. "Did you ever hear of a Jensen?"

"Did she ever hear of a speed limit?"

"Oh, *Dad*."

"It isn't funny, Buddy," he said.

10 I stood there and he stood there and then he said, "Where'd you go?"

I didn't want to tell him then. He wasn't in the greatest mood, and I didn't want to open that whole can of worms at the end of a beautiful evening.

"We just rode around."

"Rode around at eighty miles an hour?"

15 "She wasn't doing eighty."

"She was close to it," he said. He took a drag on his cigarette and twirled his car keys in his hand. "Buddy, if your social calendar isn't too full, I'd appreciate it if you'd do something with Streaker tomorrow."

"I work until two," I said.

20 "And after two?"

"I was going clamming* with Ollie."

"Take Streaker with you," he said. "Okay?"

"Okay," I agreed.

"Streaker hangs around his mother too much," my father said.

25 "I know that. Okay."

He gave me one of his friendly punches and opened his car door. "I've never even heard of a Jensen," he said.

"Neither had I," I said.

"Well, anyway, did you have a good time?"

30 "Yeah."

"Your mother's asleep on the couch," he said. "Don't wake her up, she's beat. We started to panel the playroom tonight."

The playroom was actually the garage. My father had built a wooden floor there, and they were fixing it up for Streaker and me.

35 "See you tomorrow," I said.

*Clamming: Looking for clams in the sand near the sea. Clams are a popular food in many parts of the world.

1. Who are the people in the passage?

2. Where are they?

3. What happened before this in the story?

4. What do you think will happen after this?

Gentlehands

Passage 2

She was all in blue, right down to her sandals. I guess she specialized in wearing all one color, and she had this great perfume on, and that smile, and she just stood there and I just stood there, and the jukebox was roaring out some rock number, and the whole place was babbling around us,
5   waiters calling out: "Two over easy, o.j., and one black."
"I came to get you," she said.
"I'm working," I said.
"I'm shopping," she said. "What time are you through working?"
"Two," I said.
10   "I'm going to take you for a swim," she said. "Would a swim make you happy, Buddy?"
"I guess it would," I said.
"Don't guess with me, Buddy," she said.
"BUDDY!" I could hear Kick behind me.
15   "Someone's calling you," she said. "I'll be parked outside at two sharp. Okay?"
"Okay," I said.
Before I'd left the house that morning, I'd stuck a note up in Streaker's bunk telling him to be ready at two thirty.
20   So much for promises, and clamming.

5. When does this part of the story take place?

6. Who are the people in this passage?

7. Where are they?

8. What happened before this in the story?

9. What is meant by "So much for promises, and clamming"?

10. What do you think will happen after this?

11. What can you guess about Buddy after reading both passages?

12. What can you guess about Buddy's family?

Building a Powerful Vocabulary

Building a powerful vocabulary means more than learning new words. It means learning new ways to think about words. In this unit, you'll learn thinking skills that will help build your vocabulary. You'll learn to guess the meaning of unknown words. You'll learn how to use synonyms and pronouns to help you understand what you read.

Using the Context

The context is the sentence or sentences around a word. The context can tell you a lot about a new word. It can tell you what kind of word it is—noun, verb, adjective, or adverb. It can also give you some idea of the meaning of the word. Then you don't have to stop reading and look in a dictionary. You can read much more quickly this way, and you can understand more.

Guessing unknown words from the context

In the following exercises, you'll use the context to guess which word belongs in each blank space.

Example:

First read the passage all the way to the end. Then look at the words in the box below. Use the context to help you choose a word to write in each space.

Last week was Henry's birthday. He was twenty-one years old. His girlfriend bought

him a new ________________. His brother and ________________ gave him a party. Henry's
(1)   (2)

mother made a special chocolate birthday ________________, and all of Henry's good
(3)

friends came to his ________________. They danced all ________________. Henry really
(4)   (5)

enjoyed his birthday.

watch	cake	night	house	sister

Now check your answers below.

(1) watch   (2) sister   (3) cake   (4) house   (5) night

First read the passage all the way to the end. Then look at the words in the box below. Use the context to help you choose a word to write in each space.

Oprah Winfrey

Oprah Winfrey is a successful actress, TV producer, and the first African-American billionaire in the United States. She was born in Kosciusko, Mississippi, a small ______________ (1) in America's south. She lived with her ______________ (2) until she was six years old. The ______________ (3) was very poor. At a very young ______________ (4), Oprah learned to read aloud ______________ (5) her family. Her skills in reading and ______________ (6) helped her all her life.

speaking	family	town	to	grandmother	age

Show your work to another student. Do you agree on the answers?

First read the passage all the way to the end. Then look at the words in the box below. Use the context to help you choose a word to write in each space.

Oprah's Childhood

When she was six years old, Oprah was sent to live ___________ (1) her mother in Milwaukee, Wisconsin. Her mother was ___________ (2) poor and uneducated, and Oprah ___________ (3) unhappy there. At age thirteen, she ___________ (4) away from home. The police ___________ (5) her to a special home for ___________ (6) who run away. But she couldn't ___________ (7) there because it was ___________ (8) full. She had to ___________ (9) to Nashville, Tennessee, to live with her ___________ (10), Vernon Winfrey.

Life with her father was ___________ (11) easy for Oprah. He was very ___________ (12) from her mother. He believed that Oprah ___________ (13) follow his rules very closely. For ___________ (14), she had to be home ___________ (15) every night. She also had to ___________ (16) a book every week and she had to write a ___________ (17) about it. Oprah's father wanted her ___________ (18) to do her best. He would not let ___________ (19) do less than her ___________ (20).

<table>
<tr><td>her</td><td>read</td><td>best</td><td>very</td><td>was</td><td>report</td><td>father</td></tr>
<tr><td>sent</td><td>example</td><td>children</td><td>ran</td><td>always</td><td>should</td><td>with</td></tr>
<tr><td>go</td><td>early</td><td>stay</td><td>too</td><td>not</td><td>different</td><td></td></tr>
</table>

Show your work to another student. Do you agree on the answers?

In this exercise, you have to think of the words to write in the spaces. First read the passage all the way to the end. Then use the context to help you think of a word to write in each space.

Oprah's Success

Oprah started work as a reporter on a radio station in Nashville. Then she went to _______________ (1) at a TV station. At _______________ (2) same time she _______________ (3) to Tennessee State University and _______________ (4) Speech and Performing Arts. Since _______________ (5), she has worked on TV talk shows and in _______________ (6) films.

Today, Oprah lives and _______________ (7) in Chicago. She is _______________ (8) owner of HARPO Productions, a company that makes _______________ (9) shows and movies. (If you _______________ (10) at the word "HARPO", you _______________ (11) see it is "OPRAH" backwards.) Millions of _______________ (12) watch her TV _______________ (13), and she is rich and famous. _______________ (14) Oprah remembers that _______________ (15) used to be poor, and she _______________ (16) to help other people. _______________ (17) example, she remembers how important _______________ (18) were for her. So she _______________ (19) "Oprah's Book Club" to encourage people to _______________ (20). Books on Oprah's Book Club List often become best-sellers. Oprah also gives $100,000 _______________ (21) year to people who _______________ (22) others.

Show your work to another student. Do you agree on the answers?

Guessing word meanings from the context

When you want to guess the meaning of a new word, use the context. When you do the following exercises, you should work alone. Don't use a dictionary, and don't ask other students or the teacher about the words. Try to guess the meanings from the context. After you finish each exercise, you may check your answers with another student, your teacher, or a dictionary.

Example:

Read the sentences below and guess the meaning of glue. *Write the meaning in English. It does not have to be exact. A general meaning is okay.*

I can't find the *glue*. Do you know where it is? I used it yesterday to put together a broken cup. Now I need to fix this broken toy. I can't do it without *glue*.

What does *glue* mean? ____

____

Now check your answer.

Glue is something we use to put together or fix broken things.

For each item, guess the general meaning of the word from the context. Write the general meaning in English.

1. Last winter there was a big storm with lots of snow. One of the old trees came down. It fell on the wall around the garden. Now there is a *gap* in the wall. We'll have to build the wall up again.

   What does *gap* mean? _______________________________________

   ____

2. We brought our boat into the *harbor* just before the storm started. It was a small *harbor*, and it was crowded with other boats. But it was safe from the strong winds.

   What does *harbor* mean? _______________________________________

   ____

3. A lot of Greek art shows *naked* men and women. The Greeks believed that the human body was beautiful. They wanted to show the whole human body in their art.

   What does *naked* mean? _______________________________________

   ____

4. That's not true! You're a *liar*. You didn't see a fish in the swimming pool. It's not possible! There aren't any fish in the swimming pool!

   What does *liar* mean? _______________________________________

   ____

5. George was standing by the closed door. He was very tired, so he started to *lean* against the door. Suddenly, the door opened and George almost fell down.

   What does *lean* mean? _______________________________________

   ____

6. Sondra didn't understand everything that the man said. But she got the *gist*. She understood that she had better leave quickly because it was dangerous there.

   What does *gist* mean? _______________________________________

   ____

Now check the meanings of the words with another student, your teacher, or a dictionary.

For each item, guess the general meaning of the word from the context. Write the general meaning in English.

1. When the war started, many people left Rwanda. They lived in big camps for *refugees* in Zaire and Burundi. Life was hard for the *refugees* in these camps.

   What does *refugees* mean? ____

   ____

2. Today I received some letters from Malaysia. There were some beautiful stamps on the envelopes. I took them off and gave them to my brother. He *collects* stamps from all over the world.

   What does *collects* mean? ____

   ____

3. Hitler was one of the most *evil* people in history. He was a powerful man, and he used his power the wrong way. He caused many millions of people to suffer and die.

   What does *evil* mean? ____

   ____

4. Sir Cavendish continued to stand there. The King was very angry. "Why are you on your feet?" he shouted. "You must *kneel* before the King!"

   What does *kneel* mean? ____

   ____

5. Paulo played the drums in high school. In his last year, he decided to *join* the school band. But he didn't really like playing band music. He preferred rock and roll.

   What does *join* mean? ____

   ____

6. Mrs. Sweeny was ready to *retire* from her job. She was sixty-five years old, she was tired of working, and she wanted to have more time at home.

   What does *retire* mean? ____

   ____

Now check the meanings of the words with another student, your teacher, or a dictionary.

For each item, guess the general meaning of the word from the context. Write the general meaning in English.

1. George likes to *boast* about how well he can play tennis. He says he can beat any of us! He thinks he's the best tennis player in town!

   What does *boast* mean? _______________________________

   ____

2. I sat down on the grass to rest. Then I felt something on my leg. It was a little black *ant*. There were many more of them running all over my feet. I jumped up quickly.

   What does *ant* mean? _______________________________

   ____

3. Jimmy's medicine had a *nasty* taste. He took it the first time, but he didn't want to take it again. His mother had to put some sugar in it.

   What does *nasty* mean? _______________________________

   ____

4. You can get to Mercer Island by small boat taxis or by *ferry*. The *ferry* can also carry cars. In good weather, it takes about half an hour.

   What does *ferry* mean? _______________________________

   ____

5. It didn't rain for months, and the weather was very hot. Soon there was a terrible *drought* in the country. The farmers couldn't grow any food, and wild animals died.

   What does *drought* mean? _______________________________

   ____

6. Miriam was *enthusiastic* about dancing. She loved her dance classes, and she told everyone she wanted to be a dancer.

   What does *enthusiastic* mean? _______________________________

   ____

Now check the meanings of the words with another student, your teacher, or a dictionary.

In this exercise, some of the items are phrases (groups of words). For each item, guess the general meaning of the word or phrase from the context. Write the general meaning in English.

1. When Suki heard that her mother couldn't come, she *burst into tears*. I told her that her mother would come the next day. But Suki only cried harder.

   What does *burst into tears* mean? _______________________________________

   ____

2. My mother was an *absentminded* person. She was always thinking about something else, so she often didn't pay attention to things. One day, she went to work with two different shoes on!

   What does *absentminded* mean? ____

   ____

3. Sahita always *goes along with* everything I say. I'm sure she doesn't really agree with me all the time. But she always says "yes!" I don't understand. Is she afraid of me?

   What does *goes along with* mean? _______________________________________

   ____

4. The exam had a few difficult parts. But *on the whole* it was not hard, and almost all the students did well.

   What does *on the whole* mean? ____

   ____

5. Hello? This is Jonathan. I'm calling from my mobile phone. Can you come and help me? I drove off the road because of some ice. Now my car is *stuck* in the snow. I can't get back on the road.

   What does *stuck* mean? ____

   ____

6. Did you leave a *tip* for the waiter? I usually leave about 15 percent of the price of the meal. But he was a very good waiter, and he was very nice. We should leave 20 percent.

   What does *tip* mean? ____

   ____

Now check the meanings of the words with another student, your teacher, or a dictionary.

In this passage, the underlined words may be new to you. Read the passage all the way to the end. Use the context to guess the meaning of the words you don't know. Don't use a dictionary, and don't ask anyone about the words.

Ballooning

The first kind of air <u>transportation</u> was not a plane. It was a <u>balloon</u>. People traveled by balloon a hundred years before there were planes or jet <u>aircraft</u>. Those early days of ballooning were exciting, but they were also dangerous. Sometimes the balloons fell suddenly. Sometimes they burned. However, the danger did not stop the <u>balloonists</u>.

The first real balloon flight was in France in 1783. Two Frenchmen, the Montgolfier brothers, made a balloon. They filled a very large cloth bag with hot air. Hot air is lighter than cold air, so it goes up. The Montgolfiers' hot air balloon went up 1,000 feet in the sky.

Later that same year, two other Frenchmen <u>ascended</u> in a basket under a balloon. They built a fire under the balloon to make the air hot. This made the balloon stay up in the air for a few hours. But their balloon was tied to the ground. So it could not go anywhere.

The first free balloon flight was in December 1783. The balloon flew for twenty-five minutes over Paris. It traveled about five and one half miles. Flying a balloon is not like flying a plane. The balloon has no engine and therefore no power of its own. The wind directs the balloon. It goes where the wind blows. The <u>pilot</u> can <u>control</u> only the <u>altitude</u> of the balloon. He or she can raise and lower the balloon to find the right wind direction. That is how a good pilot controls where the balloon goes.

Soon balloonists tried longer flights. A <u>major</u> event in the history of ballooning was the first long flight over water. In 1785, an American and a Frenchman flew over the English Channel. They left England on a cold, clear January day. After about an hour, their balloon began to <u>descend</u> toward the water. They threw out some <u>equipment</u> and food to make the balloon lighter. The balloon continued to fall, so they threw out almost everything in the basket—even some of their clothes. Finally, after about three hours, they landed in France, cold but safe.

During the nineteenth century, ballooning became a popular sport. There were balloon races in Europe. Balloons were also used by scientists to study the air and by armies in wartime. After the airplane was <u>invented</u>, people lost interest in balloons. Planes were much faster and easier to control. But some people today still like to go up in balloons. High up in the balloon basket, they find quiet. They have a wonderful view of the world below.

Column 1

1. transportation _____
2. balloon _____
3. aircraft _____
4. balloonists _____
5. ascended _____
6. pilot _____
7. control _____
8. altitude _____
9. major _____
10. descend _____
11. equipment _____
12. invented _____

Column 2

a. important
b. distance above the earth
c. way of traveling
d. a machine for traveling by air
e. go down
f. person who flies a plane or balloon
g. special things you need to do something
h. people who travel in a balloon
i. went up
j. made for the first time
k. a bag full of air
l. make something do what you want it to do

New Words

____

____

____

____

____

____

____

Definitions

____

____

____

____

____

____

____

Read the passage all the way to the end. Use the context to guess the meaning of the words you do not know. Don't use a dictionary, and don't ask anyone about the words.

The Story of Photography

The history of photography began long ago. In ancient times, the Greeks already knew how to make a kind of camera. In the fifteenth century, painters used a simple camera without film. It helped them see better what they were painting.

In the early nineteenth century, two Englishmen made the first pictures with cameras. These were very simple pictures made by sunlight on paper. Then in 1827, a French scientist named Niepce made the first photograph on metal. But this photograph was not very clear.

Niepce and Daguerre, a French painter, worked together to make better photographs. In 1837, Daguerre took a picture of his studio. He used a new kind of camera and a different process. In his picture, you could see everything clearly, even the smallest details.

Soon, other people began to use Daguerre's process. They called this kind of photograph a *daguerreotype*. Travelers took cameras with them and brought back daguerreotypes from all around the world. People photographed famous buildings, cities, and mountains.

In about 1840, the process was improved. Then photographers could take pictures of people and moving things. But the process still was not simple. The photographers had to carry lots of film and processing equipment. But this did not stop the photographers, especially in the United States. After 1840, daguerreotype artists were popular in most cities.

Matthew Brady was one well-known American photographer. He took many portraits of famous people. The portraits were unusual because they were lifelike and full of personality. Brady was also the first person to take pictures of a war. His 1862 Civil War pictures showed dead soldiers and ruined cities. They made the war seem more real and more terrible.

In the 1880s, new inventions began to change photography. Photographers could buy film ready-made in rolls, so they did not have to make the film themselves. Also, they did not have to make the photos immediately. They could bring the film back to their studios and develop it later. They did not have to carry lots of equipment. And finally, the invention of the small handheld camera made photography less expensive.

With the small camera, anyone could be a photographer. People began to use cameras just for fun. They took pictures of their families, friends, and favorite places. They called these pictures *snapshots*.

Documentary photographs became popular in newspapers in the 1890s. Soon magazines and books also used them. These pictures showed true events and people. They were much more real than drawings.

Some people also began to think of photography as a form of art. They thought that photography could do more than show the real world. It could also show ideas and feelings, like other art forms did.

A. Guess the meanings of the underlined words in the passage. The underlined words are in Column 1. The meanings are in Column 2. Write the letter of the best meaning after each word. You may look back at the passage. Work with another student.

Column 1	Column 2
1. studio _____	a. a way of doing something
2. process _____	b. what makes people who they are
3. details _____	c. completely fallen down, useless
4. improved _____	d. showing how things really are
5. portraits _____	e. kind or type
6. personality _____	f. without waiting, right away
7. ruined _____	g. change film into photographs
8. immediately _____	h. made better
9. develop _____	i. small, important parts
10. documentary _____	j. pictures of people
11. form _____	k. a place for artists and photographers to work

B. Read the passage again. Are there any other words that are new to you? Write them on the lines below. Then write the definitions from the dictionary. Ask your teacher to check your definitions.

New Words   **Definitions**

_____________________   ____

_____________________   ____

_____________________   ____

_____________________   ____

_____________________   ____

_____________________   ____

_____________________   ____

_____________________   ____

C. Show your new words to another student. Does he or she know your words? Explain the definitions of your words.

Using Pronouns and Synonyms

Writers try not to use the same word again and again. That wouldn't be interesting for the reader. Writers can use a **pronoun** instead of repeating a noun or phrase (group of words). Or they can use a **synonym** (another word that means the same thing).

Pronouns

Pronouns can be used instead of nouns. Pronouns are small words, but they are very important when you are reading. These small words tie ideas to each other in a passage. You'll understand more of what you read if you pay attention to pronouns.

Some pronouns:

he, him, his	we, us, our	you, your	I, me, my, mine
she, her, hers	they, them, their	it, its	this, that, these, those

In the following examples, the pronouns are underlined:

Example a:

Sharon Yee lives in Taiwan. <u>She</u> has an apartment near the National Museum. <u>She</u> likes to walk to the museum. Sometimes two or three friends go with <u>her</u>. At the museum, <u>she</u> learns about <u>her</u> country's past.

All the underlined pronouns take the place of the noun *Sharon Yee*. The noun *Sharon Yee* is called the **referent**, because the pronouns refer to it.

Example b:

Swimming and bicycling are popular sports. People like <u>them</u> because <u>they</u> are easy to do. <u>These</u> sports also help people make their hearts and lungs stronger. <u>They</u> are good, too, because <u>they</u> are not dangerous, and people can enjoy <u>them</u> with friends.

All of the underlined pronouns take the place of the phrase *swimming and bicycling*. The **referent** is *swimming and bicycling*.

In each of the following sentences, the pronoun is underlined. Circle the referent.

Example:

Running is not a new sport. People were doing <u>it</u> hundreds of years ago.

1. Runners know that a good diet is important. <u>They</u> eat healthy foods, especially before a race.

2. During a race, people along the road give water to the runners. <u>It</u> helps keep the runners from becoming too thirsty.

3. In Kenya and other parts of Africa, running is part of everyday life. <u>It</u> is a usual way for people to travel.

4. Many Africans are good runners. <u>They</u> often win marathons and races in the Olympics.

5. In some races, the winners get large amounts of money. In other races, <u>they</u> only get their picture in the newspaper.

Runners in the Boston Marathon.

**In this passage, the pronouns are underlined. Read the passage all the way to the end.
Then write the pronouns and their referents on the lines below.**

The Boston Marathon

Every year, in the middle of April, thousands of people go to Boston. <u>They</u> go to run in the Boston Marathon. <u>This</u> is one of the oldest road races in the United States. <u>It</u> began in 1897.

Each year, more runners join the Boston Marathon. <u>They</u> come from every part of the
5 world. In the 2003 marathon, there were 20,223 runners from almost every country in the world. About 17,500 of <u>them</u> finished <u>it</u>.

The Boston race is 26.2 miles, or 42 kilometers. <u>It</u> starts in Hopkinton, Massachusetts, and ends in the center of Boston. The runners go through 13 more towns during the race. Crowds of people watch <u>them</u> as <u>they</u> go through the towns. <u>They</u> cheer
10 for <u>them</u> and often offer <u>them</u> water.

Pronoun	Line Number	Referent
They	*1*	*people*

Underline the twenty pronouns in this passage. Write each pronoun, its line, and its referent below.

Figure Skating

Figure skating is a special kind of ice skating. It is a very popular sport in many countries. Every year, skating contests are shown on television. People around the world watch them and cheer for their favorite skaters.

The figure skaters wear beautiful clothes in the contests. They skate to music in a
5 kind of dance on ice. The skaters smile and try to look relaxed. They try to make the skating look easy. But, in fact, it is very difficult and they are usually very nervous. Even a small mistake can be terrible. It means they will lose points in the contest.

In each part of the contest, the skater must do many difficult jumps and turns. A group of special judges watches her carefully. They look at several things. First, they look
10 to see if the skater makes any mistakes. They also watch the way she moves. At the end of the contest, they decide how many points to give her.

Often there are lots of people watching the skating contest. When their favorite skaters finish, they throw flowers on the ice. The skaters are very tired, but they have to wait until the judges give them their points.

Pronoun	Line Number	Referent
It	1	ice (figure) skating

More about pronouns

Sometimes a pronoun can take the place of several words or phrases, or even a sentence.

Example a:

Anita and Helena couldn't find their car in the parking lot at the mall. <u>That</u> is why they were so late for dinner.

Pronoun	**Referent**
That	couldn't find their car

Example b:

Lilly and Harry had to clean the kitchen, shop for food, and cook dinner. They had to get <u>it</u> done before their mother returned home from her trip.

Pronoun	**Referent**
it	clean the kitchen, shop for food, and cook dinner

EXERCISE 13

Some pronouns in these passages are underlined. Circle the referents.

Example:

Two Frenchmen went up in a basket under a balloon. <u>They</u> built a fire to make the air hot. <u>This</u> made the balloon stay up in the air.

1. The pilot of a balloon can control its altitude. <u>He</u> or <u>she</u> can raise and lower the balloon to find the right wind direction. <u>That</u> is how a good pilot can control where the balloon goes.

2. Early photographers had to carry film and heavy equipment everywhere <u>they</u> went. But <u>this</u> did not stop them.

3. Helen Keller was deaf and blind. <u>She</u> could not speak until she was seven years old. <u>That</u> did not stop her. <u>She</u> became a famous writer and teacher.

4. A tornado is a dangerous storm. <u>It</u> brings strong winds, and <u>it</u> travels very fast. The strong winds can turn over cars, destroy houses, and kill people. And <u>this</u> happens in just a few minutes.

5. Tornadoes blow dust and dirt into the air. <u>They</u> make a cone shape in the sky. When people see <u>this</u>, <u>they</u> get ready for the storm.

6. When tornadoes touch the ground, <u>they</u> move along at about 35 to 45 kilometers per hour. No one knows which way <u>they</u> will go.

7. In a small town, a tornado can destroy an entire street of homes and stores. Many families lose their homes. The government tries to help <u>them</u> when <u>this</u> happens.

8. Tornadoes are common in Kansas, Arkansas, Nebraska, Iowa, and Missouri. People in <u>those</u> states worry when they see a cone-shaped cloud in the sky. <u>It</u> tells <u>them</u> a tornado is coming.

9. The wind of a tornado is strong. No one knows exactly how fast <u>it</u> is in the center. The wind always breaks the machines used to measure <u>it</u>!

Synonyms: General and specific

Synonyms are different words or phrases that refer to the same idea. A writer uses synonyms to tie ideas together. You can understand more if you pay attention to synonyms. Read the following sentences:

Sam and Susan Diamond visited London, Edinburgh, and Glasgow last year. They enjoyed the many museums in <u>those cities</u>. It was their first visit to <u>that part of the world</u>.

"Those cities" is a synonym for "London, Edinburgh, and Glasgow." "That part of the world" is another synonym for "London, Edinburgh, and Glasgow."

1. **Specific:** "London, Edinburgh, Glasgow"
2. **Less specific:** "those cities"
3. **General:** "that part of the world"

EXERCISE 14

Put the following synonyms in order from specific to general. Write "1" above the most specific word or phrase. Write "2" above the less specific word or phrase. Write "3" above the most general word or phrase.

Example:

    1   3   2

  dog   animal   pet

1. music, rock music, twentieth-century music

2. Japanese mountain, Mount Fuji, mountain

3. problems, water pollution problems, pollution problems

4. plant, flower, rose

5. violin, musical instrument, stringed instrument

6. Chile, country, South American country

7. man, Dr. Diamond, dentist

8. place, Montreal, city

9. The *New York Times*, newspaper, reading material

10. group, Diamond family, people

In each passage, there is a word underlined. Find and circle the synonym(s) for it in the passage.

Example:

Liz and Jeff moved to Paris last month. They like the (city) very much.

1. Chrys was born in London, but she lives in Glasgow now. She has learned to love Scotland. It is her new home.

2. Hiroko has a very old violin from Italy. The sound of this stringed instrument is very special.

3. The president of the city council gave a long speech. As the leader, she has to plan many new projects.

4. The tornado hit a small town in Kansas. The storm swept down the main street. Terrible winds destroyed homes, stores, and cars on the street.

5. Lemons, limes, and oranges are all delicious to eat. These citrus fruits are also healthy for you. They are a good source of vitamin C.

6. Many Americans skip breakfast. They say they do not have time for food in the morning. This is a mistake. The human body needs that meal.

7. Yesterday we looked at an apartment with a very nice kitchen. It was a large room with lots of sunlight and lots of space for cooking.

8. We saw a lion with three little cubs at the wild animal park. They were lying on the rocks in the warm afternoon sun. It was nice to see a whole family of these beautiful cats.

9. In some countries, the winter is long and cold. It is not a popular season. Some people are so unhappy at that time of the year that they get sick.

10. Astronauts all have one problem: They get motion sickness. This illness makes it difficult to do their work. Doctors and scientists are working on this problem.

Learning to Look for the Topic

What Is a Topic?

A **topic** is a word or phrase (a few words) that tells what something is about. For example, a friend might ask you, "What's this book about?" Your friend doesn't want to know everything about the book. He or she just wants to know the topic. You would answer your friend with something like, "It's about mountain climbing," or "It's about the Second World War."

In this unit, you'll learn to look for the topic when you read. The topic is the key to understanding what you read. It also helps you remember. A good reader always asks, "What is this about? What is the topic?"

Finding the Topic

In the groups of words in the following examples, one of the words is the topic for all the other words. You will choose which word is the topic. You may not know the meaning of all the words, but don't use a dictionary when you work on these exercises. Work with another student and try to guess the meaning of any new words. After you finish each exercise, you may look in the dictionary to get the meaning of words you couldn't guess.

Example a:

Sometimes the topic is the name of a group of things.

Which word is the topic? Clrcle the topic and write it on the line. Don't use the dictionary.

1. The topic is _sports_. (The other words are names of sports.)

   football   baseball   tennis   (sports)   skiing

2. The topic is ________________.

   carrots   peas   potatoes   vegetables   onions   beans

Example b:

Sometimes the topic is the name of something with many parts.

Which word is the topic? Circle the topic and write it on the line. Don't use the dictionary.

1. The topic is _Europe_. (The other words are parts of Europe.)

   France   Germany   Italy   (Europe)   Belgium   Austria

2. The topic is ________________.

   nose   ears   eyes   mouth   head   chin

Circle the topic in each group of words. Then write the topic on the line. Work with another student. Don't use the dictionary.

1. Topic: _______________

   mother   sister   uncle   brother   aunt   family

2. Topic: _______________

   nine   sixteen   number   eighty   thirty-two   seventy-seven

3. Topic: _______________

   dog   elephant   lion   animal   horse   mouse

4. Topic: _______________

   bedroom   bathroom   house   dining room   kitchen   living room

5. Topic: _______________

   refrigerator   oven   microwave   kitchen   stove   sink

6. Topic: _______________

   Paris   Moscow   Tokyo   Beijing   Los Angeles   City

7. Topic: _______________

   bread   fruit   vegetables   food   cheese   meat

8. Topic: _______________

   music   food   people   games   party   laughing

9. Topic: _______________

   table   furniture   chair   chest   sofa   bed

10. Topic: _______________

    shirt   skirt   suit   clothes   dress   socks

Check the dictionary for any words that you couldn't guess.

EXERCISE 2

Circle the topic in each group of words. Then write the topic on the line. Work with another student. Don't use the dictionary.

1. Topic: _______________

   milk   orange juice   coffee   drink   water   tea

2. Topic: _______________

   dollar   euro   yen   ruble   money   peso

3. Topic: _______________

   bus   airplane   train   travel   boat   ship

4. Topic: _______________

   engine   windows   doors   car   brakes   tires

5. Topic: _______________________
   river   lake   water   ocean   sea   pond

6. Topic: _______________________
   teacher   students   books   classroom   pencils   desks

7. Topic: _______________________
   doctor   nurse   hospital   beds   patients   medicine

8. Topic: _______________________
   happy   sad   feeling   excited   angry   bored

9. Topic: _______________________
   keyboard   hard drive   monitor   computer   mouse   software

10. Topic: _______________________
    oxygen   nitrogen   helium   neon   hydrogen   gas

Check the dictionary for any words that you couldn't guess.

Thinking of the Topic

In the following exercises, the topic is not included in the group of words. You must think of a topic for the words.

Read all the words in each group. What is the topic? Write it on the line. Work with another student. Don't use the dictionary.

Example:

Topic: *Things for eating and drinking* _______________
knife   spoon   cup   bowl   fork   chopsticks

1. Topic: _______________________
   subway   metro   bicycle   car   train   bus

2. Topic: _______________________
   hospital   factory   library   restaurant   hotel   bank

3. Topic: _______________________
   table of contents   index   title page   chapters   cover   pages

4. Topic: _______________________
   red   purple   pink   green   blue   yellow

5. Topic: _______________________
   physics   chemistry   astronomy   biology   geology   biochemistry

6. Topic: _______________________________________
   cheese   milk   ice cream   butter   cream   yogurt

7. Topic: _______________________________________
   morning   afternoon   noon   midnight   dusk   evening

8. Topic: _______________________________________
   bicycling   running   swimming   skating   skiing   gymnastics

Check the dictionary for any words that you couldn't guess.

EXERCISE 4

Read all the words in each group. What is the topic? Write it on the line. Work with another student. Don't use the dictionary.

1. Topic: _______________________________________
   apples   bananas   papayas   oranges   plums   pears

2. Topic: _______________________________________
   Mercury   Venus   Saturn   Mars   Jupiter   Uranus

3. Topic: _______________________________________
   dollar   quarter   penny   dime   nickel   silver dollar

4. Topic: _______________________________________
   driveway   expressway   highway   street   turnpike   avenue

5. Topic: _______________________________________
   Nevada   California   Arizona   Wyoming   New Mexico   Montana

6. Topic: _______________________________________
   homesickness   joy   anger   sadness   pride   fear

7. Topic: _______________________________________
   Kennedy   Washington   Clinton   Carter   Bush   Lincoln

8. Topic: _______________________________________
   war   hunger   sickness   many poor people   few jobs   crime

Check the dictionary for any words that you couldn't guess.

Read the words in each group. One word does not belong with the others. Cross out the word that does not belong. Then write the topic on the line. Work with another student. Don't use the dictionary.

Example:

Topic: *Cities in the United States*

Boston   New York   Chicago   ~~Paris~~   San Francisco   Los Angeles

1. Topic: _______________________________
   ice cream   cake   carrots   cookies   chocolate   pudding

2. Topic: _______________________________
   Amazon   Ganges   Danube   Atlantic   Nile   Yangtze

3. Topic: _______________________________
   hat   gloves   swimsuit   scarf   mittens   jacket

4. Topic: _______________________________
   February   April   March   June   January   Tuesday

5. Topic: _______________________________
   television   radio   piano   CD player   MP3 player   boom box

6. Topic: _______________________________
   teacher   scientist   lawyer   husband   doctor   taxi driver

7. Topic: _______________________________
   box   bag   pocket   table   backpack   basket

8. Topic: _______________________________
   roof   wall   chair   window   door   floor

Check the dictionary for any words that you couldn't guess.

Finding Two Topics

Divide each group of words into the two topics given. Then write the words under the topics. Work with another student.

Example:

ladder	concert	sports	movie
stairs	elevator	quiz show	escalator

Topic A Ways to go up

Topic B Things to watch on TV

1.

Zimbabwe	Buddhist	Ethiopia	Catholic	Muslim
Jewish	Nigeria	Christian	Zambia	Kenya

Topic A African countries

Topic B World religions

2.

mountains	ocean	lake	forest	prairie
desert	river	stream	field	sea

Topic A Bodies of water

Topic B Geography

3.

| Mexico | Australia | Guatemala | Ireland | El Salvador |
| Honduras | Scotland | England | Costa Rica | Canada |

Topic A Spanish-speaking
        countries

Topic B English-speaking
        countries

_______________________   _______________________
_______________________   _______________________
_______________________   _______________________
_______________________   _______________________
_______________________   _______________________

4.

| hour | baggage claim | check-in | waiting area | minute |
| security | month | year | century | gate |

Topic A Ways to measure time

Topic B Parts of an airport

_______________________   _______________________
_______________________   _______________________
_______________________   _______________________
_______________________   _______________________
_______________________   _______________________

5.

| cold | wind | octagon | triangle | ice |
| rectangle | rain | square | circle | snow |

Topic A Weather

Topic B Geometric shapes

_______________________   _______________________
_______________________   _______________________
_______________________   _______________________
_______________________   _______________________
_______________________   _______________________

Divide each group of words into two topics. Write the two topics. Then write the words under the topics. Work with another student.

1.

| armchair | table | book | bookcase | magazine |
| newspaper | lamp | sofa | letter | map |

Topic A ___________________________ **Topic B** ___________________________

___________________________ ___________________________

___________________________ ___________________________

___________________________ ___________________________

___________________________ ___________________________

___________________________ ___________________________

2.

| scream | loud | talk | easy | shout |
| good | tell | beautiful | difficult | whisper |

Topic A ___________________________ **Topic B** ___________________________

___________________________ ___________________________

___________________________ ___________________________

___________________________ ___________________________

___________________________ ___________________________

___________________________ ___________________________

3.

| foot | arm | stomach | leg | heart |
| liver | kidneys | lungs | hand | neck |

Topic A ___________________________ **Topic B** ___________________________

___________________________ ___________________________

___________________________ ___________________________

___________________________ ___________________________

___________________________ ___________________________

4.

| actors | telephone | file cabinet | camera operators | musicians |
| computer | director | producer | chair | desk |

Topic A _______________________________   **Topic B** _______________________________

_______________________________   _______________________________

_______________________________   _______________________________

_______________________________   _______________________________

_______________________________   _______________________________

5.

| jazz | classical | drum | accordion | folk |
| trumpet | guitar | rock | blues | piano |

Topic A _______________________________   **Topic B** _______________________________

_______________________________   _______________________________

_______________________________   _______________________________

_______________________________   _______________________________

_______________________________   _______________________________

Working with Topics

Now you will write the words for some topics. You may use a dictionary for this exercise.

EXERCISE 8

Think of words for these topics. Write the words on the lines below. Then talk to another student about his or her words. Are they the same as yours?

1. Topic: Interesting jobs

____

____

____

____

____

2. Topic: Parts of a bus

____

____

____

____

____

3. Topic: Reasons for learning English

____

____

____

____

____

4. Topic: _______________________________
(Now you write the topic.)

____

____

____

____

____

Understanding Paragraphs

What Is a Paragraph?

A **paragraph** is a group of sentences. Every sentence in a paragraph is about the same topic. In this unit, you'll first learn how to find the topic of a paragraph. Then you'll learn how to find the main idea of a paragraph. The topic and the main idea are important. They help you to understand the meaning quickly and help you to remember what you read.

Example:

This is a good paragraph. All of the sentences are about one topic: the violin family of instruments.

There are several instruments in the violin family. The violin is the most popular. It is an important instrument in the classical orchestra. It is also played in jazz and country music groups. The cello and the viola have the same shape as a violin, but they are bigger. They are used mostly in classical music. The biggest stringed instrument is the bass. It's so big you have to stand up when you play it. The bass is played in classical orchestras, and it is also often played in jazz groups.

This is <u>not</u> a good paragraph. The sentences are <u>not</u> about one topic.

Violins are made of wood. The best old pianos were made in Germany. Musicians spend a lot of time practicing. Sometimes they play for eight hours a day. Most violinists stand up when they play alone. Taking music lessons can be expensive. The kind of wood in a violin is important. Many famous musicians started to study at an early age.

Read each group of sentences. Remember, in a good paragraph, every sentence is about the same topic. Which ones are good paragraphs? Check (✓) Yes or No. If you check Yes, write the topic. Work with another student.

1.   It's easy to make a good cup of tea. The first people to grow coffee beans lived in the Middle East. Most of the oranges for juice grow in Florida. California is another place for growing oranges. That is how people in other parts of the world learned about rice. Cover the pot and wait a few minutes.

Is this a good paragraph? Yes _____ No _____

If yes, what is it about? ____

2.   A doctor's job is not easy. Doctors often spend many hours with patients. There are usually more patients waiting. So doctors don't have much free time during the day. They often have to work all night in the hospital, too. They must also read about new ways of taking care of patients, and they must write reports about people in their care.

Is this a good paragraph? Yes _____ No _____

If yes, what is it about? ____

3.   In the United States, sports stars make a lot of money. It's not unusual for a basketball player to get $6 million a year. Some baseball players are also paid millions of dollars. These sports stars also get extra money from sporting equipment companies. For example, manufacturers pay sports stars to wear the shoes they make.

Is this a good paragraph? Yes _____ No _____

If yes, what is it about? ____

4.   In some countries, students can go to college for free. It's often difficult to get a good job in a small town. Students often leave small towns to study in the city. The populations of most countries are growing quickly. Many families have five or six children. In the winter, there is always a lot of snow in Maine.

Is this a good paragraph? Yes _____ No _____

If yes, what is it about? ____

Choosing the Best Topic

A good reader always asks, "What is this paragraph about? What is the topic?"

The best topic is one that is not too specific and not too general. When you buy a new pair of shoes, you choose a pair that is just right. Not too small, and not too large. And when you choose a topic, you must choose one that is not too specific (too small) and not too general (too large).

Example:

Read this paragraph. Ask yourself, "What is it about?"

Miami is a popular place for tourists, especially in winter. In fact, this part of Florida always has warm, sunny weather. Miami is on the seaside, and it has beautiful beaches. These beaches are one important reason why people go to Miami. But the city is also fun to visit. There are brightly colored homes and hotels along many streets. There are many interesting museums, and there are dozens of restaurants with great food.

What is the topic? Circle the letter of the topic. Then write "too specific" or "too general" after the other two topics.

a. Restaurants in Miami   *too specific*

b. Popular places for tourists   *too general*

c. Why tourists like Miami   ___________________

The best choice is *c, Why tourists like Miami.* It tells what the paragraph is about. Every sentence tells something that tourists like about Miami. Choice *a* is too specific. There is only one sentence in the paragraph that is about food. Choice *b* is too general. The paragraph is not about every popular place for tourists. It is only about Miami.

Read each paragraph. Ask yourself, "What is it about?" Circle the letter of the topic. Then write "too specific" or "too general" after the other two topics. Work with another student.

The Florida Everglades

1. The Everglades is in the center of south Florida. It is a wild area with no towns or houses. The Everglades is famous for its wildlife and plants. Some of these plants and animals live only in the Everglades. They live there because of the warm climate and water. In fact, the Everglades has lots of water. In the middle of the Everglades is a very wide river, called the "River of Grass." It changes with the seasons. In the rainy season (May through October) it is 50 miles (80 kilometers) wide in some places.

a. The climate of Florida ___________________

b. Plants and wildlife   ___________________

c. The Florida Everglades ___________________

2.   The animals in the Everglades have to move with the seasons. During the
dry season, from November to April, most of the river is dry. Snakes, fish, frogs,
and other water animals move to the deeper pools of water. Alligators stay near
the pools to eat the fish. Some birds make their nests nearby so they can also
eat the fish in the pools. Then, in May, the spring rains begin. The animals
start moving to other parts of the Everglades. They know there will be more
water and food everywhere.

   a. Animals in the Everglades   ____________________

   b. The dry season in the Everglades   ____________________

   c. Why Everglades animals move   ____________________

3.   Water is very important to plants and wildlife in the Everglades. But these
days, there is less water for the Everglades. The population of Florida is
growing fast. Nine hundred people move to the state every day. To get water
for all these people, the towns and cities of south Florida are digging lots of
deep wells. They are also taking water from the River of Grass. Because of this,
the river is becoming smaller, even in the wet season. These changes are not
good for the wildlife of the Everglades. Many plants and animals could die.

   a. Florida's growing population   ____________________

   b. Water problems in Florida   ____________________

   c. Animal and plant life   ____________________

Read each paragraph. Ask yourself, "What is it about?" Circle the letter of the topic. Then write "too specific" or "too general" after the other two topics. Work with another student.

Forests

1.   Some of the largest trees in the world are in California. These are called *redwood trees*. Redwood National Park is a large forest of redwood trees. Visitors in the park can walk and drive through the forest to look at the trees. Some redwoods are hundreds of years old. They are very tall and are very wide at the bottom. One tree has a large hole at the bottom of it. The hole is so big you can drive a car through it.

   a. Parks in California   _______________________

   b. Redwood trees in California   _______________________

   c. The age of redwood trees   _______________________

2.   In many hilly areas of Scotland, there once were large forests. These forests had rich dirt that was good for plants. The trees in the forest kept the dirt in place. But over many years, people cut down the trees. They needed the wood for burning and they needed the land for farming. With no trees, a lot of the good dirt was washed away by the rain. The land became rocky and not good for farming. Now the Scottish government wants to make the land better again. It is planting new trees. These new forests look nice and green. They also will improve the land for the future.

   a. Forests in the future   _______________________

   b. Rocky hills in Scotland   _______________________

   c. The forests of Scotland   _______________________

3.   Large forests are important to us in many ways. They give us wood for building and heating. They are a home for many kinds of plants and animals. For many city people, forests are a place to go for a vacation. There they can learn about nature, breathe fresh air, and sleep in a quiet place. There is one more reason why forests are important for everyone. The leaves on trees help clean the air. Dirty air is a serious problem in many parts of the world. Without our forests, this problem might be even worse.

   a. The importance of forests   _______________________

   b. Taking vacations in forests   _______________________

   c. Large forests around the world   _______________________

Thinking of the Topic

In Exercises 4 through 7, the topic is not given. Read each paragraph and ask yourself, "What is this about? What is the topic?" Think carefully—the topic should not be too specific or too general.

Example:

Read the paragraph and then write the topic on the line below.

The earth is getting warmer. This is called *global warming.* Scientists have done research on the temperature of places around the world. They say that the earth's temperature is higher now than it was years ago. As a result, the climate is changing in many countries. There are more storms, and the storms are stronger. The summers are hotter in some places, and the winters are colder.

Topic: *Changes in the earth's climate*

The topic for this paragraph should include the idea of climate and the idea of change. There are a number of ways you could say this. *Changes in the earth's climate* is one possibility. Other answers are possible if they give the same ideas and are not too specific or too general. For example, *Temperatures around the world* is too specific and *Weather problems* is too general.

EXERCISE 4

Read each paragraph. Working with another student, decide on the topic. Be sure your topic is not too general or too specific. Write the topic below the paragraph.

Some Facts about Weather

1. When there is a heavy rainstorm, you sometimes see lightning, which is a bright flash of light in the sky. In the past, people thought lightning came from an angry god. In the 1700s, Benjamin Franklin found out that lightning was electricity. Storms with lightning really are electrical storms. Scientists today still do not know everything about lightning, however. They do not know exactly what it comes from, and they never know where and how it will hit the earth.

    Topic: ____

2. All clouds are made of many little drops of water. But not all clouds are alike. There are three kinds of clouds. Cirrus clouds are one kind. These are made of ice drops. They look soft and light. Cumulus clouds are another kind of cloud. They are large and deep and flat on the bottom. We usually see cumulus clouds on warm summer days. Finally, there are stratus clouds, which cover the whole sky. These clouds make the sky gray, and the sun does not shine at all.

    Topic: ____

3.   Fog is really a cloud near the ground. Both fog and clouds are made of many little drops of water. These drops stay in the air because they are so small. You cannot see each drop, but fog can make it hard to see other things. It can be dangerous if you are driving, for example. Sometimes where there is a lot of fog you cannot see the road. Sailors also have trouble when there is fog. Boats may get lost and hit rocks or beaches in the fog,

Topic: ____

Read each paragraph. Working with another student, decide on the topic. Be sure your topic is not too general or too specific. Write the topic below the paragraph.

The Use of Water

1.   In the United States, drinking water comes from a few different places. Many cities get their drinking water from special lakes called *reservoirs*. Other cities get their water from lakes and rivers. For example, the drinking water for New Orleans comes from the Mississippi River. In some areas, people get their water from the mountains. The water from mountain snow is delicious and clean. In other areas, people dig deep holes in the ground for water. These holes are called *wells*. Outside of cities, most people get their water this way.

Topic: ____

2.   Many American scientists are worried about the drinking water in the United States. They think that soon there may be no more clean drinking water. Dirt, salt, and chemicals from factories can get into the water, making it unsafe to drink. This is already true in some places. One example is a small town in Massachusetts. Many children in this town became sick because of chemicals in the water. Another place with water problems is California. The water near old air force airports is not safe to drink. Chemicals from rockets got into the ground and then into the water.

Topic: ____

3.   It's important to use water carefully. Here are some ways you can use less water. First, be sure to turn off faucets tightly. They should not drip in the bathroom or kitchen sink. Second, do not keep the water running for a long time. Turn it off while you are doing something else. For example, it should be off while you are shaving or brushing your teeth. It should also be off while you are washing the dishes. Finally, in the summer you should water your garden in the evening. That way you will not lose a lot of water. During the day, the sun dries up the earth too quickly.

Topic: ____

Read each paragraph. Working with another student, decide on the topic. Be sure your topic is not too general or too specific. Write the topic below the paragraph.

Galileo Galilei

1.   Galileo Galilei was one of the first modern scientists. He was born in Pisa, Italy, in 1564. At first he studied philosophy, but later he studied mathematics and astronomy. He was interested in the way the earth and other planets move around the sun. He found out several important facts about our world. He also started a new way of working in science. Before Galileo, scientists did not do experiments. They just guessed about how something happened. Galileo was different. He did not just make guesses. He did experiments and watched to see what happened.

Topic: ____

2.   Galileo is famous for his study of gravity (how and why things fall). He was the first person to do experiments about this problem. Before, people thought that heavy things always fell faster than light things. He found out that this was not true. He took a heavy ball and a light ball and he dropped them both from a high place. They fell at the same speed. This meant that weight was not important. This is the law of falling bodies. It is an important law for understanding our world.

Topic: ____

3.   The life of a scientist was not always easy in the 1500s. In fact, Galileo got into trouble because of his scientific ideas. His ideas were not the same as the religious ideas at the time. Many religious people did not agree with him. During his whole life, he had to worry about this. He even went to prison for a while. But no one could stop him from thinking. He continued to look for scientific answers to his questions about the world.

Topic: ____

This exercise is a bit different. In each paragraph, one sentence does not belong with the others. Cross out that sentence. Then write the topic below the paragraph. Work with another student.

Travel by Train

Example:

There are several reasons why people travel by train. Some people use the train to go to work every day. It's faster and easier than driving a car. ~~Some cars now have a special map to help you.~~ Tourists often travel by train when they go on vacation. In European countries, for example, the train is a good way to visit different cities. Some people take the train just because they love trains. Their hobby is traveling on the railroads of the world.

Topic: *Reasons why people travel by train*

1. The Trans-Siberian Railroad in Russia is the longest continuous rail line on earth. It's almost 6,000 miles (or about 10,000 kilometers) long. Tourists ride this train because it is a very special experience. They get on the train in Moscow and get off seven days later in the Far East. Or if they want, they can stop and visit places on the way. Other tourists stay in Moscow to visit museums and churches.

   Topic: ____

2. One of the most exciting train rides in Europe is the trip from Geneva, Switzerland, to Milan, Italy. Geneva is a city near the Alps Mountains. In Geneva, the United Nations has many offices. The train goes around tall mountains, and then it goes through a tunnel. When the train comes out of the tunnel, it is in the middle of the Alps! The view from the window is too beautiful for words.

   Topic: ____

3. Not all train travel is for tourists or railroad fans. In the United States, most train travel is for commuting to work. Many Americans commute more than an hour each way to work. Commuting by train can be pleasant. People can read, work, drink coffee, chat with other passengers, or sleep. It's important to get a good night's sleep. On some commuter trains, small groups of people get to know each other. Sometimes they play cards or chat as they commute to work.

   Topic: ____

Main Ideas of Paragraphs

The *main idea* of a paragraph is usually stated in one sentence. It tells the writer's idea about the topic. The main idea sentence is important. There can be many paragraphs about the same topic, but they do not all have the same main idea.

Example a:

In this example, the topic is *elephants*. The three sentences below are three different main ideas about the topic, elephants. Can you think of another one?

1. Elephants live in Africa and Asia.
2. Elephants are killed for their ivory tusks.
3. Elephants can cause serious problems for farmers.

Write another main idea sentence about elephants. (Make sure that you write a complete sentence, not just a topic.)

____

____

Example b:

In this example, the topic is *television shows*.

Write three different main idea sentences about television shows. Then show your sentences to another student. Are they the same as yours?

1. ____

2. ____

3. ____

Example c:

In this paragraph, the topic is *bicycles*. What is the author's main idea about bicycles?

> In some parts of the world, many people use bicycles for transportation. First of all, they are much cheaper than cars. They also do not need gas to make them go. And bicycles are easy and cheap to fix. In cities, bicyclists don't have to wait in traffic. They can always go around a traffic jam. Finally, bicycles don't need parking spaces. They can be parked anywhere.

Circle the letter of the best main idea. Work with another student.

a. Bicycles are cheaper than cars.

b. Bicycles are a problem in traffic.

c. Bicycles are good for transportation.

The best choice is *c, Bicycles are good for transportation*. This is the writer's main idea about bicycles. All the information in the paragraph is about this idea. Choice *a* is not correct because it is too specific. It is only one part of the paragraph. Choice *b* is not correct because the paragraph does not say bicycles are a problem in traffic. In fact, it says that bicycles have no problems with traffic.

Choosing the Best Main Idea

Read each paragraph. Ask yourself, "What is the topic? What is the writer's main idea about the topic?" Circle the letter of the best main idea. Work with another student.

Some Ideas about Clothes

1. Clothes can tell you a lot about a person. Some people like very colorful clothes. They want everyone to look at them. They want to be the center of things. Other people like to wear nice clothes, but their clothes are plain, not colorful or fancy. They don't like people to look at them. There are also some people who wear the same thing all the time. They don't care if anyone looks at them or not. They don't care what anyone thinks about them.

    a. Some people wear colorful clothes.

    b. Clothes can tell you a lot about a person.

    c. Some clothes are nice, but very plain.

2. It's important to bring the right clothes when you travel. If you're traveling to a cold country, you should bring warm clothes. Be sure you have a hat and gloves, too. If you're going to a hot country, you need different clothes. You don't want heavy or dark clothes. In hot weather, light clothes are best. If you're going to a city, you may need some nice clothes. You may want to go to a special restaurant or a concert. It's different if you're traveling by bicycle in the country. Then you'll want comfortable clothes. One rule is the same for all travelers, however. Do not bring too many clothes!

    a. The right clothes are important when you travel.

    b. Warm clothes are very important.

    c. Be sure to bring enough clothes when you travel.

3. Today's clothes are different from the clothes of the 1800s. One difference is the way they look. For example, in the 1800s all women wore dresses with long skirts. Today women don't always wear dresses with long skirts. Sometimes they wear short skirts, and sometimes they wear pants. Another difference between the 1800s and today is the cloth. In the 1800s, clothes were made only from natural kinds of cloth, such as cotton, wool, silk, and linen. Today, there are many kinds of man-made cloth, such as nylon, rayon, and polyester. A lot of clothes are made from these kinds of cloth.

    a. Clothes of the 1800s looked very different from today's clothes.

    b. A lot of clothes are made of man-made cloth today.

    c. Clothes today are different from the clothes of the 1800s.

Read each paragraph. Ask yourself, "What is the topic? What is the writer's main idea about the topic?" Circle the letter of the best main idea. Work with another student.

Chemistry in the Past

1.   Chemistry is an old science. People were always interested in chemicals. People who worked on chemicals before the 1700s are called *alchemists*. They did not study chemistry like modern chemists. Their kind of chemistry was called *alchemy*. They had some strange ideas. For example, they believed they could make gold by mixing together the right things. For hundreds of years, alchemists tried to do this. Of course, no one ever made gold this way.

   a. Alchemists never made gold.

   b. Alchemists lived before the 1700s.

   c. Alchemists studied chemicals in strange ways.

2.   Robert Boyle (1627–1691) is sometimes called the "father of chemistry." He started out as an alchemist, but he began to think in a different way. For example, alchemists thought that everything was made of four things—earth, air, fire, and water. But Boyle found that things are made up of many different *elements*. In fact, he wrote a definition of what an *element* is. He said that an element is something that cannot be broken into smaller parts. Boyle's work marked the end of alchemy as a science.

   a. Robert Boyle helped build the science of alchemy.

   b. Robert Boyle said everything is made of four elements.

   c. Robert Boyle helped to start the science of chemistry.

3.   Antoine Lavoisier (1743–1794) is important in the history of modern chemistry. In about 1776, he began to use a new way to study chemicals. Before Lavoisier, scientists just looked at something and thought about it. However, Lavoisier did experiments. He studied the size and weight of many different things. He found out something important. He found out that nothing really goes away. It just changes into something else. For example, when water boils, it doesn't go away. It becomes steam, a cloud of water. This was an important idea for the future of chemistry.

   a. Antoine Lavoisier used experiments to study chemicals.

   b. Antoine Lavoisier studied the size and weight of water.

   c. Antoine Lavoisier lived in the 1700s.

Read each paragraph. Ask yourself, "What is the topic? What is the writer's main idea about the topic?" Circle the letter of the best main idea. Work with another student.

Immigrants

1.   In some countries, jobs are hard to find. Many people can't find work, and they are very poor. But in other countries, especially in the United States, Canada, and Europe, there are more jobs. So the poor people move to these countries to look for work. They may leave their homes and families only for a few months or years. That's what some people from Romania and Ukraine do in Italy and Germany, for example. But many other people never return home. They decide to stay in their new country, and they become immigrants. That's what happens in the United States for many workers from Mexico and Central America.

a. Jobs are hard to find.

b. Many people look for work in foreign countries.

c. Some foreign workers never return home.

2.   When workers move to a new country, they often have problems. The first problem, of course, is language. Sometimes the immigrants can find jobs with other people from their home country. Then learning the language is not so important. But usually they need to know the language in order to work. The immigrants may also have problems with the people they meet. They may have trouble with neighbors or people at work because they are different. People may feel afraid of them because they have a different religion or a different skin color.

a. Immigrants learn new languages.

b. Immigrants can have problems in the new country.

c. Immigrants may have a different religion or skin color.

3.   When immigrants have children, they may be in a difficult situation. The parents usually continue to speak their native language at home. But when the children go to school, they soon learn the new language. So they speak one language at home and another language at school and with their friends. When they are older, however, they may not want to speak their parents' language anymore. They may want to be like their friends. Their parents may not be happy about this. And so there may be family problems and fights.

a. Immigrant children speak two languages.

b. Immigrant families have lots of children.

c. Immigrant parents and children may not agree.

Writing the Main Idea Sentence

The main idea can be written in several ways. Remember, the main idea must be a complete sentence. It must tell both the topic and the author's idea about the topic.

Read each paragraph. Ask yourself, "What is the topic? What is the writer's main idea about the topic?" Then write a main idea sentence.

What Science Tells Us about the Earth

1.   The earth is always changing. Some of the changes are caused by the weather. For example, in a desert, the wind blows the sand around. It makes the desert look different every year. Rain also causes changes. It washes away the dirt and even changes the shape of some rocks. Another kind of change is caused by rivers. When a river goes down a mountain, it cuts into the mountain. After a long time, the mountain is lower and the land is flatter.

Main idea: ____

____

2.   Mt. Vesuvius in Italy and Mt. St. Helens in the United States are both famous mountains, and they are similar. They are both volcanoes. A volcano is a mountain that is open at the top. Smoke and hot air come out of the hole. Sometimes, very hot rock also comes out of the hole. That can mean trouble for people nearby. This is what happened with Mt. Vesuvius and Mt. St. Helens. Hot rock poured out of Mt. Vesuvius and covered the city of Pompeii in 79 C.E. Many people in the city were killed. The Mt. St. Helens volcano didn't kill many people because there were no cities close to the mountain. However, the hot rock killed a large part of the forest on the mountain, and a lot of dust fell on cities many miles away.

Main idea: ____

____

3.   Scientists may know a lot about the outside of the earth, but they still are not sure about the inside. For example, they understand how mountains are made and what a volcano is, but they do not know when a volcano will send hot rock into the air. Scientists also are not sure about how the earth was made. They have many different ideas about this. There are still many difficult questions for scientists who study the earth.

Main idea: ____

____

Show your work to another student. Do you agree on the main ideas?

Read each paragraph. Ask yourself, "What is the topic? What is the writer's main idea about the topic?" Then write a main idea sentence.

Classified Ads in the Newspaper

1.   Not all newspaper ads are for selling things. Some ads are about people. The "Help Wanted" ads give information about jobs. All kinds of jobs are found in this part of the newspaper. There are ads for secretaries and electricians, doctors and professors. Another kind of ad about people is the "personal" ad. These ads are not about work. They are written by people who are looking for friends. Sometimes these people are even looking for husbands and wives. Newspaper ads are a good way to get people together.

Main idea: ____

____

2.   We can learn a lot about a country from the personal ads. These ads tell us about people and their problems. One example of this is from Spain. One small town in Spain had 42 men and not many women living in it. The men wanted to find wives, so they put a personal ad in a city newspaper. Some women living in the city were not happy living alone and answered the ad by telephone. They wanted to find out more about the town and the men. The women did not go to live in the town, however. They did not really want to work on farms. They did not really want to marry small-town men. So the men did not find wives, and the women are still alone. Not all men and women in Spain are like these people, but this ad may tell us something about larger problems in Spain.

Main idea: ____

____

3.   Personal ads are usually written for good reasons. Most of the people who write them really do want a friend. Sometimes though, people write personal ads for other reasons. They may write the ad as a joke. This is not a nice thing to do. The people who answer the ads may be unhappy. They may need a friend very much. Some of the people who write the ads can cause worse problems. They may want to hurt someone. So, if you answer a personal ad, you should be careful. The ad may not mean what it says.

Main idea: ____

____

Show your work to another student. Do you agree on the main ideas?

Finding the Pattern of Organization

Study these pictures for sixty seconds. Your teacher will time you. After sixty seconds, turn the page.

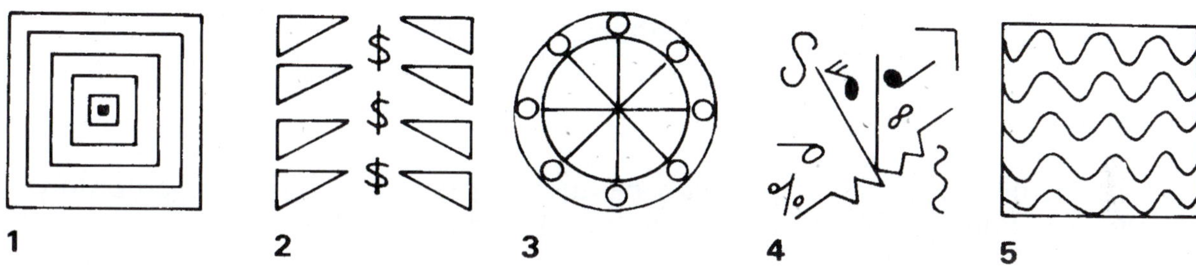

1   2   3   4   5

Now look back and check your drawings.

Which picture was the most difficult to remember?

Why?

Pictures 1, 2, 3, and 5 were easy because they have a pattern of organization. Picture 4 does not have a pattern, so it is more difficult to remember.

Introduction to Patterns

Patterns are important. We use them to help us understand and remember. In fact, without patterns, we could not live! For example, we know the pattern of our home—we can even find things in the dark. And we also have a time pattern in our daily lives—we don't have to decide every day when to have our meals and when to look for the mail. We follow the usual patterns.

The night sky is filled with millions of stars. People noticed long ago that they could see patterns in the stars. For thousands of years, travelers and sailors have used those star patterns to find their way.

In languages there are patterns, too, but each language has different patterns. To read well in English, you must be able to find the patterns used in English. They will help you understand and remember what you read.

In this unit, you'll learn how to recognize four patterns: *listing, time order, comparison,* and *cause/effect.* You'll learn the signal words that are used in each pattern.

The Listing Pattern

In this pattern, the writer gives a list of details to explain the main idea. The details are usually reasons or examples, and the writer uses a signal word to point out each detail.

Signal Words for the Listing Pattern:

first	and	one	last
second	also	another	finally
third	too	other	for example

Example a:

Read this paragraph. Find out why diamonds are expensive. Find the topic and main idea. Answer the question below.

Diamonds are expensive for several reasons. <u>First</u>, they are difficult to find. They are found in only a few places in the world. <u>Second</u>, they are useful. People use diamonds to cut other stones. <u>Third</u>, diamonds do not change. They stay the same for millions of years. <u>Finally</u>, diamonds are beautiful.

Topic: *Diamonds*

Main idea: *Diamonds are expensive for several reasons.*

How many reasons are given? *Four*

The main idea sentence tells you that this paragraph will give a list of reasons. The underlined words are signal words. They help you recognize the listing pattern. There is a signal word for each reason, so it is easy to find them.

Signal Words	Details (reasons)
first	*difficult to find*
second	*useful*
third	*do not change*
finally	*beautiful*

Example b:

Read this paragraph. How many different kinds of pollution does it mention? Find the topic and main idea. Underline the signal words and write them below.

There are many different kinds of pollution. One kind is air pollution. This is caused by burning oil, coal, and gas. It also comes from factories. Water pollution is another problem. Waste and chemicals are found in many rivers, lakes, and oceans. Pollution of the earth is also a very big problem. Farms, factories, and hospitals all add dangerous chemicals to the earth. Yet another kind of pollution is noise pollution. This is especially a problem near big cities and airports.

Topic: *Pollution*

Main idea: *There are many different kinds of pollution.*

Write the signal words.

Signal Words	Details (kinds of pollution)
___________	*air pollution*
___________	*water pollution*
___________	*pollution of the earth*
___________	*noise pollution*

Read each paragraph. Write the topic and main idea. Underline the signal words and then write the signal words and details.

Computers Today

1. Computers are helpful in many ways. First, they are fast. They work with information much more quickly than a person's brain can work. Second, computers can work with lots of information at the same time. Third, they keep information for a long time. They don't forget things the way people do. Also, computers are almost always correct. They are not perfect, of course, but they usually do not make mistakes.

Topic: ____

Main idea: ____

____

Signal Words   **Details**

______________________   _______________________________

______________________   _______________________________

______________________   _______________________________

______________________   _______________________________

2. Computers come in all shapes and sizes. For example, large computers are used in many places. Big office buildings have special large computers. These computers take care of the lights, heat, and air-conditioning. Other, smaller computers are found in homes and offices. They are used for work, for information, or for fun. Many people have small personal computers called *notebooks* or *laptops*. They are especially useful for people who need computers when they travel. Finally, many new computers are so tiny that you cannot see them at all. These computers are everywhere: in telephones, televisions, cameras, cell phones, and cars.

Topic: ____

Main idea: ____

____

Signal Words   **Details**

______________________   _______________________________

______________________   _______________________________

______________________   _______________________________

Read each paragraph. Write the topic and main idea. Underline the signal words and then write the signal words and details.

Computers and Communication

1. There are many programs that let computers "talk" to each other. For example, in many workplaces, the computers are in a network. People can use them to work together on a job. The computer cash registers in supermarkets also work together. These computers "tell" a computer in the main office about the business. Then the owners of the supermarket can find out what people like to buy. Finally, people can connect their home computers to the Internet. The Internet makes it possible for computers around the world to connect with each other and "talk."

Topic: ____

Main idea: ____

____

Signal Words   **Details**

_________________   _____________________________

_________________   _____________________________

_________________   _____________________________

2. Computer language can be funny at times. For example, we say computers have a "memory." We know they do not really remember or think. But we still say "memory." Also, computer programs have "menus." Of course, we are not talking about restaurants or food. This is a different kind of menu, one for choosing a program or section of the memory. Another example is the "mouse" we use to "talk to" the computer. It's hard not to think about a real mouse when you hear the word. But there are no little gray animals in the machine.

Topic: ____

Main idea: ____

Signal Words   **Details**

_________________   _____________________________

_________________   _____________________________

_________________   _____________________________

Read each paragraph. Write the topic and main idea. Underline the signal words and then write the signal words and details.

Using Computers for Fun

1.   People find many ways to use their home computer for fun. First of all, there are thousands of computer games. These can be played by one or two people, or even in groups. Second, people can use the DVD on their home computer to watch movies. They can also download movies from the Internet and watch them at home. And last, probably the most popular way computers are used for fun is sharing music with friends. Music that is on a friend's computer can be sent over the Internet to many people.

Topic: ____

Main idea: ____

____

Signal Words   **Details**

________________________   ________________________

________________________   ________________________

________________________   ________________________

2.   Because of the Internet, people can use their computer to meet other people around the world. One way that they do this is by visiting a chat room. There are chat rooms about every subject. Sometimes people who meet in a chat room want to meet in person. Sometimes people even get married to someone they met in a chat room. Another way to meet other people is by signing up on a list serve. Everyone on the list can send messages to everyone else on the list. You can find people who are interested in the same things you are. The problem with a list serve is that you might get hundreds of e-mail messages every day!

Topic: ____

Main idea: ____

____

Signal Words   **Details**

________________________   ________________________

________________________   ________________________

Writing exercise: *On a separate piece of paper, write a paragraph using the listing pattern. Write about one of these topics, or choose a topic of your own. Remember to use the signal words for the listing pattern in your paragraph.*

- My favorite places to go for a vacation
- The importance of a good night's sleep
- Special holiday foods
- My favorite computer games

The Time Order Pattern

In the time order pattern, the writer tells how one thing follows another. A writer uses this pattern in two ways: to tell a story and to explain the steps in doing something.

Signal Words for the Time Order Pattern:

- Dates and times (years, ages, days)
- Other words:

first	before	soon	while	at last
next	after	then	during	finally
last		later		

Example a: Events in a story

Read this time order paragraph. Answer the questions below.

Albert Einstein lived and worked as a physicist in several countries. He was born in <u>1879</u> in Ulm, Germany. At the <u>age of twenty-six</u>, he graduated from the University of Zurich in Switzerland. In the <u>same year</u>, he did his most famous work in physics. In <u>1921</u>, he won the Nobel Prize for Physics. Between <u>1919 and 1933</u>, he lived in Germany. He also traveled a lot to talk with other scientists. <u>Then</u> he had to leave Germany because of Hitler and the Nazi Party. He moved to the United States in <u>1933</u> and began working in Princeton, New Jersey. Einstein died there on <u>April 18, 1955.</u>

What is the topic of this paragraph? _______________________________________

What is the main idea? _______________________________________

The time order signal words are underlined. Each signal word points to a major event in the life of Albert Einstein.

Here are the signal words. Write the details.

Signal Words	Details (events)
_1879_	_Albert Einstein was born in Ulm, Germany._
age of twenty-six	
same year	
_1921_	
1919 and 1933	
Then	
_1933_	
April 18, 1955	

Example b: Steps in doing something

Read this time order paragraph. Answer the questions below.

Big companies in Florida make orange juice entirely by machine. <u>First</u>, the oranges are placed in a big washing machine. The oranges move slowly through the machine and are washed with strong soap. <u>After</u> they're washed, the oranges roll into the juicing machines. The juicing machines press and squeeze about 100 oranges per minute. <u>Then</u>, the oranges go through a long tube with holes in it. That's how the juice is separated from the orange skins. The skins can't go through the holes, so they come out at the end of the tube. <u>Next</u>, the orange juice goes into another machine that takes out the seeds and other tiny objects. <u>Last</u>, the orange juice goes into a packing machine. In this machine, the juice is poured into bottles or cartons. The bottles or cartons are closed, and the juice is ready to be sold.

What is the topic of this paragraph? ___________________________________

What is the main idea? ____

The time order signal words are underlined. Each signal word points to a step in making orange juice by machine.

Here are the signal words. Write the details.

Signal Words	Details (steps)
First	
After	
Then	
Next	
Last	

Read each paragraph. Write the topic and main idea. Underline the signal words and then write the signal words and details.

The Vietnam War

1.   The Vietnam War began in 1946, soon after World War II. It was a war between the Vietnamese and the French. The government of Vietnam was French. But the Vietnamese people wanted the French to leave so they could have their own government. For nine long years, the Vietnamese fought hard, and slowly they won more and more land. By 1953, the French Army realized that they were in trouble. They were not winning the war. French soldiers were dying, and the war was costing a lot of money. So, in 1954, the French Army stopped fighting and left Vietnam. That was the end of the first part of the Vietnam War.

Topic: ____

Main idea: ____

____

Signal Words   *Details*

2.   The second part of the Vietnam War began in 1954. At that time, the French Army left, and there were two Vietnams: North Vietnam and South Vietnam. There were also two governments. Both governments wanted to be the only government for all of Vietnam. So from 1954 until 1960, the North and the South fought all the time. The North Vietnamese slowly grew stronger. By the beginning of 1965, the North Vietnamese were winning the war. But the United States government did not want the North Vietnamese to win. So in March of 1965, the United States began to help South Vietnam. They sent guns, airplanes, and a few soldiers to help the South. Then the United States sent more soldiers. By July 1965, there were about 75,000 American soldiers in Vietnam.

Topic: ____

Main idea: ____

____

Signal Words   *Details*

Read each paragraph. Write the topic and main idea. Underline the signal words and then write the signal words and details.

The American War in Vietnam

1.   In 1965, the Vietnam War became an American war. That year, the United States sent airplanes with bombs over North Vietnam. The North Vietnamese were moving into South Vietnam, and the U.S. government wanted to stop them. More and more bombs were used each year. The bombs killed thousands of North Vietnamese men, women, and children. Thousands more lost their homes and their land. The United States also sent more soldiers every year. By the end of 1967, there were almost 510,000 Americans in Vietnam. However, the North Vietnamese were still winning the war.

Topic: ____

Main idea: ____

____

Signal Words   **Details**

_______________   _______________________

_______________   _______________________

_______________   _______________________

_______________   _______________________

_______________   _______________________

2.   In the United States, some people did not want the war. In the early 1960s, only a few people felt this way. But by the late 1960s, many people believed Americans should not be fighting in Vietnam. The United States government had to listen to these people. In May 1968, the American government began to talk to the North Vietnamese government about stopping the war. For the next few months, fewer bombs were used against the North. By the end of the year, the bombing stopped. It still took a long time to end the war. American soldiers started to go home in 1970. The last Americans left five years later.

Topic: ____

Main idea: ____

____

Signal Words   **Details**

_______________   _______________________

_______________   _______________________

_______________   _______________________

_______________   _______________________

_______________   _______________________

_______________   _______________________

Read each paragraph. Write the topic and main idea. Underline the signal words and then write the signal words and details.

The Hawaiian Islands

1. The Hawaiian Islands first appeared in the Pacific Ocean about 30 million years ago. They were made by the explosion of underwater volcanoes (mountains that explode at the top). For many years, the islands were just rocks, with no plants or animals. Then birds discovered the islands. They carried seeds from other places. After a while, the seeds grew into plants and trees. The birds built their nests on the islands. There were no other animals to eat the birds or their eggs, so there were soon many birds, of many different kinds. Finally, about 1,500 years ago, the first humans came to the islands, bringing animals with them.

Topic: ______________________________________

Main idea: ____________________________________

____

Signal Words   **Details**

______________   ______________________________
______________   ______________________________
______________   ______________________________
______________   ______________________________
______________   ______________________________

2. When people from other islands came to the Hawaiian Islands, they had to learn to live in peace together. The first people came from the Marquesa Islands to live in the Hawaiian Islands in about 500 C.E. During the next few hundred years, groups of people came there from other islands. For many years, they all lived together in peace. Then, in about 1200 C.E., a new group of people arrived from Tahiti. These Tahitians were not peaceful people. For a while, the different groups fought each other. But as time passed, the fighting slowly stopped. However, the different groups still had separate kings on separate islands. Finally, in 1810, after a short war, Kamehameha became the first king of all the islands.

Topic: ______________________________________

Main idea: ____________________________________

____

Signal Words   **Details**

______________   ______________________________
______________   ______________________________
______________   ______________________________
______________   ______________________________
______________   ______________________________
______________   ______________________________
______________   ______________________________

3.   In 1778, the Hawaiian Islands changed forever. In that year, the first European, Captain James Cook, sailed into a port on the island of Hawaii. Soon after that, news about the islands reached England and the United States. By 1819, two ships full of Europeans and Americans had arrived. Some came to hunt for whales. Others came to teach Hawaiian people about Christianity. Still others came to start big sugar farms and make money. During these years, many Hawaiians became ill and died from diseases brought to the islands. During the nineteenth century, many more Europeans and Americans moved to Hawaii. Slowly, the Hawaiian people lost control over their islands. Finally, in 1893, the United States took over the islands from the last Hawaiian queen, Liliuokalani.

Topic: ____

Main idea: ____

____

Signal Words	**Details**
________________	________________
________________	________________
________________	________________
________________	________________
________________	________________
________________	________________
________________	________________

EXERCISE 8

Read each paragraph. Write the topic and main idea. Underline the signal words and then write the signal words and details.

Old Hawaiian Traditions

1.   The *lei* is a kind of necklace of flowers. It's a popular Hawaiian tradition. Making a lei is not easy, and it takes time to make one well. First, you have to buy a lot of beautiful, fresh flowers. Next, you have to put the flowers in water to keep them fresh. Then you choose a pattern for the lei. After you decide on a pattern, you can begin to work on it. The lei is made by sewing the flowers in a large circle of string. This takes about an hour of careful work. At the end, you'll have a beautiful Hawaiian lei.

Topic: ____

Main idea: ____

____

Signal Words	**Details**
________________	________________
________________	________________
________________	________________
________________	________________
________________	________________

2.   Surfing is a water sport that started in Hawaii many years ago. It's not an easy sport, but it's very exciting to do. If you're a good swimmer, you can learn to ride a surfboard. First, swim out from the beach with your surfboard. Then wait for a good, strong ocean wave. When a good wave comes to you, stand up on the board. Then, as the wave rises under you, keep your balance and try not to fall down. While you ride the wave, use your feet to control the direction of the board. Try to keep it heading for the beach. Finally, if you're lucky, you can ride the wave all the way to the beach. But it's not easy to stay on your feet!

Topic: ____

Main idea: ____

____

Signal Words   **Details**

_________________   __________________________

3.   The Hawaiian hula dance has a long history. Many years ago, it was part of the Hawaiian religion. Hawaiians believed that a goddess named Laka taught the dance. At that time, only men were allowed to do it. Later, women began to dance the hula, too. Then, in the 1800s, Europeans and Americans came to Hawaii. They didn't like the hula because it was very different from their way of dancing. They tried to stop Hawaiians from dancing the hula. For some years, the hula was almost forgotten. During that time, few people remembered how to dance it. But later in the 1800s, King Kalakaua decided that the hula was important for the islanders. He started a special hula dance group, and the dance was saved. Today, many Hawaiian children learn the hula at a young age. It is an important part of the island traditions.

Topic: ____

Main idea: ____

____

Signal Words   **Details**

_________________   __________________________

Writing exercise: *On a separate piece of paper, write a paragraph using the time order pattern. Write about one of these topics, or choose a topic of your own. Remember to use the signal words for the time order pattern in your paragraph.*

- Learning to drive
- Making a good cup of coffee
- A busy weekend
- Getting ready for an exam

The Comparison Pattern

A writer uses a comparison pattern to show how two things are alike and how they are different. *In a comparison paragraph, the topic is always about two things.*

Signal Words for the Comparison Pattern:

Words that Show Likeness	**Words that Show Difference**
alike	different
similar	unlike
same	more than
also	less than
both	but
too	however
	on the other hand

Example a:

Compare the United States to Canada.

How are they alike?

Both are on the same continent, North America.

Both have many people from around the world.

The United States is a large country, and Canada is too.

Both have land on the Atlantic and the Pacific Oceans.

They have a similar history: both were part of the British Empire.

How are they different?

Canada has two official languages, but the United States has no official language.

The United States has more people than Canada.

Canada has more land than the United States.

Canada is a younger nation than the United States.

Canada and the United States have different laws.

Compare the United States to another country. ________________________
(Country)

How are they alike?

____

____

____

____

____

How are they different?

____

____

____

____

____

Example b:

Sometimes a writer uses the comparison pattern to show only *how two things are alike*. This paragraph tells how two fruits are alike. It does not tell any differences.

Read this comparison paragraph and underline the signal words. Answer the questions below.

Lemons and limes are similar kinds of fruit. Both grow in warm places. Both have hard skins and soft insides. They are also eaten in a similar way. People don't usually eat whole lemons and limes because both of them have a very sour taste. The two fruits are often used in desserts and main dishes. People make juice from lemons and also from limes. Finally, lemons and limes have the same vitamin in them—vitamin C.

What is the topic? (What is this paragraph comparing?) ________________________

Main idea: ____

____

Signal Words	**Details (likenesses)**
Both	grow in warm places
Both	have hard skins and soft insides
similar	way of being eaten
both	have a sour taste
The two	are used in cooking
and also	people make juice from them
same	vitamin

Example c:

Sometimes a comparison tells only about the differences between two things. This paragraph tells *only differences* between two fruits.

Read this comparison paragraph and underline the signal words. Answer the questions below.

Lemons and limes are citrus fruits, but they are quite different. First of all, lemons are yellow, but limes are green. The taste is a little different, too. Lemons are grown all over the world, but limes are grown in only a few places. This is because people knew about lemons thousands of years ago. Limes, on the other hand, are a new fruit. They are really a special kind of lemon. Scientists made them from lemons only about 50 years ago.

What is the topic? (What is this paragraph comparing?) ______________________

Main idea: ____

____

Signal Words	**Details (differences)**
but	*yellow, green*
different	*taste*
but	*where they are grown*
on the other hand	*lemons are old; limes are new*

EXERCISE 10

Read each paragraph. Write the topic and main idea. Underline the comparison signal words. Then write the likenesses and/or differences.

Food

1. The food in India is similar to the food in China. First of all, in both countries, rice is an important food: It is served at almost every meal in India and China. Both Indian and Chinese dishes can be spicy. They are also alike because they both use many different vegetables. In both countries, meat is not always the most important part of the meal. India and China are large countries. In the different areas of these countries, people have very different traditions about food. So, in both countries, there are many different kinds of food and ways of cooking.

Topic: ____

Main idea: ____

____

Likenesses

____

____

____

____

____

2.   In Paris today, people can shop for food at supermarkets or at small shops.
The supermarkets and small shops are similar in some ways. In both places, you
can buy meat, bread, fruits, vegetables, and other foods. Both supermarkets and
small shops are found in every neighborhood. They both have the kinds of food
that Parisians enjoy. However, their differences are important. While the
supermarkets are open every day and in the evening, small shops are open
fewer hours. Often the food is more expensive in small shops. But many
Parisians say that the food there is often fresher and tastier in the small shops.

Topic: ____

Main idea: ____

____

Differences   **Likenesses**

__________________________   __________________________

__________________________   __________________________

__________________________   __________________________

**Read each paragraph. Write the topic and main idea. Underline the comparison signal
words. Then write the likenesses and/or differences.**

Medical Care

1.   French and English doctors sometimes have different ideas about medical
care. In France, doctors often give strong medicine to move blood to the brain.
However, doctors in England do not think that is helpful. French doctors often
worry about a patient's liver and diet. But English doctors do not. And French
doctors take stomach illnesses very seriously. They often give their patients
magnesium, calcium, and vitamin D. But in England, doctors often say that
stomach problems are not serious at all. They usually think the stomach
problems are caused by worrying too much. French doctors are usually
interested in trying out a variety of new treatments. English doctors, however,
first wait to see if the new treatments really work.

Topic: ____

Main idea: ____

____

Differences

____

____

____

____

2.   Medical care in the United States and Canada is similar in some ways. The doctors and hospitals in both countries are excellent. They have the same medicines and ideas about how to take care of patients. However, the way people pay for medical care is very different. In Canada, everyone, rich or poor, has health care. People pay a tax to the government, and the government pays the doctors and hospitals. In the United States, on the other hand, insurance companies pay the medical bills. People have to pay a lot of money to the insurance companies. Many poor people cannot afford to pay for insurance, so they don't have good medical care.

Topic: ____

Main idea: ____

____

Differences   ***Likenesses***

_______________________________   _______________________________

_______________________________   _______________________________

_______________________________   _______________________________

_______________________________   _______________________________

EXERCISE 12

Writing exercise: *On a separate piece of paper, write a paragraph using the comparison pattern. Write about one of these topics, or choose a topic of your own. Remember to use the signal words for the comparison pattern in your paragraph.*

- Two friends
- Two teachers
- Two cities
- Two cars

The Cause/Effect Pattern

The writer uses a cause/effect pattern to show how one thing causes another.

Signal Words for the Cause/Effect Pattern:

If the CAUSE COMES FIRST IN A SENTENCE, **C** --------➤ **E**, use these signal words:

so	can make	is a cause of
leads to	makes	can result in
can cause	can effect	results in
causes	effects	had an effect on
can help	can stop	
helps	stops	

If the EFFECT COMES FIRST IN A SENTENCE, **E** ◄-------- **C**, use these signal words:

because	is the effect of	is made by
because of	is caused by	
is due to	results from	

Example:

The sentences in Box A and Box B express the same idea. In Box A, the <u>cause</u> comes first. In Box B, the <u>effect</u> comes first.

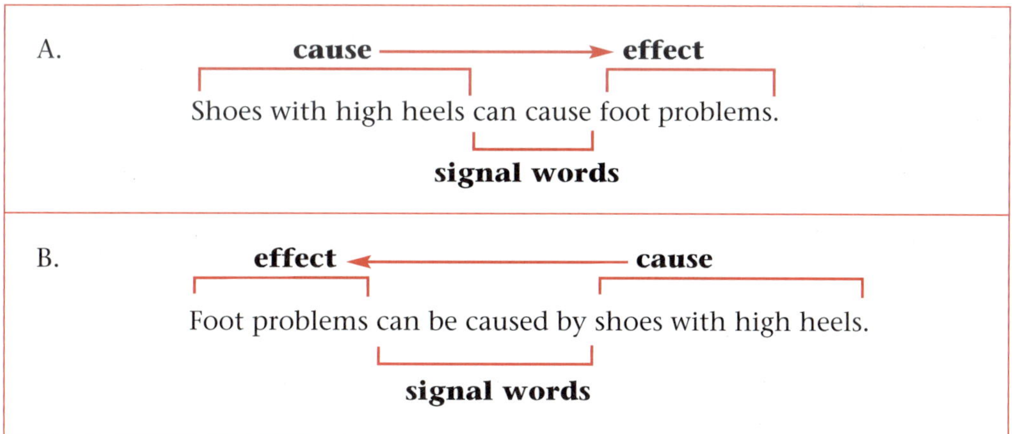

Under each sentence, write "C" under the cause and "E" under the effect. Draw an arrow (→ or ←) from the cause to the effect. Then underline the signal word(s).

Example:

Exercise <u>can make you</u> thirsty.

C ——————→ E

1. Eating uncooked meat can result in illness.

2. Many car accidents happen because of ice and snow on the road.

3. Bad food and not enough sleep are two reasons for poor health.

4. Doctors tell us that smoking cigarettes often leads to cancer.

5. Some people become nervous because of drinking coffee.

6. Many fires in homes are due to careless smokers.

7. Heart disease is sometimes the result of eating too much.

8. Bright sunlight can cause your eyes to hurt.

9. High insurance costs are one result of car accidents.

10. Serious family problems can cause illness.

Under each sentence, write "C" under the cause and "E" under the effect. Draw an arrow ($\rightarrow$ or $\leftarrow$) from the cause to the effect. Then underline the signal word(s).

1. Sam won a prize because he had the highest score.

2. Some students go to college because they want to play on a sports team.

3. Reading for pleasure can result in a larger vocabulary.

4. Helen found a job quickly because of her English skills.

5. As a result of your phone call, I could not go back to sleep.

6. The students made too much noise, so he called the police.

7. She received an award because of her computer program.

8. Eating too much chocolate can result in weight gain.

9. Doctors say that good health comes from regular exercise.

10. The football team lost all their games because they were playing badly.

Finding causes and effects in paragraphs

Example a:

Sometimes, one cause has many effects.

Read this cause/effect paragraph and look for the effects of a cold winter in Florida. The signal words are underlined.

A cold winter <u>can cause</u> serious problems in Florida. The farmers there grow a lot of oranges. Very cold weather <u>causes</u> orange trees to die. Cold weather also <u>results in</u> fewer tourists. There are many hotels and vacation places in Florida. These places are in trouble if there are fewer tourists. Finally, very cold weather <u>can cause</u> health problems. Many people do not have heating in their homes, and they become ill from the cold.

Topic: *cold winter in Florida*

Main idea: *A cold winter can cause serious problems in Florida.*

Cause	Signal Words	Effects
cold winter	*can cause*	*problems*
	causes	*orange trees die*
	results in	*fewer tourists*
	can cause	*health problems*

Example b:

Sometimes, one effect has many causes.

Read this cause/effect paragraph and look for the causes of car accidents. The signal words are underlined.

Car accidents are a big problem in the United States. Some accidents <u>are caused by</u> bad weather. When roads are icy or wet, it can be difficult to control the car. Other accidents <u>result from</u> problems with the car. Even a small problem like a flat tire can be serious if the car is going fast. Bad roads are another <u>cause of</u> accidents. Some accidents happen <u>because</u> the driver falls asleep. But the most common <u>cause of</u> accidents is drunk driving. Drivers who have had too much alcohol cause many injuries and deaths.

Topic: *Car accidents*

Main idea: *Car accidents are a big problem in the United States.*

Causes	Signal Words	Effect
bad weather	*are caused by*	*car accidents*
car problems	*result from*	
bad roads	*cause of*	
driver falls asleep	*because*	
drinking alcohol	*cause of*	

Read each paragraph. Write the topic and main idea. Underline the signal words and then write the causes and effects.

Staying Healthy

1.   In the United States, many people take vitamin pills. In fact, they spend millions of dollars on them every month! Americans buy vitamins and special health products because they want to keep their bodies healthy. They don't always eat healthy food, so they take vitamins instead. The big spending on vitamins is also the effect of advertising. Big companies advertise vitamins as the quick and easy cure to many health problems. People believe these ads, even though they are not always true. As a result, Americans buy more and more vitamins.

Topic: ____

Main idea: ____

____

Causes   **Effects**

_______________________   _______________________

_______________________   _______________________

_______________________   _______________________

2.   Aspirin is a simple drug. It has many useful effects. It can stop a headache or an earache. It helps take away pain in the fingers or knees. Aspirin can stop a fever if you have the flu, and it can make you feel better if you have a cold. Some doctors believe that aspirin also can result in a healthy heart. They say that some people should take an aspirin every day. For those people, aspirin could prevent heart disease. Many doctors say that people should take an aspirin immediately after a heart attack. It could save their life.

Topic: ____

Main idea: ____

____

Causes   **Effects**

_______________________   _______________________

_______________________   _______________________

_______________________   _______________________

_______________________   _______________________

_______________________   _______________________

_______________________   _______________________

Read each paragraph. Write the topic and main idea. Underline the signal words and then write the causes and effects.

The Problem of Being Overweight

1. Today, more than half of all Americans are too fat. They are more than twenty pounds (9.1 kg.) overweight. This problem is caused by the way Americans eat. They like to eat "fast foods" like hamburgers, French fries, and pizza. These foods have lots of fat, salt, and sugar in them. People also become fat because of the amount of food they eat. Americans eat much more than they need at meals. Many Americans also eat chips and sweets between meals. Doctors say that being overweight is partly caused by too little exercise. Many Americans like driving everywhere instead of walking. In their homes, they often lie on the couch and watch TV. They don't get any regular exercise.

Topic: ____

Main idea: ____

____

Causes

____

____

____

Effects

____

____

____

2. If you are very overweight, you may soon have serious problems with your health. A group of doctors wrote a report about some of the effects of too much fat. One important effect is stress on the heart. If you are overweight, your heart has to work harder. This may lead to a heart attack or to other heart problems. Extra fat can also change the amount of sugar in your blood. This can cause serious diseases, such as diabetes. High blood pressure is another possible result of being overweight. Even cancer can sometimes be a result. More studies are needed about all these problems, but one thing is clear: Extra fat may make your life shorter.

Topic: ____

Main idea: ____

____

Causes

____

____

____

____

____

Effects

____

____

____

____

____

Writing exercise: *On a separate piece of paper, write a paragraph using the cause/effect pattern. Write about one of these topics, or choose a topic of your own. Remember to use the signal words for the cause/effect pattern in your paragraph.*

- Effects of marriage on ______'s (or my) life
- Causes of traffic jams
- How very hot weather can cause health problems
- The effects of cell phones on our lives

Using All Four Patterns

Example:

What is the pattern of organization in this paragraph? Write the letter(s) of the pattern from the list of abbreviations below. Then read the sentences below the paragraph. One of the sentences is missing from the paragraph. Decide which one fits best in the paragraph and write the letter for that sentence.

Shakespeare was born in Stratford-on-Avon on April 16, 1564. For a few years, he studied at a school near home. He moved to London when he was still young. By the age of 35, he was already well-known. He continued to work in London until about 1613. Then he returned to Stratford and lived there until his death in 1616.

Pattern: ___To___   Sentence: ___b___

Patterns:

L—*listing*   **TO**—*time order*   **CE**—*cause/effect*   **C**—*comparison*

Missing sentences:

a. Shakespeare wrote poetry, but he is best known for his plays.

b. At the age of 18, he married Ann Hathaway.

c. People still love his plays because the people in them are very real.

The best pattern for this paragraph is *time order*. The signal words are: *April 16, 1564; For a few years; when; By the age of 35; until about 1613;* and *in 1616.*

The best missing sentence for this paragraph is *b*. That sentence also has a time order signal: *At the age of 18.*

In each paragraph below, there is a different pattern and a missing sentence. Working with another student, decide what the pattern is and which sentence fits best. The patterns and missing sentences (plus one extra) are listed below. After each paragraph, write the letter(s) of the pattern and the letter of the missing sentence.

William Shakespeare

1. Two great writers were born in England in 1564. One was William Shakespeare. The other was Christopher Marlowe. Shakespeare lived until the age of fifty-two, but Marlowe died suddenly when he was only twenty-nine. Both were famous in their time, and both are still loved today.

    Pattern: _____   Sentence: _____

2. During his lifetime, Shakespeare was very successful as a writer. This was mainly because of his genius. He knew how to write about life, and he had a wonderful way with words. But Shakespeare's success was also due to the special time when he lived. In those days, the English were very interested in new ideas. They loved music, art, plays, and poetry.

    Pattern: _____   Sentence: _____

3. Shakespeare wrote plays, but they were not all alike. He wrote three kinds of plays. One kind was the history play. One example of this is his play called *Henry V*, about a king of England. Another kind was the tragedy, such as *Macbeth*.

    Pattern: _____   Sentence: _____

Patterns:

L—listing   **TO**—time order   **CE**—cause/effect   **C**—comparison

Missing sentences:

a. He also wrote many comedies, such as *A Midsummer Night's Dream*.

b. Shakespeare wrote many plays and some poetry, but Marlowe finished only four plays.

c. A genius like Shakespeare had a chance to use his great mind.

d. Some people think Shakespeare's plays were written by someone else.

In each paragraph below, there is a different pattern and a missing sentence. Working with another student, decide what the pattern is and which sentence fits best. The patterns and missing sentences (plus one extra) are listed below. After each paragraph, write the letter(s) of the pattern and the letter of the missing sentence.

The New Zoos

1.   Zoos in the United States are changing. The old zoos had lots of cages. Even large animals were kept in cages. Often, the cages had nothing in them except an animal, and the animal looked very sad and lonely. Many animals live together in these cages. In fact, they're not like cages at all. They are full of trees, flowers, rocks, and water. They look like real wild areas.

      Pattern: _______   Sentence: _______

2.   The new zoos teach people a lot about animals. They show people how the animals really live. They also show the way the animals have families and how the mothers take care of the babies. These zoos even show how animals form groups and live together. In addition, the animals in the new zoos do not look sad. Are they really happy? They cannot tell us, of course, but they look healthier.

      Pattern: _______   Sentence: _______

3.   Zoo workers say that some animals change after they come to the big new cages. For example, a young gorilla named Timmy was born at the Cleveland Metroparks Zoo. For years he lived in a small cage in a dark building. Then he was moved to the Bronx Zoo, to a large cage outside. He sat on some rocks because he didn't like the feeling of the grass on his feet. Then he started to move around a lot. Later, he became very friendly with the other gorillas in the cage. After only a few months, he became a father!

      Pattern: _______   Sentence: _______

Patterns:

L—listing   **TO**—time order   **CE**—cause/effect   **C**—comparison

Missing sentences:

a. People can see the way they eat and sleep.

b. Soon many other countries will have new zoos, too.

c. The new zoos still have cages, but they are very big.

d. For the first few days, he just sat in one place.

In each paragraph below, there is a different pattern and a missing sentence. Working with another student, decide what the pattern is and which sentence fits best. The patterns and missing sentences (plus one extra) are listed below. After each paragraph, write the letter(s) of the pattern and the letter of the missing sentence.

Cloth Around the World

1.   Cloth can be made from many different things. For example, some cloth is made from plants. Linen is made from the flax plant, and cotton is made from the cotton plant. People also make cloth from the wool of animals. In different parts of the world, people use wool from sheep, goats, rabbits, llamas, and camels. These days, it's also possible to make cloth from chemicals. That's how nylon and polyester are made. Finally, another modern kind of cloth is called *fleece*. It's made from old plastic bottles.

    Pattern: _____   Sentence: _____

2.   India and Egypt both produce a lot of cotton cloth. Both countries also have a lot of workers to pick the cotton and make the cloth. There are machines for picking cotton, but in these countries a lot of work is still done by hand. However, the cotton cloth from India is quite different from the cotton cloth from Egypt. In India, much of the cotton cloth is very thin. It's usually brightly colored. Often, Indian cotton is made into tablecloths, colorful clothes, and bedding. Egyptian cotton, on the other hand, is often made into thick towels and fine shirts.

    Pattern: _____   Sentence: _____

3.   The Chinese first began to make silk more than 27,000 years ago. Silk is a very interesting cloth because it comes from silkworms. First, tiny silkworms are spread out and covered with a thin cloth. The worms eat the leaves and grow bigger. After six weeks, the worms are ready to build a small nest called a *cocoon*. Each worm makes its cocoon with a single thread. Eight days later, the silk maker boils the cocoons to kill the worms. At last, after the silk from each cocoon is taken out, it can be made into silk thread and then silk cloth.

    Pattern: _____   Sentence: _____

L—listing   **TO**—time order   **CE**—cause/effect   **C**—comparison

Missing sentences:

a. The climate in both countries is good for growing cotton.

b. Next, mulberry leaves are put on top of the cloth.

c. Modern factories make cloth like nylon and rayon.

d. Silk is another kind of cloth that comes from an animal, the silkworm.

Skimming

Speed is often important when you are reading. You may have a lot to read but not much time. In fact, you probably don't need to read everything carefully. You don't need to know and remember all of the facts and ideas. You only need to get the general meaning of a chapter, article, or passage. You can do this by **skimming.**

You usually skim:

- articles in newspapers and magazines.
- parts of library books (to see if they'll be useful to you).
- tests and exams (to see what there is to do and to plan your time).
- the first few pages of a new pleasure reading book (to find out if you want to read it).

Skimming for Point of View

Skimming is helpful when you want to find out quickly about the writer. You can skim to find out what the writer thinks about something. This is the writer's **point of view.**

When you want to know the writer's point of view, you don't need to read everything. You need to read only a few important words or phrases.

Example a:

Skim this paragraph quickly. Answer the question by putting a checkmark (✓) beside the answer.

Dogs are often a problem at home. Many dogs are noisy and dirty. They may even be dangerous for small children.

Is this writer for or against dogs at home?

For ______   Against __✓__

You didn't need to read all the sentences to learn this. You only had to read a few key words: *problem, noisy, dirty,* and *dangerous.* From those words, you could tell the writer's point of view. This writer is against dogs at home.

Example b:

Skim this paragraph quickly. Answer the question by putting a checkmark (✓) beside the answer.

An apartment looks much nicer with some plants. The green leaves make it seem cooler in summer. The flowers give it a happy feeling.

Is this writer for or against plants in an apartment?

For ______   Against ______

How do you know this? What are the key words?

Skim these paragraphs quickly. Ask yourself, "Is the writer for or against the idea?" Put a checkmark (✓) beside the answer. You should work very fast.

1. Too much fruit juice can be bad for children. It is especially bad for children's teeth. If children drink too much fruit juice, they will have problems later.

    For _____   Against _____

2. Sport-utility vehicles (SUVs) often cause serious accidents. They can't turn quickly and they often go off the road. These cars are big and heavy, so they are very dangerous for other, smaller cars.

    For _____   Against _____

3. In San Francisco, the air is always a comfortable temperature. It is never too hot or too cold. In winter, it never snows and it's often sunny. There is pleasant weather all year.

    For _____   Against _____

4. Some people take too many vitamin pills every day. These people believe lots of vitamin pills are good for their health. But they're wrong. Too many vitamin pills can hurt your health.

    For _____   Against _____

5. There is something sad about animals in the zoos. They never really look happy. Maybe they're thinking about their real home. Maybe they don't like people looking at them all the time.

    For _____   Against _____

6. Children often watch television for six or more hours a day. This is not a good use of their time. It's not good for their health because they get very little exercise. Also, they don't read or play games.

    For _____   Against _____

7. Computers may cause serious problems in our world. There's a lot of important information on computers. If bad people get that information, they can be dangerous.

    For _____   Against _____

8. Sometimes there is a good reason to give children a small amount of sugar or candy. When they have to take medicine, for example, sweets can help.

    For _____   Against _____

Skim these paragraphs quickly. Ask yourself, "Is the writer for or against the idea?" Put a checkmark (✓) beside the answer. You should work very fast.

1. Many people believe that they should eat meat every day. This isn't true. You don't need to eat meat at all. In fact, you may be more healthy if you don't eat any meat.

   For _______   Against _______

2. Air travel isn't much fun any more. You have to arrive at the airport two or three hours early. There are always long lines, and flights are often very late.

   For _______   Against _______

3. Digital cameras make it very easy to take good pictures. You can check to see if you like a picture before you decide to keep it. Then, it's easy and cheap to print the pictures on your computer.

   For _______   Against _______

4. Traveling by bicycle is the best way to see a country. A bicycle doesn't need gas and it's not expensive. Also, you get some exercise while you travel.

   For _______   Against _______

5. Bicycles can be dangerous. You can hurt yourself by falling off a bicycle. You can also get seriously hurt if you are hit by a car.

   For _______   Against _______

6. Everyone should learn another language. Knowing a second language is useful these days. It also may teach you something about other people and places.

   For _______   Against _______

7. It's not easy to move to another country. There may be problems with language or culture. It may be difficult to find a job or a place to live. In another country, you don't have family or friends to help.

   For _______   Against _______

8. Music often makes you feel better about life. It can make you happy if you are sad. It can make you relax when you are tense.

   For _______   Against _______

Skimming for Pattern of Organization

Sometimes you need to find out quickly how a passage is organized. You want to know its pattern. You don't need to know the details for this, so you don't need to read all the words. You can read just the signal words. They will tell you the pattern.

Example a:

Which pattern of organization will you find in this paragraph? Skim to find the signal words. Put a checkmark (✓) beside the best answer.

Whales look for food most of the day and night. That's because whales are very large animals . . .

Listing _____   Time order _____   Cause/effect ✓__   Comparison _____

The signal word is *because*. The pattern is *cause/effect*.

Example b:

Which pattern of organization will you find in this paragraph? Skim to find the signal words. Put a checkmark (✓) beside the best answer.

This book has a lot of information about Poland. First, it tells about the history. It also explains . . .

Listing _____   Time order _____   Cause/effect _____   Comparison _____

EXERCISE 3

Here are the first few lines of some paragraphs. Skim them to find the signal words for the pattern of organization. Put a checkmark (✓) beside the best answer.

1. A parakeet is a small bird that lives in tropical forests. The parrot is similar to a parakeet, but it is larger . . .

   Listing _____   Time order _____   Cause/effect _____   Comparison _____

2. Some kinds of birds cannot fly. The penguin is one of these birds. It lives mostly in the very cold Antarctic climate. Another kind of bird that cannot fly is the ostrich . . .

   Listing _____   Time order _____   Cause/effect _____   Comparison _____

3. When you're reading, it's a good idea to follow certain steps. First, you should preview the passage . . .

   Listing _____   Time order _____   Cause/effect _____   Comparison _____

4. Headaches are often the result of psychological causes. For example, worrying about something can cause a headache . . .

   Listing _____   Time order _____   Cause/effect _____   Comparison _____

5. The clambake is a popular New England dinner. It usually includes many different kinds of seafood. Clams are the most common kind of seafood at a clambake. There may also be . . .

   Listing _____   Time order _____   Cause/effect _____   Comparison _____

6. Digital cameras are easier to use than the old cameras. It's also cheaper to print photos from a digital camera.

   Listing _____   Time order _____   Cause/effect _____   Comparison _____

7. Gold was first found in California in about 1840. The next 10 years in American history were called the California Gold Rush. By 1850, there were . . .

   Listing _____   Time order _____   Cause/effect _____   Comparison _____

8. Cola and ginger ale are both kinds of soft drinks. Both these drinks have a lot of sugar in them, but cola has caffeine in it and ginger ale . . .

   Listing _____   Time order _____   Cause/effect _____   Comparison _____

EXERCISE 4

Here are the first few lines of some paragraphs. Skim them to find the signal words for the pattern of organization. Put a checkmark (✓) beside the best answer.

1. Leif Ericsson visited North America in about the year 1000. He was probably the first European to see America. Then, in . . .

   Listing _____   Time order _____   Cause/effect _____   Comparison _____

2. The Spanish kings and queens sent many people to find out about America. Christopher Columbus was one of these people. Another was . . .

   Listing _____   Time order _____   Cause/effect _____   Comparison _____

3. Leif Ericsson and Christopher Columbus were both early visitors to North America. However, Ericsson lived much earlier than Columbus. He sailed from a different . . .

   Listing _____   Time order _____   Cause/effect _____   Comparison _____

4. Many American Indians died soon after the Europeans arrived. There was one important reason for this . . .

   Listing _____   Time order _____   Cause/effect _____   Comparison _____

5. Many Europeans came to America because they wanted religious freedom. They couldn't practice their religion in their home country, so . . .

   Listing _____   Time order _____   Cause/effect _____   Comparison _____

6. It took a long time for the first Europeans to make a home in America. First they had to find food and water. Next, they had to build houses . . .

   Listing _____   Time order _____   Cause/effect _____   Comparison _____

7. The first group of English people in America had a very hard time. The main reason for this was the fact that they arrived in early winter.

   Listing _____   Time order _____   Cause/effect _____   Comparison _____

8. Many American history books leave out some important information. For example, they often do not tell much about the American Indians. They also . . .

   Listing _____   Time order _____   Cause/effect _____   Comparison _____

Skimming for Ideas

You should skim when you want to find out the general idea quickly. Speed is important for this kind of skimming, too. You should skim at least two times faster than you usually read.

When you skim for the general idea, you must change the way you read. You can't read every word or even every sentence. You have to skip over a lot. In fact, you should skip over everything except a few important words. These are the words that tell you the general idea.

Guidelines for Skimming for Ideas

1. Read the first sentence or two at your usual speed. Ask yourself, "What is this about?"

2. As soon as you guess the general idea, go to the next paragraph. Remember, you don't need to know the details. You only need to learn something very general about the passage.

3. Read only a few words in each paragraph after that. You should look for the words that tell you about the general idea. Often they are at the beginning of the paragraph, but they may also be at the end.

4. Always work quickly. Remember that details are not important.

You can skim an article from a newspaper or a magazine to find the general ideas.

Most of the words in this passage have been blacked out. Read the words and sentences that are left. They will help you find the general ideas. Read as quickly as you can. Then answer the questions below.

A Taste of Thailand

by Susan Alexander

Thai restaurants are very popular in the United States these days. One reason is that many people from Thailand ▓▓▓▓▓▓ immigrants ▓▓ ▓▓▓▓▓▓▓▓▓▓▓▓▓▓▓▓▓▓▓▓

But ▓▓▓▓▓▓▓▓▓▓ also popular ▓▓▓▓▓▓▓▓▓▓▓ not from Thailand. ▓▓▓▓▓▓▓ ▓▓▓▓▓▓▓ special dishes ▓▓▓▓▓ unusual spices.

▓▓▓▓ also ▓▓▓▓▓▓▓▓▓▓▓▓ reasonable prices. ▓▓▓▓ ▓▓▓▓ especially popular ▓▓▓▓ Students ▓▓▓▓▓▓▓▓▓▓▓

Thai restaurants ▓▓▓▓▓ good, friendly service ▓▓ peaceful ▓▓▓▓▓▓ ▓▓▓ visit to Thailand.

1. What is one reason why Thai restaurants are popular?

2. What is special about Thai restaurants?

3. Are Thai restaurants only for immigrants?

Show your answers to another student. Do you have the same answers? Did you get the general ideas? Now turn the page and read the whole article.

A Taste of Thailand

by Susan Alexander

Thai restaurants are very popular in the United States these days. One reason is that many people from Thailand live there. These immigrants like eating the food of their home country.

But the restaurants are also popular with people who are not from Thailand. They love the food because of the special dishes cooked with unusual spices.

People also like to eat in Thai restaurants because of their reasonable prices. In fact, that's why Thai food is especially popular near universities. Students can afford to have a full, tasty meal with a traditional dessert.

Thai restaurants are known for good, friendly service in a peaceful setting. For many people, it's like a visit to Thailand.

Example b:

A book review gives you some information about a book. You can skim a book review to help you decide if you want to read the book.

In this example, some parts are underlined. Read only these underlined parts. They will help you find the general ideas. Read as quickly as you can. Then, answer the questions below.

Murder in the Language Lab

by M. L. Allen

This book is an unusual detective story. It begins with a crime, a murder. A scientist is killed in a laboratory. No one knows who killed the scientist. Inspector Barker is the detective. He must find the killer, but he needs help.

He gets help from Sally, a chimpanzee who lives in the laboratory. In this laboratory, scientists are studying language. They are interested in how animals like Sally can learn some language. Sally is one smart chimpanzee. She cannot talk, but she understands many words. She answers questions by using a computer. Sally saw the murder. She is afraid of Inspector Barker at first, but she wants to help. So she tells Inspector Barker who the murderer is.

If you like detective stories, you will enjoy this one. But you probably will be very surprised when you learn who the murderer is!

1. Why is this story unusual?

2. Does Inspector Barker find out who the murderer is?

3. Who is Sally?

Show your answers to another student. Do you have the same answers? Did you get the general ideas? Check your answers by reading the whole review.

Skim this book review to get the general idea. You should read only a few sentences and words. Read as quickly as you can. Then, answer the questions below.

The Hot Zone

A Terrifying True Story

by Richard Preston

Around the world, people are catching strange and horrible illnesses. This problem began in the 1980s and 1990s, and it is even worse today. The new illnesses are caused by tiny viruses. The illnesses are a big problem because no one knows how to cure them. Most people who catch these viruses die.

This book tells the story of how the killer viruses are moving around the world. Sometimes people carry them. Sometimes monkeys carry them. The stories in this book are true, but they are hard to believe because they are so terrible.

The author writes vivid descriptions of the illnesses. The reader can almost see the sick patients as they die horrible deaths, with blood coming out of their ears, nose, and mouth.

Near Washington, D.C., a special laboratory works on these dangerous viruses. In one of the best parts of this book, Preston tells how scientists at that lab work very carefully. They wear special clothes that make them look like astronauts. A tiny hole in their clothes could let a killer virus inside!

This book is perfect for people who like exciting stories and is not for people who are easily scared.

1. Is this book about the past or the present?

2. Where are the killer viruses?

3. What is special about the scientists in the laboratories?

Show your answers to another student. Do you have the same answers? Check your answers by reading the whole review.

Skim this magazine article to get the general ideas. Remember, you need to read only a few sentences and words. Read as quickly as you can. Then, answer the questions below.

Burning Trees to Save a Forest

by Liz Westfield

Burning trees to save a forest! Strange as it sounds, that is the United States Forest Service's new idea for saving America's forests.

For more than a hundred years, Americans were taught that fires in a forest were always bad. When trees burned in the forest, it was a disaster which would ruin the forest. The Forest Service promoted this idea in many ways. They even invented a character named Smokey the Bear, who always said, "Remember, only <u>you</u> can prevent forest fires."

In the past, whenever there was a fire in the forest, the rangers immediately put it out. No fires were allowed to burn, even in places where many of the trees were dead or diseased. This did not help the forests, however. In fact, with so many dead and diseased trees, the forest fires in the western United States have been far worse in recent years.

The new chief of the U.S. Forest Service recently explained that there is a new and better way to save our forests. He said, "Small, limited fires are part of nature. That is the way that old, dead, and diseased trees are cleared away to make room for new trees."

Now the Forest Service has new plans. They will start small fires in forests, but they will control the fires. The fires will be started in parts of the forest which are old and full of diseased trees. The rangers plan to burn about 30,000 acres a year for the next 20 years.

As the chief said, "It took many years for the forests to become old and diseased, and so it will take more than 20 years to correct the problem by using controlled fires."

1. In the past, what did Americans think about forest fires?

2. What happened in the past when there was a forest fire?

3. What is the new plan of the Forest Service?

Show your answers to another student. Do you have the same answers? Check your answers by reading the whole article.

Skim this magazine article to get the general ideas. Remember, you need to read only a few sentences and words. Read as quickly as you can. Then, answer the questions below.

The Secret of a Good Violin

by Susan Austen

Most musicians agree that the world's best violins were made in Cremona, Italy, about 300 years ago. These violins sound better than any others. They even sound better than violins made today. Violin makers and scientists now try to make instruments like the Italian violins, but they are not the same. Musicians still prefer the old ones. Why are these old Italian violins so special? No one really knows, but many people think they have an answer.

Some people think it is the age of the violins. They say that today's violins will also sound wonderful someday. The problem with this answer is that not all old violins sound wonderful. Only some old violins have a special sound. So age cannot be the reason. Other people think the secret to those violins is the wood. The wood of the violin is important. It must be from certain kinds of trees. It must not be too young or too old. Perhaps the violin makers of Cremona knew something special about wood for violins.

Other people say that the kind of wood is not so important and that it is more important to cut the wood a special way. The wood for a violin must be cut very carefully. It has to be the right size and shape. The smallest difference will change the sound of the violin. Some musicians think that the violin makers from Cremona knew a secret about cutting wood.

However, size and shape may not be the answer, either. Scientists measured the old violins from Cremona very carefully. They can make new ones that are exactly the same size and shape. The new violins still do not sound as good as the old ones. Other scientists think the secret may be the varnish. Varnish is what covers the wood of the violin. It makes the wood look shiny. It also helps the sound of the instrument. No one knows what the Italian violin makers used in their varnish. So no one can make the same varnish today.

There may never be other violins like the violins of Cremona. Their secret may be lost forever. Young musicians today hope this is not true. They need fine violins, and there are not very many of the old violins left. Also, the old violins are very expensive. Recently, a famous old Italian violin was sold for several million dollars!

1. Do people agree about what makes a good violin?

2. What are some of the possible reasons why the old violins are better than the new violins?

3. What problem do young musicians have today?

Show your answers to another student. Do you have the same answers? Check your answers by reading the whole article.

Skim this magazine article to get the general ideas. Remember, you need to read only a few sentences and words. Read as quickly as you can. Then, answer the questions below.

Changes in Family Life

by Jacob Sand

Family life in the United States has changed. Forty or fifty years ago, the wife was called a "housewife." She cleaned, cooked, and cared for the children. The husband earned the money for the family. He was usually out working all day. He came home tired in the evening, so he didn't do much housework. And he didn't see the children very much, except on weekends.

These days, however, many women work outside the home. They can't stay with the children all day. They, too, come home tired in the evening. They don't want to spend the evening cooking dinner and cleaning up. They don't have time to clean the house and do the laundry. So who is going to do the housework now? Who is going to take care of the children?

Many families solve the problem of housework by sharing it. In these families, the husband and wife agree to do different jobs around the house, or they take turns doing each job. For example, the husband always cooks dinner, and the wife always does the laundry. Or the wife cooks dinner on some nights, and the husband cooks dinner on other nights.

Then there is the question of the child care. In the past, many families got help with child care from grandparents. But now, many grandparents are still working at their jobs, and they can't help with regular child care. Also, many families in the United States don't live near their relatives. The grandparents often are too far away to help.

More often, parents have to pay for child-care help. The help may be a babysitter or a day-care center. The problem with this kind of help is the high cost. It is possible only for couples with jobs that pay well.

Parents may get another kind of help from the companies they work for. Some companies now let employees work part-time. Other companies have child care at work. This way, children are near the parents and can spend more time with them during the day.

There is still another way families can organize their lives. If the father earns less than the mother, the father can stop working. He can stay home with the children and become a "househusband."

These changes in the home are not always easy for the family. Some parents have very little time to spend with their children. This doesn't make the children happy. In a lot of homes, the wife still does most of the housework, and she goes out to a job all day, too. So she may feel unhappy. Sometimes husbands and wives can't agree about how to organize their lives, and they decide to separate. But many families find good things in the changes, and they find new ways of being a family together.

1. What is different about family life today?

2. What are some new problems that families have today?

3. What are some of the effects of these changes?

Show your answers to another student. Do you have the same answers? Check your answers by reading the whole article.

Skim this magazine article to get the general ideas. Remember, you need to read only a few sentences and words. Read as quickly as you can. Then, answer the questions below.

Some Problems with E-mail at Work

by Yuki Shibata

Everyone knows the advantages of using e-mail. It's much faster than ordinary mail. It's much cheaper than the telephone. And it's easier than trying to meet with someone in person. However, it is not always good to use e-mail at work. Some companies are limiting the use of e-mail in their offices for several reasons.

One reason is that e-mail is only one-way. You send out your message and then you have to wait for an answer. This is not a problem if you need to send simple information. You may only need to know that the message was received. But if the message is more complicated, e-mail is not so good. It's not good, for example, if you need to make a decision or a plan. It can take many messages and a lot of time to decide something by e-mail. In that case, it's better to talk on the phone. Or, if you're in the same building, you should go meet in person. Then you can also take a little walk and you can get to know each other better.

There is another problem with e-mail: You don't get much information from the message. You have only the words themselves. This doesn't matter if the message is just about facts or if it is not important. But it might cause trouble if the message is about something important. You can't tell much about the person who sent the message. You have no idea what she was thinking or feeling. You may put your own feelings into the message. And this can lead to communication problems in a company.

In England, psychologists did some research about using e-mail at work. They studied office workers opening their e-mail. The psychologists measured the blood pressure of the workers. They found that certain kinds of messages made blood pressure go up. It went up if the messages seemed angry or negative. It also went up if the messages were from the boss. It went up the highest when the messages were both negative and from the boss.

The psychologists said that people should be careful how they use e-mail at work. This is especially true for the people with top jobs in a company. Their messages can easily hurt or upset people. They should never send important news by e-mail. They should always meet face to face with the person. Then everyone will understand each other better and will work together better.

1. What are some problems with e-mail at work?

2. What did psychologists in England do research about?

3. Why should people be careful about using e-mail?

Show your answers to another student. Do you have the same answers? Check your answers by reading the whole article.

PART 3

Thinking Skills

How to Think in English

If you want to read English well, you must think in English. The Thinking Skills exercises in this part will help you learn to think in English.

Example:

This paragraph is not complete: The ending is missing. Read the paragraph and the four possible endings. Decide which is the best ending and circle the letter.

Henry went to the doctor because he couldn't see well. The doctor told him he should get a new pair of

a. eyes.
b. pants.
c. gloves.
d. glasses.

The correct ending is *d*. Henry needs to get new glasses. He couldn't see well, and a new pair of glasses will help him see better. Ending *a* is not correct because Henry can't get new eyes. It doesn't make sense. Endings *b* and *c* are not correct because pants and gloves will not help Henry see better.

Guidelines for Thinking Skills Exercises

1. Do some Thinking Skills exercises every week.

2. Work quickly. Your first guess will often be the right one!

3. Don't use a dictionary. Try to guess the meaning of new words from the context.

4. Don't translate the words. You can follow the ideas better—and get the right answer—if you think in English!

5. When you finish an exercise, check your answers with your teacher.

6. Write the date and the number of questions you answered correctly in the Thinking Skills Progress Chart below.

Thinking Skills Progress Chart

Write the date and number of questions you answered correctly.

Exercise	1	2	3	4	5	6	7	8	9	10	11	12	13	14	15	16	17	18	19	20	21	22	23	24	25
Number Correct																									
Date																									

Choose the best ending for each paragraph.

1. The driest place on the earth is the Atacama Desert in Chile. Scientists say that in this desert there is never any
   a. sun.
   b. wind.
   c. rain.
   d. sand.

2. In the past, people traveled across the Atlantic by ship. The trip took months. But now a plane can cross the Atlantic in
   a. a few months.
   b. a long time.
   c. a few hours.
   d. more time.

3. The easiest way to get somewhere is to walk. It's not the fastest way, but it's cheap. You don't need anything special. You only need
   a. two feet.
   b. a ticket.
   c. a car.
   d. gas.

4. On special days, the whole family has dinner at our house. Everyone came last week for my father's
   a. parents.
   b. family.
   c. house.
   d. birthday.

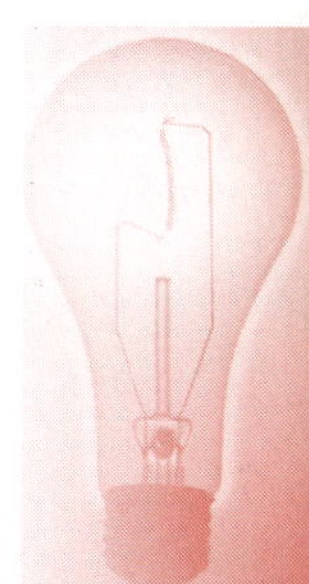

5. In the morning, the language lab was full of people. Many students were waiting for a seat. Jill decided to come back later when the lab was
   a. closed.
   b. busy.
   c. more crowded.
   d. less crowded.

Choose the best ending for each paragraph.

1. In very hot countries, the sun can hurt your eyes. It's a good idea to wear a hat when you are outside. You should also wear
   a. shoes.
   b. sunglasses.
   c. a swimsuit.
   d. gloves.

2. New York City is one of the biggest cities in the world. It has about seven million people. Tokyo is even larger. It has
   a. a million people.
   b. thousands of people.
   c. as many people.
   d. eight million people.

3. Curtains on the windows can make a room cooler in the summer. They let air come into the room, but they
   a. stop the wind.
   b. keep out the sun.
   c. stop the flies.
   d. keep out the rain.

4. Some plants grow in very dry places. These desert plants can live for a long time with no
   a. flowers.
   b. sun.
   c. food.
   d. water.

5. Clocks were first made in Europe in about 1500. Before then, people looked at the sun
   a. to tell the time.
   b. to get places.
   c. in the morning.
   d. to read.

Choose the best ending for each paragraph.

1. Every year, the flu kills many people in the United States. It is especially dangerous for older people. The flu can lead to health problems and
   a. other countries.
   b. younger people.
   c. new medicines.
   d. even death.

2. Parents should not let small children eat candy often. It's not good for their teeth, so it could mean expensive bills from the
   a. supermarket.
   b. babysitter.
   c. dentist.
   d. doctor.

3. People used to think that the sun moved around the earth. They thought the earth stayed in one place and the sun
   a. went around the moon.
   b. moved across the sky.
   c. never moved.
   d. also stayed still.

4. Many farmers in Florida grow oranges. They also grow lemons, limes, and grapefruit. Florida is famous for its
   a. apples.
   b. vegetables.
   c. weather.
   d. fruit.

5. The people who work on the orange farms in Florida often work in terrible conditions. They are paid very little and they
   a. don't like oranges.
   b. like working on farms.
   c. don't have to work hard.
   d. have to work very hard.

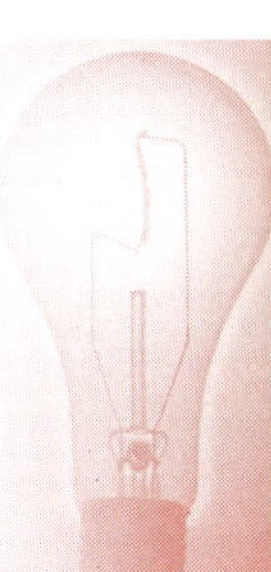

EXERCISE 4

Choose the best ending for each paragraph.

1. Pittsburgh, Pennsylvania, used to be a very dirty city. The dirt came from the steel factories. Everything in the city was covered with
   a. new grass.
   b. clean sand.
   c. big signs.
   d. black dust.

2. Jazz started in the United States around 1900. Now there are jazz musicians around the world. But the most famous jazz musicians are
   a. English.
   b. dead.
   c. European.
   d. American.

3. The Wright brothers are famous in the history of flying. In 1903, they flew 120 feet in the world's first
    a. automobile.
    b. machine.
    c. airplane.
    d. wings.

4. Last week, Mr. Thomas rented a new apartment. He does not have a table, chairs, or any other furniture yet. The apartment looks
    a. empty.
    b. full.
    c. comfortable.
    d. crowded.

5. In the past, people used the sun to tell time. They went to bed when it was dark, and they got up when it was light. When the sun was highest, they knew it was
    a. midnight.
    b. morning.
    c. noon.
    d. late.

EXERCISE 5

Choose the best ending for each paragraph.

1. Big windows can be dangerous for birds. They don't understand that there is glass. They see sky or trees in the windows and they crash into
    a. other birds.
    b. the glass.
    c. the ground.
    d. airplanes.

2. People used to learn the news from the newspaper. But today many people don't read the paper. They prefer to learn the news from
    a. television.
    b. a movie.
    c. books.
    d. friends.

3. Every country has a national holiday. This holiday usually is an important date in the history of
    a. the United States.
    b. the summer.
    c. the world.
    d. that country.

4. Whales are the largest animals in the ocean, but some whales eat only very tiny fish. That means they must
   a. eat larger fish.
   b. drink a lot of water.
   c. eat a lot of fish.
   d. travel far.

5. In a cold climate, plants grow quickly in the spring and summer. This is partly because the weather is warmer. It is also because the days are longer and plants get more
   a. air.
   b. sunlight.
   c. water.
   d. leaves.

EXERCISE 6

Choose the best ending for each paragraph.

1. Coffee grows in places with a warm climate. In some parts of the world, the land is good for growing coffee, but the winters are too
   a. cold.
   b. dry.
   c. short.
   d. cloudy.

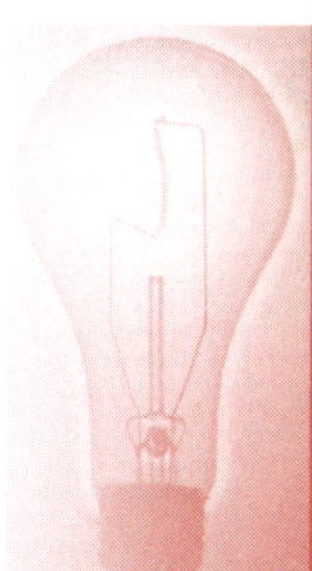

2. In Sweden, the summer days are long, and the sun shines for many hours. But the winter is very dark. The days are short because the sun rises late and sets
   a. late.
   b. beautifully.
   c. at midnight.
   d. early.

3. Forest Park is in the city of Portland, Oregon. It is the biggest natural park in a United States city. It doesn't have baseball fields, gardens, or snack bars. The whole park is a
   a. city.
   b. forest.
   c. field.
   d. camp.

4. Penguins are unusual birds. They can swim very well. But they are heavy and have very small wings, so they cannot
   a. sing.
   b. talk.
   c. fish.
   d. fly.

5. I'm reading a book about the life of Tolstoy, the famous Russian writer. He had a
   very interesting life. His wife helped him a lot by
   a. playing the piano.
   b. speaking French.
   c. reading his stories.
   d. going to Moscow.

EXERCISE 7

Choose the best ending for each paragraph.

1. Alexander Graham Bell made the first telephone in 1876 in the United States.
   Now the telephone is international. You can use it to talk to someone anywhere
   a. in the city.
   b. in the world.
   c. in history.
   d. on time.

2. Cooking can be dangerous. You can cut yourself with the kitchen knife. Or you
   can burn yourself
   a. on the stove.
   b. with a glass.
   c. in the sink.
   d. with a fork.

3. In California, the time is three hours earlier than the time in New York. If it is
   eleven o'clock in New York, it must be
   a. three o'clock in California.
   b. eight o'clock in California.
   c. two o'clock in California.
   d. eleven o'clock in California.

4. Did you know that fish can make noises? There are many ways for them to do
   this. For example, some kinds of fish use their teeth to
   a. move around.
   b. bite people.
   c. get food.
   d. make noises.

5. Thousands of years ago, people loved gold. They wore gold rings, earrings, and
   bracelets. Today, people still like to wear jewelry made of
   a. rings.
   b. gold.
   c. bracelets.
   d. wood.

Choose the best ending for each paragraph.

1. A bicycle is useful in the city. It's faster than walking. It can go more places than a car. Also, with a bicycle, you don't have to look for a
   a. parking space.
   b. road.
   c. wheel.
   d. driver.

2. In New York, one thing hasn't changed for fifty years. A piece of pizza costs the same as a ride on the subway. In the 1950s, they both cost fifteen cents. Today,
   a. they both cost two dollars.
   b. the subway is expensive.
   c. they still both cost fifteen cents.
   d. pizza costs more than the subway.

3. The best way to learn about a new city is to walk around. You can watch people and listen to their conversations. You can look at things in the shop windows. This way you will get to know
   a. the price of food.
   b. the language.
   c. how the people live.
   d. the history of the city.

4. Denver, Colorado, is next to the Rocky Mountains. In fact, the city is partly in the mountains. That is why it is called the
   a. "low city."
   b. "mile-high city."
   c. "flat city."
   d. "city of dreams."

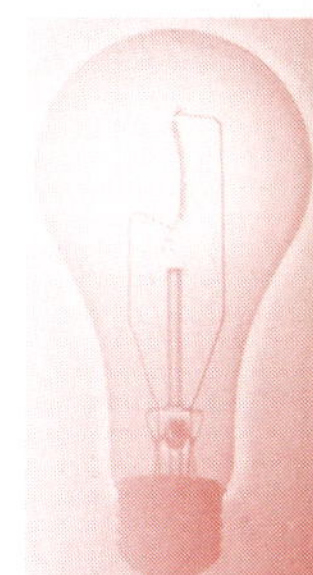

5. Are you going out? The weather report says that a rainstorm is coming later tonight. Before you leave the house, please be sure to
   a. watch the news.
   b. close the windows.
   c. lock the door.
   d. read the newspaper.

Choose the best ending for each paragraph.

1. The Marais is a nice neighborhood to visit in Paris. It doesn't have big museums and fancy shops. It's a quiet, old neighborhood, with nice buildings and
   a. a beautiful park.
   b. dirty streets.
   c. too many cars.
   d. a big supermarket.

2. You can tell a horse's age by looking at its teeth. You can learn about its health by looking at its eyes. So before you buy a horse, look carefully at its
   a. chest.
   b. feet.
   c. tail.
   d. head.

3. Summer sports are popular even in northern countries with short summers. For example, in Sweden, sailing is an important national sport. So is
   a. ice skating.
   b. tennis.
   c. cooking.
   d. skiing.

4. Doctors say that your body needs lots of water all day. They say it's a good idea to drink
   a. nothing during the day.
   b. only tea in the afternoon.
   c. several glasses of water a day.
   d. water only in the morning.

5. "April showers bring May flowers." People say this in places where April is a rainy month. The rain helps plants grow. Then, in May, many plants
   a. have flowers.
   b. are finished.
   c. have fruits.
   d. are still seeds.

Choose the best ending for each paragraph.

1. Many people are afraid of new things. This is not a new fear. In the nineteenth century, the first trains terrified people. They said that the trains went too fast and were
   a. necessary.
   b. comfortable.
   c. dangerous.
   d. beautiful.

2. Some birds fly many miles every year. In the fall, they leave their homes in the north and fly south to warmer places. In the spring, they leave their winter homes and go back
   a. north.
   b. south.
   c. around.
   d. away.

3. One hundred years ago, there were no radios, CD players, or televisions. If people wanted to hear music, they had to go to a concert, or they had to
   a. go to the city.
   b. play music themselves.
   c. change the station.
   d. stay home.

4. Franz Joseph Haydn wrote music in the 1700s. He lived to be seventy-seven years old. Many younger musicians loved him, and they learned a lot from him. To them, Haydn was like
   a. a son.
   b. a violinist.
   c. other old men.
   d. a father.

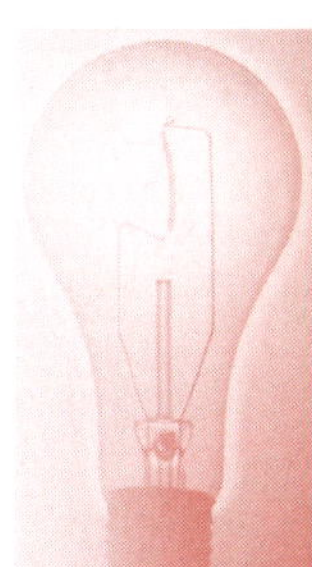

5. Many great singers are Italian. In fact, singing is an important part of Italian culture. Some people say that even the Italian language sounds
   a. like English.
   b. like music.
   c. different.
   d. the same.

Choose the best ending for each paragraph.

1. In the 1930s, Shirley Temple was a child movie star. She was very popular when she was very young. She was also very rich. She became a millionaire
   a. in the 1940s.
   b. when she was ten.
   c. after she died.
   d. in a movie.

2. In the twentieth century, millions of Russians were sent to Siberia. It was very cold there, and there was very little food. Most of them
   a. lived a long life.
   b. wrote books about it.
   c. were happy there.
   d. didn't live very long.

3. Two hundred years ago, corn was grown only in South and North America. Now it is an important food all around the world. It is even grown
   a. in South America.
   b. on farms.
   c. in China.
   d. in the United States.

4. Europeans discovered tomatoes in South America in the sixteenth century. At first they thought this new fruit was not healthy to eat. They believed that tomatoes made you
   a. live longer.
   b. hungry.
   c. fatter.
   d. sick.

5. Sometimes distant mountains look blue. When you look closer, you see that they are not blue. They just look blue when they are
   a. near the sky.
   b. under the clouds.
   c. large.
   d. far away.

Choose the best ending for each paragraph.

1. Queen Victoria was born in 1819. She became queen in 1837 and she remained queen until her death in 1901. She ruled England for most of the nineteenth century. In fact, the second half of that century is called the
   a. royal period.
   b. Elizabethan period.
   c. Victorian period.
   d. English period.

2. In the United States, many children watch TV for hours every day. They never read books, except at school. It is not surprising that these children
   a. have no books.
   b. go to school.
   c. can read well.
   d. cannot read well.

3. In cold weather, it's important to wear a hat. In fact, without a hat, you lose 25 percent of your body heat through your
   a. hands.
   b. head.
   c. hat.
   d. body.

4. New Yorkers generally love city life. They like noisy places and bright lights. They often aren't happy in the country. For many of them, the country seems too
   a. noisy.
   b. loud.
   c. quiet.
   d. bright.

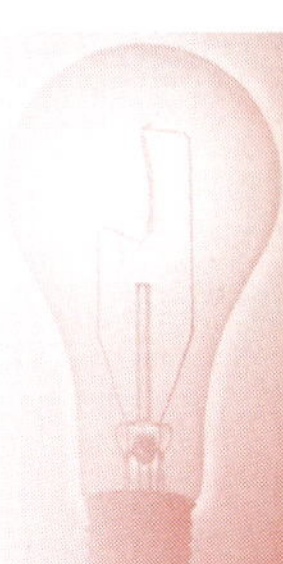

5. Cooking is different in the mountains. You have to cook things longer. For example, it usually takes about an hour to bake bread. But in the mountains, it may take
   a. an hour and a half.
   b. half an hour.
   c. less time.
   d. forty-five minutes.

Choose the best ending for each paragraph.

1. Seagulls are birds that usually live near the ocean. But you can also find seagulls near cities. Their favorite food is fish, but they will eat
   a. at the beach.
   b. only fish.
   c. near the ocean.
   d. almost anything.

2. In New England, the weather changes often. It may be sunny in the morning. Then it can be very cold and rainy in the afternoon. That is why a famous writer said, "If you don't like the weather in New England,
   a. go home."
   b. wait a few hours."
   c. bring an umbrella."
   d. listen to the radio."

3. Nineveh was an important city in the Middle East in the seventh century. It was famous for its gardens, its religious buildings, and its library. It was a rich and
   a. empty city.
   b. ugly city.
   c. beautiful city.
   d. modern city.

4. In a civil war, people in the same country fight each other. This can be the most terrible kind of war. Sometimes even people from the same family
   a. work together.
   b. fight each other.
   c. live near each other.
   d. move to another country.

5. Why are some people afraid of airplane travel? In fact, it is much more dangerous to ride in a car. There are very few airplane accidents, but every year there are
   a. thousands of airplane accidents.
   b. very few car accidents.
   c. thousands of car accidents.
   d. very few bicycle accidents.

Choose the best ending for each paragraph.

1. The idea of flying is old. Thousands of years ago, people watched birds in the air. They studied the birds' wings, and they made wings with bird feathers. Then they
    a. flew like birds.
    b. tried to fly.
    c. will fly someday.
    d. told stories.

2. What is your favorite color? If it is red, you may be a lively kind of person. If you like blue, you may be a person who likes peace and quiet. Your favorite color tells something about
    a. colors.
    b. life.
    c. you.
    d. peace.

3. Sputnik was the first spaceship. The Russians sent it up into space in 1957. Soon after that, the Americans sent up a spaceship, too. That was the beginning of the
    a. Scientific Age.
    b. Space Age.
    c. Nuclear Age.
    d. Industrial Age.

4. Jules Verne is called the "father of science fiction." He wrote novels in the 1800s. In his novels, he described many things that really happened later. For example, he told about airplanes and submarine ships. He also told about a trip to
    a. the moon.
    b. the seaside.
    c. America.
    d. the sun.

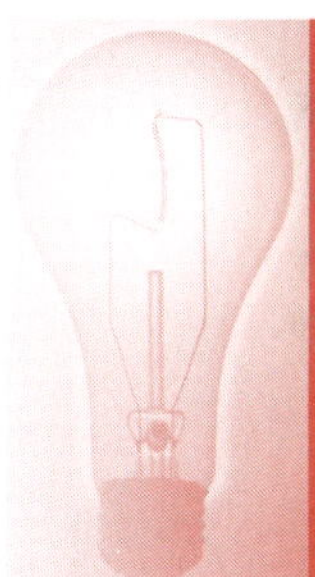

5. On weekends, people in New York City like to go away. They go to the country, to the mountains, or to the sea. Every Friday evening, the roads going out of New York City are
    a. empty.
    b. crowded.
    c. wet.
    d. wide.

Choose the best ending for each paragraph.

1. The whale swims like a fish and lives in the ocean, but it is not a fish. A fish stays under water all the time. A whale must have air. It can go down deep in the ocean for many minutes, but it always needs to
   a. find a fish to eat.
   b. swim a long way.
   c. act like a fish.
   d. come up again for air.

2. On some days, the clouds are thin and high in the sky. These clouds may mean rain in the next few days. On other days, there are heavy, dark clouds. They often mean rain is coming soon. Clouds can tell you a lot about the
   a. sky.
   b. air.
   c. weather.
   d. temperature.

3. Around the world, the roads near cities are full of cars every day. This traffic is not good for the cities for a number of reasons. One of the worst effects of daily traffic is
   a. fresh air.
   b. dirty water.
   c. dirty air.
   d. clean water.

4. If you work on a computer, you can work anywhere. You don't need to work in an office. In fact, many people now go to the office only for meetings. They do most of their work
   a. for the company.
   b. at school.
   c. in the office.
   d. at home.

5. In the early nineteenth century, Italy was not really a country. The area had many small countries with different governments. In 1870, all these small countries came together. Then
   a. modern Italy died.
   b. modern Italy was born.
   c. the old Italy was born.
   d. they started a war.

Choose the best ending for each paragraph.

1. The Hebrides Islands are in the northwest of Scotland. The sea is beautiful there, but the water is cold, even in summer. It is not a good place to go
   a. fishing.
   b. swimming.
   c. shopping.
   d. walking.

2. Tweed is a special kind of woolen cloth. The Scottish island of Harris is famous for its tweed. All around the world, people pay a lot of money for
   a. Scottish bread.
   b. woolen cloth.
   c. the island of Harris.
   d. Harris tweed.

3. Today, some fishing boats are like factories. They can catch and freeze large amounts of fish. But they catch too many fish, in fact. Now, some areas of the oceans have
   a. very dirty water.
   b. lots of ice left.
   c. lots of fish left.
   d. very few fish left.

4. A violin maker has to choose the wood carefully. For a good violin, she needs very special wood. A violin made from the wrong wood will
   a. sound better.
   b. sound the same.
   c. not sound as nice.
   d. have no sound at all.

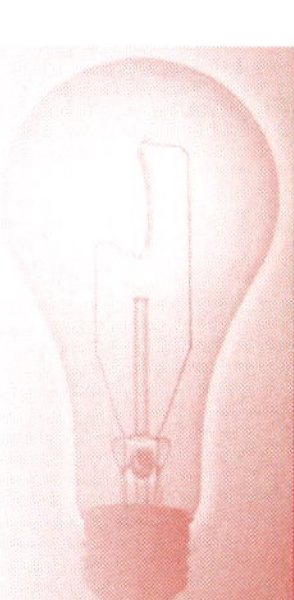

5. Some birds travel long distances. They may fly thousands of miles to a winter home. Then they fly back to their old home in the spring. They always return to the same place. No one knows how they do it. Scientists think these birds have
   a. a language in their heads.
   b. a map in their heads.
   c. special feathers on their wings.
   d. longer lives than other birds.

Choose the best ending for each paragraph.

1. Louis XIV was king of France from 1643 until 1715. He was called the "Sun King" because he was a very powerful and rich king. But he was not a very clean king. He had a bath
   a. every day of his life.
   b. in a gold bathroom.
   c. many times in his life.
   d. only three times in his life.

2. Some scientists used to have strange ideas about the size of a person's head. They thought that people with large heads were the smartest and that people with smaller heads were
   a. not as smart.
   b. also smart.
   c. the smartest.
   d. even smarter.

3. Strong muscles are less important than a strong heart. A healthy and strong heart is necessary for a long life. People with weak hearts usually
   a. live longer.
   b. die at a younger age.
   c. get better.
   d. do not die young.

4. Doctors often say that you should not smoke cigarettes, you should not be fat, and you should not work too hard. All these things can give you heart trouble. Some doctors get heart attacks. Maybe they don't
   a. smoke cigarettes.
   b. work too hard.
   c. do what they say.
   d. eat what they cook.

5. Every year, more people move to cities. They think they will find better jobs in the city. They don't want to work on farms and live in small towns. Cities are growing larger all the time, and
   a. more people are living on farms.
   b. people are more interesting.
   c. there are no jobs in small towns.
   d. fewer people are living on farms.

Choose the best ending for each paragraph.

1. All living things change over time. It may take many thousands or millions of years. Often, the changes are caused by the place where they live. For example, some fish live in rivers deep underground. There is no light where they live, so these fish have no
   a. food.
   b. eyes.
   c. eggs.
   d. babies.

2. The American Civil War was a difficult time. The northern states were fighting the southern states. Sometimes families who lived in the central states were divided by the war. In some cases, one son fought for the North and another
   a. for the South.
   b. left the state.
   c. stayed home.
   d. for the family.

3. Brighton Beach is a neighborhood in New York City. There are many Russian people living there, and many of the shops and restaurants are Russian. In fact, the neighborhood is sometimes called
   a. "Little New York."
   b. "Little Odessa."
   c. "Little Beach."
   d. "Little Tokyo."

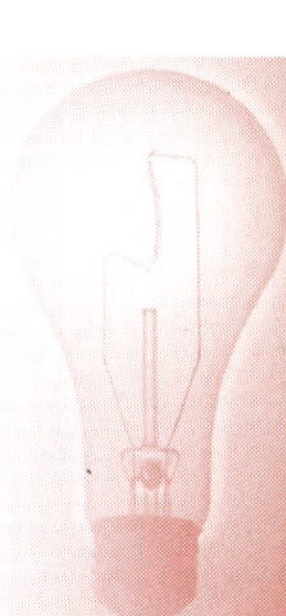

4. Every year, the Italian neighborhood in New York City has a special holiday, San Gennaro. On that day, people sell Italian food in the street. There are Italian songs and dances. There are games and exciting rides. The streets are
   a. full of Chinese people.
   b. very quiet that day.
   c. full of people.
   d. empty all day.

5. World War I ended in 1918. It was a terrible war that killed millions of people. Many Europeans believed there would be no more wars. They called World War I
   a. "the first of many."
   b. "the war to end all wars."
   c. "only the beginning."
   d. "a war to be proud of."

Choose the best ending for each paragraph.

1. Two thousand years ago, the Romans ruled much of the Western world. The city
of Rome was in the center. Writers like to say that in those days
   a. "no roads led to Rome."
   b. "all roads led to Rome."
   c. "all roads led to the West."
   d. "all roads led to the East."

2. Sir Edmund Hillary was the first person to reach the top of Mt. Everest. But he
was not alone. He was with a man from Nepal named Tenzing Norgay. Many
people know Hillary's name, but few people
   a. remember Norgay.
   b. know about Mt. Everest.
   c. go mountain climbing.
   d. like the people in Nepal.

3. The violin, viola, and cello all belong to the same family of musical instruments.
The violin is the smallest, with the highest sound. The viola is larger, with a
lower sound. The cello is largest, with the lowest sound. In this family,
   a. larger instruments have lower sounds.
   b. the size makes no difference to the sound.
   c. large instruments have higher sounds.
   d. the sizes are all the same.

4. The Koruba are people who live in Brazil. Their homeland is deep in the jungle
near the Amazon River. They live the same way they have always lived. They
don't know anything about
   a. life in the jungle.
   b. the modern world.
   c. the Amazon River.
   d. the Koruba people.

5. Most European languages came from the same language thousands of years ago,
so in some ways they are alike. But Hungarian and Finnish are different from
the other European languages. In fact, they
   a. came from the same language as the others.
   b. are spoken all over Europe.
   c. are also alike in some ways.
   d. came from a different language.

Choose the best ending for each paragraph.

1. One hundred years ago, the British Empire was very large. The British sent ships and soldiers to North and South America, Africa, and Asia. There were British ships all around the world. The British were proud of this. They liked to say, "The sun never sets
   a. in England."
   b. in our hearts."
   c. on the far side of the world."
   d. on the British Empire."

2. In some cowboy movies, the cowboys are all either good or bad. The good cowboys are great men who help everyone. The bad cowboys are robbers and killers. But in real life, most cowboys were just like other men—not all good or bad. The idea of cowboys we get from movies is
   a. very true.
   b. not true.
   c. good.
   d. helpful.

3. On average, Americans move to a new home every seven years. However, some Americans never move. They live all their lives in the same place. So there must be other Americans who
   a. move to new homes.
   b. move very often.
   c. never move.
   d. move every seven years.

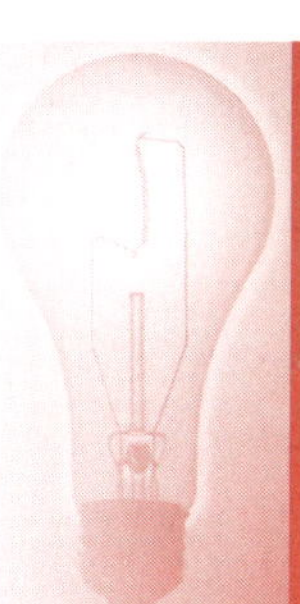

4. Some people say that it's harder to learn things when you get older. They say your brain doesn't work as quickly. That is why they sometimes say, "You can't teach
   a. a young dog anything."
   b. an old dog new tricks."
   c. a young dog new tricks."
   d. a dog when you are young."

5. The Potato Famine happened in Ireland in the 1840s. The Irish people were poor. They couldn't buy meat or bread because they were too expensive. They ate mostly potatoes. Then a disease killed many of the potato plants. With no potatoes to eat, the people
   a. were happier.
   b. ate meat instead.
   c. died of hunger.
   d. were ill.

Choose the best ending for each paragraph.

1. Kinkajous are small animals that live in South America. Few people have seen a kinkajou because these animals live high up in trees and they
   a. sleep during the day.
   b. sleep during the night.
   c. come down every day.
   d. are friendly with children.

2. "An apple a day keeps the doctor away." That's what mothers used to say to their children. People believed that it was good to eat lots of apples, but they didn't know why. Now, scientists know that this is true, and they know why. Apples really are
   a. good for your health.
   b. bad for your teeth.
   c. very unhealthy.
   d. good for your doctor.

3. John Logie Baird sent the first television picture in 1925. He didn't send it very far. It went just from one office to another office in London. Two years later, he sent a picture from London to Glasgow. Then, in 1928, he sent a picture much farther away, from London to
   a. London.
   b. New York.
   c. Scotland.
   d. his house.

4. The plains zebra lives in large groups in Africa. Every year, these groups travel about 300 miles in a big circle. They follow the seasons and the rain. When one area becomes too dry, they
   a. are afraid of lions.
   b. move to another area.
   c. wait for the rain.
   d. move to the desert.

5. In the United States, there are many people from Central and South America. More people arrive from this area every year. They come from many different countries, but the largest group comes from
   a. China.
   b. Miami.
   c. Mexico.
   d. Texas.

Choose the best ending for each paragraph.

1. Hong Kong is an interesting mixture of people and ideas. It is now part of China, but it belonged to Great Britain in the past. In some ways, it seems British. But in many other ways, it is
    a. Chinese.
    b. Western.
    c. new.
    d. American.

2. Many of the most famous marathon runners are from Africa. Young African men and women work very hard at running. They practice long hours and become very strong. That's why they
    a. started running races.
    b. don't eat any meat.
    c. win so many races.
    d. travel so much.

3. Today, people run much faster than they did in the past. Until 1954, the fastest time for running a mile was over four minutes. That year, Roger Bannister ran a mile in less than four minutes. Since then, many other runners have also
    a. run a mile very slowly.
    b. been able to run a mile.
    c. run a mile in over four minutes.
    d. run a mile in less than four minutes.

4. Many English words come from Greek words. For example, the Greek word for *star* is *aster*. So the scientists who study the sky are called
    a. philosophers.
    b. sky-gazers.
    c. astronomers.
    d. archaeologists.

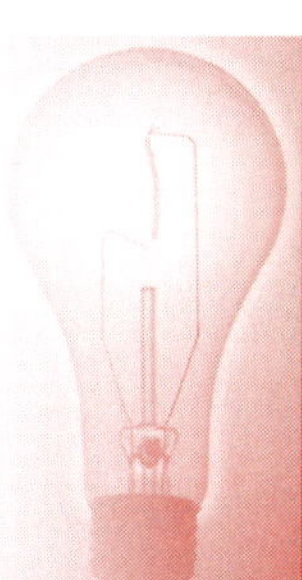

5. In the last few years of his life, Beethoven could not hear. In his earlier life, he always tried out his music on the piano. Later, however, he could not do that. When he wrote his music, he had to
    a. listen to an orchestra.
    b. play the violin.
    c. sing it to someone.
    d. think it in his head.

Choose the best ending for each paragraph.

1. Many New Yorkers live in tall apartment buildings. The nicest apartments with the best views are the ones at the top. These are called penthouse apartments. Everyone wants these apartments, of course, but they are usually
   a. empty.
   b. the most expensive.
   c. the last ones to be rented.
   d. the least expensive.

2. In the 1920s, scientists discovered the remains of Peking Man in China. He lived more than 400,000 years ago. He was not a modern human being, but he was very similar. He probably used fire, and he
   a. walked on two feet.
   b. walked on four feet.
   c. couldn't walk at all.
   d. didn't eat meat.

3. One very large apartment building in New York is like a small city. In the building, you can shop for food, meet friends in a restaurant, go for a swim, or get a haircut. If you live there, you never need to go
   a. shopping.
   b. outside.
   c. home.
   d. to New York.

4. Strange things happen when there is a full moon. More babies are born. Cats and other pets become restless. Some people cannot sleep. So it is not surprising that when the moon is full there are
   a. fewer letters in the mail.
   b. more car accidents.
   c. more stars in the sky.
   d. fewer car accidents.

5. In the country, you can see many things in the night sky. If you know some astronomy, you can find stars, the Milky Way galaxy, and sometimes some planets. In the city, it is different. You can't see many stars, because
   a. they are too far away.
   b. there is not enough time.
   c. there are no stars near cities.
   d. the city lights are too bright.

Choose the best ending for each paragraph.

1. In the U.S. state of Indiana, there is a town called Peru. Every summer, something special happens in this town. The whole town puts on a circus. The children and young people are in the circus. Their relatives and friends are
    a. at home.
    b. in the audience.
    c. at the zoo.
    d. on vacation.

2. Do you like crime stories with happy endings? Then you'll like the books by Sue Grafton. They're about a smart, young detective named Kinsey Millhone. In these books, someone is usually killed, and Kinsey
    a. always finds the killer.
    b. never finds the killer.
    c. often kills someone, too.
    d. sometimes goes to New York.

3. Tea is a popular drink in many countries. In Russia, the people use a special pot to boil water for tea. It's called a *samovar*. This pot is important to Russian families. Even a poor family usually
    a. has a samovar.
    b. drinks milk.
    c. boils water.
    d. makes tea.

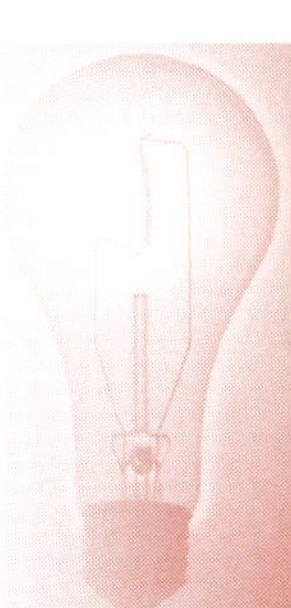

4. People who live alone sometimes feel ill and unhappy. Their doctors may tell them to get a pet. Their "medicine" can be a dog, cat, bird, or goldfish. These people are not sick. They just need
    a. some medicine.
    b. a new doctor.
    c. something to love.
    d. to find a new job.

5. Elephants and whales are a lot alike. Elephants are the largest animals on land. Whales are the largest animals in the sea. People hunt and kill both whales and elephants, and now there are many fewer than in the past. Someday,
    a. elephants will not be large anymore.
    b. there may be more whales and elephants.
    c. there may not be any more whales or elephants.
    d. whales will move to different parts of the sea.

Choose the best ending for each paragraph.

1. Nutella is a popular Italian food. It's made from chocolate, nuts, and sugar. Someone invented it after World War II. At that time, chocolate was very hard to get and very expensive. Nutella was a great success because it tasted like chocolate but it
   a. was cheaper.
   b. was terrible.
   c. wasn't cheap.
   d. was very hard to get.

2. On a map, Italy looks like an old-fashioned, knee-high boot. The top of the boot is the border with France, Switzerland, and Austria. The bottom of the boot goes out into the Mediterranean Sea, and it seems to have a
   a. hand and finger.
   b. heel and toe.
   c. shoe.
   d. mountain.

3. In 1895, Louis Lassen was a cook in New Haven, Connecticut. Some sailors from Hamburg, Germany, went to his coffee shop. They told him how to make a special kind of meat sandwich. Louis started selling the sandwich at his coffee shop. Soon it became very popular. Louis wanted to thank his sailor friends, so he called it a
   a. meat sandwich.
   b. new havener.
   c. hamburger.
   d. frankfurter.

4. Napoleon was a famous leader. He became the emperor of France, and he had a large army. He wasn't afraid of any people. But he was afraid of one kind of small animal. He was terribly afraid of
   a. cats.
   b. lions.
   c. war.
   d. guns.

5. In some countries, people are likely to try new foods. The English, for example, like to eat Indian and Chinese foods. In other countries, people prefer their own food. The Italians are a good example. Most of the restaurants in Italy serve Italian food, and when Italians go to other countries, they often
   a. love the food.
   b. don't eat the food.
   c. eat Chinese food.
   d. don't like the food.

PART 4

Reading Faster

Why Read Faster?

There are three important reasons for learning to read faster:

- You can read more in less time.
- You can understand more.
- You can learn to think in English.

How is it possible to understand more when you read faster? The answer is very simple: When you read slowly, you read one word at a time. This way, you read separate words like the words below. Is it easier or harder to understand these sentences?

> What really happens when we read? Some people think we read one word at a time. They think we read a word, understand it, and then move on to the next word.

Reading separate words makes it harder to understand. The separate words become separate pieces of information. It's hard to remember lots of separate pieces of information. You may not remember the beginning of a sentence when you get to the end!

When you read faster, you read groups of words. Then your memory can work better because you are reading phrases or small ideas. It's easier to remember these ideas than a lot of separate words. It's also easier to connect these ideas together. Then you can get the larger, general idea of what you are reading. This is why you can understand better when you read faster.

Reading phrases or groups of words also helps you learn to think in English. That's because your brain is understanding ideas, not words.

How to Read Faster: Three Steps

Step 1. Check your reading habits

The following bad habits can slow down your reading. Do you . . .

- . . . try to pronounce each word as you read? Pronunciation is not necessary for comprehension. In fact, if you try to say the words, you will probably understand less.
- . . . usually move your lips while you read silently? If you do, you will never be able to read faster than about 200 words per minute. That is the fastest speed you can speak in English.
- . . . follow the words in the text with your finger or a pencil? This is another habit that can slow down your reading. It also limits the way you read. If you point at the words, your eyes will follow the lines of text. But good readers often skip parts, or they may look back at something again. Your eyes should follow your thoughts, not your finger!
- . . . translate into your native language when you are reading in English? Do you often write the words in your language next to the English words? This slows your reading speed. It also means that you are thinking in your native language and not in English!

Step 2. Skip over unknown words

In order to read more quickly, good readers often skip many words. They skip over words they do not know. They also skip unimportant words. In fact, many words are not necessary for comprehension. You can get the general meaning without them.

Read the following examples. Many words are missing. Do not try to guess the missing words. Try to understand the general meaning of the passage. Then, answer the questions below.

Example a:

Mike loves to cook. He cooks all xxxxx of food, but he likes best to xxxx cakes. He says making cakes is very xxxxxxxx. When he is cooking, he does not xxxxx about work or bad things. He xxxxxx only about the cake. He can make very beautiful xxxxx with fruit or with xxxxxxxxx. On Saturdays, when Mike has xxxxxx of time, he makes a xxxxxxxxx good cake. After dinner, the xxxxxx family sits down xxxxxxxx to enjoy Mike's cake.

1. What does Mike like to do in his free time?

2. Why does he like it?

3. What does he do on Saturdays?

Talk with another student. Do you have the same answers?

Example b:

Do you have an e-mail (electronic mail) address? Xxxxxxxx of people xxxxxx the world have e-mail addresses. With e-mail you can xxxx with people from Montevideo to Kyoto. Many xxxxxx use it for fun. They talk with their xxxxxx or family through e-mail, or they xxx e-mail to "meet" with xxxxxx who have the same interests. E-mail is also very xxxxxx for people at work. Many offices and stores now xxxx e-mail addresses. They use e-mail for all kinds of xxxxxxxx. It is much faster than xxxxxxx mail. It can take even xxxx time than a phone call.

1. Where do people use e-mail?

2. Why do people use e-mail for fun?

3. Why do people use e-mail at work?

Talk with another student. Do you have the same answers?

Step 3. Practice reading faster by timing yourself

To increase your reading speed, you can use a clock and time yourself. Then you can find out how fast you read, and you can try to push yourself to read faster. Many students have a reading rate between 50 and 200 words per minute. If you read less than 200 words per minute, you are reading word by word. That means you are probably also having trouble understanding what you read.

Use the examples on the next pages to practice timing yourself and to find out your reading rate. Be sure to *write down the exact time you start and finish reading the passage.*

Example c:

Write your starting time on the line at the top of the passage. Preview the passage and then read it all the way through to the end. Push yourself to read a little faster than usual. When you finish reading, write the time on the line at the bottom of the passage.

Alaska: Animals Everywhere

Starting time __________

Animals are everywhere in Alaska. If you go out to the wild areas, you can see a lot of wild animals. Some large animals, like the caribou, live in groups, and you can see hundreds of them. You can see other large animals, such as moose and deer. There are also bears and wolves, of course. These animals are not as dangerous as people think. If you stay away from them, they will usually stay away from you. They are usually afraid of people.

Sometimes the wild animals come to areas with people. You may see deer or moose, for example, in someone's backyard. This makes the children and the tourists happy, but it's a problem for Alaskan gardeners. These animals like to eat the plants in gardens, and they walk all over the grass and flowers.

A lot of people in Alaska have animals at home, too. Dogs are the favorite pet, especially huskies. The Eskimos use these dogs to pull sleds in the winter. Many Alaskans now keep huskies and go dog sledding as a sport. There are competitions for the most beautiful dogs and the strongest dogs. Of course, there are dogsled races, too.

Finishing time __________
Subtract your starting time − __________
Your reading time __________

Answer the questions on the following page. Do not look back at the passage.

1. This article is about
   a. wild animals.
   b. tourists in Alaska.
   c. animals in Alaska.
   d. travel in Alaska.

2. In Alaska, you can see many
   a. people.
   b. mountains.
   c. wild animals.
   d. wolves.

3. Bears and wolves
   a. often kill people.
   b. are afraid of people.
   c. stay in the mountains.
   d. usually like people.

4. You can sometimes see wild animals in
   a. the park.
   b. the zoo.
   c. backyards.
   d. houses.

5. Moose and deer sometimes eat
   a. garden plants.
   b. food in kitchens.
   c. fruit in stores.
   d. tourists in cars.

6. Many Alaskans
   a. have pets.
   b. don't like pets.
   c. have computers.
   d. eat fruit.

7. Eskimos use huskies to
   a. hunt bears and wolves.
   b. keep them company.
   c. keep away the deer.
   d. pull sleds in winter.

8. Dog sledding
   a. is fun for children.
   b. stopped years ago.
   c. is not very popular.
   d. is a popular sport.

Check your answers with your teacher. If you have any incorrect answers, read the passage again to find the correct answers. Next, find your reading rate by looking up your reading time for Example c in Reading Rate Table 1 on page 186. Then, write your rate in Progress Chart 1 on page 187.

Example d:

Write your starting time on the line at the top of the passage. Preview the passage and then read it all the way through to the end. Push yourself to read a little faster than usual. When you finish reading, write the time on the line at the bottom of the passage.

A Taste of Brazil

Starting time __________

Brazilian food is like Brazil itself. It's a rich mixture of many things from many places. Some dishes are like Portuguese dishes. That is because many Portuguese people went to live in Brazil. Other dishes are not like any European dishes. The flavors are special to Brazil. Brazilian cooks are lucky. They can get excellent fish from the ocean. They can get good meat from the farms. And they can get all kinds of tropical fruits and vegetables. These foods give Brazilian dishes their special, delicious taste.

Brazil is a large country. Each area has its own history and traditions, and so each area also has its own way of cooking. If you are in Rio de Janeiro, for example, you should try the *feijoada*. It is a very rich mixture of different meats with black beans. Brazilians usually eat it on the weekend. It's not a dish to eat in a hurry!

After your meal, you must try Brazilian coffee—*cafezinho*. The Brazilians have a special little machine for making coffee, and their coffee is special, too. It's not like American coffee or Italian coffee. It's Brazilian, and it's very good.

Finishing time __________
Subtract your starting time −__________
Reading time __________

Answer the questions on the following page. Do not look back at the passage.

1. This article is about
   a. Brazilian cooks.
   b. traveling in Brazil.
   c. Portuguese cooking.
   d. Brazilian food.

2. Brazilian cooking
   a. has mostly European flavors.
   b. mixes many different things.
   c. is just like Portuguese cooking.
   d. is not very interesting.

3. In Brazil, there
   a. are lots of good meat and fish.
   b. isn't any good meat or fish.
   c. are many Portuguese cooks.
   d. aren't any good restaurants.

4. The special taste of Brazilian food comes from
   a. the fish that cooks often use.
   b. tropical fruits and vegetables.
   c. Portuguese cooking.
   d. the Brazilian way of life.

5. The history and traditions are
   a. different in different parts of Brazil.
   b. similar all over Brazil.
   c. different from those in Argentina.
   d. like those in Rio de Janeiro.

6. *Feijoada* is a special dish from
   a. Brazil.
   b. Rio de Janeiro.
   c. all over Brazil.
   d. Europe.

7. Brazilians usually eat *feijoada*
   a. on the weekends.
   b. on holidays.
   c. at the seaside.
   d. during the week.

8. Brazilians make coffee in
   a. American coffee machines.
   b. a special kind of machine.
   c. Italian coffee machines.
   d. special coffee shops.

Check your answers with your teacher. If you have any incorrect answers, read the passage again to find the correct answers. Next, find your reading rate by looking up your reading time for Example d in Reading Rate Table 1 on page 186. Then, write your rate in Progress Chart 1 on page 187.

Guidelines for Reading Faster

1. Try to read each passage a little faster.

2. Do not look back at the passage when you are answering the questions.

3. Check your answers with your teacher. If you have some incorrect answers, look back at the passage. Think again about your answers.

4. Find your reading rate on the Reading Rate Tables on page 186.

5. For each passage, write your reading rate and comprehension score (number of correct answers) on the Faster Reading Progress Charts (pages 187–189).

6. After reading four or five passages, look at the chart and check your progress.

   - If your reading rate has stayed the same, you must push yourself to read a little faster.

   - If you have more than two incorrect answers on any passage, you might be reading too quickly too soon. Slow down a little and read more carefully.

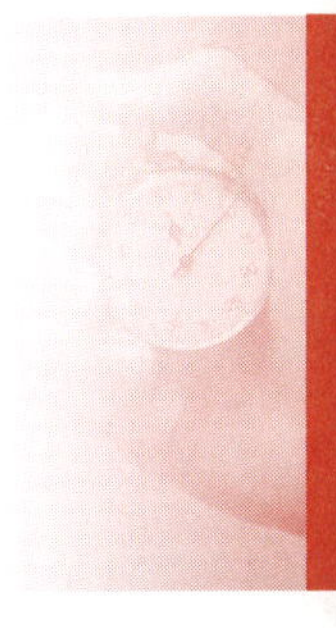

Reading Rate Tables

Table 1
Examples c and d
Unit 1, Passages 1–15

Reading Time (minutes)	Reading Rate (words per minute)
:30	400
:45	266
1:00	200
1:15	160
1:30	133
1:45	114
2:00	100
2:15	89
2:30	80
2:45	73
3:00	67
3:15	62
3:30	57
3:45	53
4:00	50
4:15	47
4:30	44
4:45	42
5:00	40

Table 2
Unit 1, Passages 16–20
Units 2 and 3

Reading Time (minutes)	Reading Rate (words per minute)
:30	800
:45	533
1:00	400
1:15	320
1:30	267
1:45	229
2:00	200
2:15	178
2:30	160
2:45	145
3:00	133
3:15	123
3:30	114
3:45	107
4:00	100
4:15	94
4:30	89
4:45	84
5:00	80
5:15	76
5:30	73
5:45	70
6:00	67
6:15	64
6:30	62
6:45	59
7:00	57

Faster Reading Progress Charts

Under the passage number, write the number of answers you had correct. Then make an "X" in the box next to your reading rate.

Faster Reading Progress Chart 1

Examples c and d
Unit 1, Passages 1–15

Passage	Examples c	Examples d	Unit 1 - 1	2	3	4	5	6	7	8	9	10	11	12	13	14	15
Number Correct																	
400																	
266																	
200																	
160																	
133																	
114																	
100																	
89																	
80																	
73																	
67																	
62																	
57																	
53																	
50																	
47																	
44																	
42																	
40																	
Date																	

Reading Rate (words per minute—WPM)

Faster Reading Progress Chart 2

Unit 1, Passages 16–20
Unit 2, Passages 21–30

Reading Rate (WPM)

Passage	Unit 1					Unit 2									
	16	17	18	19	20	21	22	23	24	25	26	27	28	29	30
Number Correct															
800															
533															
400															
320															
267															
229															
200															
178															
160															
145															
133															
123															
114															
107															
100															
94															
89															
84															
80															
76															
73															
70															
67															
64															
62															
59															
57															
Date															

Faster Reading Progress Chart 3

Unit 3, Passages 31–40

Passage	Unit 3									
	31	32	33	34	35	36	37	38	39	40
Number Correct										
800										
533										
400										
320										
267										
229										
200										
178										
160										
145										
133										
123										
114										
107										
100										
94										
89										
84										
80										
76										
73										
70										
67										
64										
62										
59										
57										
Date										

Reading Rate (WPM)

The Diamond Family

Passage 1: Susan and Sam

Starting time _________

Susan Conley Diamond and Sam Diamond live in Rosebud, a small town in New Jersey. It looks like many other towns in the United States. On Main Street, there is a post office and a police station. The drugstore and the library are down the street. There's also a shopping center, with a supermarket and a department store.

In the middle of Rosebud, near the post office, is Dr. Sam Diamond's office. Everybody in town knows Dr. Diamond. He's a good dentist. He's also a popular person. He likes to tell funny stories to his patients. They forget about their teeth when they listen to him.

Susan Conley is Sam Diamond's wife. She's a scientist with a Ph.D. in biology. She works with a group of scientists in a laboratory in New York City. They're studying the human brain and looking for ways to help people with Alzheimer's and other serious diseases.

Susan usually takes the train from Rosebud to New York. Sometimes she stays at home and works on her computer. She's very happy when she can work at home. But she likes working in the lab with interesting people, and she likes being in an exciting place like New York.

Finishing time _________   Reading time _________

Answer the questions on the following page.

1. This passage is about
    a. a town called Rosebud, New Jersey.
    b. Main Street in Rosebud, New Jersey.
    c. Sam and Susan.
    d. Susan's job in New York.

2. According to this passage, Rosebud is
    a. different from most towns in the United States.
    b. like many other towns in the United States.
    c. like no other towns in other countries.
    d. different from towns in other countries.

3. In Rosebud, there
    a. aren't many stores.
    b. aren't any drugstores.
    c. is a laboratory.
    d. is a drugstore.

4. Dr. Diamond is popular because
    a. he's a dentist in Rosebud.
    b. he listens to his patients.
    c. his office is in Rosebud.
    d. he tells funny stories.

5. Susan is
    a. Sam's wife.
    b. Sam's patient.
    c. not from Rosebud.
    d. popular in Rosebud.

6. Susan is a
    a. dentist.
    b. housewife.
    c. biologist.
    d. student.

7. Susan usually works
    a. in New Jersey.
    b. in New York.
    c. down the street.
    d. at home.

8. Susan thinks New York is
    a. a dangerous place.
    b. like other cities.
    c. not a nice place.
    d. an exciting place.

Susan and Sam live in an old, white house on Cleveland Road. They have two children, Ted and Jane. Ted and Jane are grown up now. They both live far away. Ted, a journalist, lives in Brazil with his wife, Maria. Jane, an airplane pilot, lives in Alaska. Ted and Jane's old rooms are always ready for them, and sometimes they come to visit.

Now Susan and Sam share their home with their pets: their cat, Lucky; their dog, Tuffy; and a bird named Pete. On weekends, they like to work in the yard. In the front yard, Sam grows roses and other flowers. In the back, Susan has a large vegetable garden. Sam uses the fresh vegetables in his cooking. He likes to cook special dinners and invite their friends.

In their free time, Susan and Sam also help the town of Rosebud. Every Tuesday evening, Susan goes to meetings at the town hall. The people at these meetings make important decisions about the future of the town. Every Monday evening, Sam goes to help the Rosebud Food Bank. The food bank gets food from stores and people in town. It gives the food to people without homes and jobs.

Finishing time _________   Reading time _________

Answer the questions on the following page.

1. This passage is about
   a. how families live.
   b. Rosebud, New Jersey.
   c. Susan and Sam's life.
   d. Susan and Sam's children.

2. Susan and Sam's children
   a. are grown up.
   b. live in Rosebud.
   c. live in Brazil.
   d. are very young.

3. Jane and Ted
   a. sometimes go to Alaska.
   b. have two children.
   c. have a white house.
   d. sometimes visit.

4. Susan and Sam
   a. have some pets.
   b. do not like pets.
   c. have no pets.
   d. want more pets.

5. Susan and Sam both like to work
   a. in the house.
   b. in the yard.
   c. with animals.
   d. in a store.

6. When they invite their friends for dinner,
   a. Susan cooks the meal.
   b. they cook together.
   c. they go to a restaurant.
   d. Sam cooks the meal.

7. Susan helps decide about the future of
   a. their house.
   b. New Jersey.
   c. Rosebud.
   d. her friends.

8. Sam helps poor people
   a. get enough food.
   b. in New York.
   c. plan their future.
   d. go to the bank.

Susan and Sam are different in many ways. Susan is tall and thin. Sam is short and heavy. Susan has blonde hair and blue eyes. Sam has dark hair and brown eyes. Susan is a quiet kind of person. She can work for hours alone in the laboratory. Sam loves to talk and meet people. He can talk for hours with his patients.

But Susan and Sam think the same way about many things. They both care a lot about their children and their home. They care about their work and their town. They both like to go to the seaside in the summer. At the seaside, Susan reads mystery books and Sam goes fishing. The neighbors take care of their pets and their yard back in Rosebud.

Usually, they are happy to come home to Rosebud. But sometimes they think about traveling to other parts of the world. They want to visit new places and have new experiences. They went to Hawaii once, after they were married. But that was 30 years ago!

"We're not getting any younger!" Sam often says to Susan.

"You're right," says Susan. "Let's go somewhere next year. Not now. We're too busy."

Finishing time ___________   Reading time ___________

Answer the questions on the following page.

1. This passage is about
   a. how Susan and Sam are different.
   b. Susan and Sam's life together.
   c. Susan and Sam's vacation.
   d. why Susan and Sam want to travel.

2. Susan and Sam
   a. look the same.
   b. look different.
   c. are both tall and thin.
   d. both like to work alone.

3. Sam likes to
   a. work by himself.
   b. work in a laboratory.
   c. listen to his patients.
   d. meet people and talk.

4. Susan and Sam both care about
   a. fishing at the seaside.
   b. different things.
   c. the same things.
   d. going to Hawaii.

5. In the summer, Susan and Sam
   a. go to the seaside.
   b. visit their children.
   c. travel around the world.
   d. take care of their house.

6. Susan and Sam are usually
   a. at the seaside.
   b. unhappy in Rosebud.
   c. happy in Rosebud.
   d. away from home.

7. Someday they would like to
   a. go to the seaside.
   b. get married.
   c. go to Hawaii.
   d. visit new places.

8. They can't go away now because they are
   a. too busy.
   b. too young.
   c. married.
   d. too old.

Passage 4: A Visit to the Doctor

Starting time _________

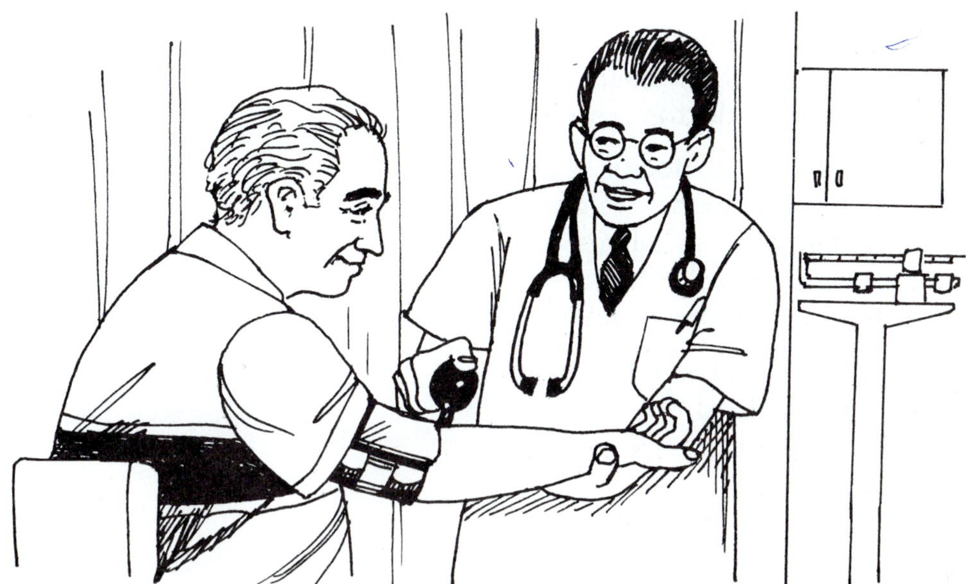

One day in March, Sam Diamond went to the doctor for his yearly checkup. He felt fine. He told the doctor he had no problems. The doctor examined him carefully and did some tests.

The next week, the doctor called Sam. He said, "I have some bad news for you. You'll have heart trouble soon if you don't change your way of life. You have to lose weight. You should exercise more, and you should get more rest."

Sam was worried. He told Susan the bad news. "What should I do?" he said. "How can I lose weight? I like good food and I don't have time to exercise!"

"Well, the doctor knows best," said Susan. She was worried, too. "You should do what he says."

"That's easy for you to say!" said Sam.

"I'll help you," said Susan. "I'll exercise with you and I'll help you cook healthy meals. Maybe we should think about some other changes, too. We're always talking about a vacation. Well, let's do it! Let's go someplace where we can both relax. I think I need a rest, too."

"We can visit Ted in Brazil!" said Sam.

"Or Jane in Alaska!" said Susan.

Finishing time _________   Reading time _________

Answer the questions on the following page.

1. This passage is about
   a. exercise and dieting.
   b. how to stay healthy.
   c. Sam's health problem.
   d. Sam's new doctor.

2. Sam went to the doctor because
   a. he wanted to lose weight.
   b. he had heart problems.
   c. the doctor called him.
   d. it was time for a checkup.

3. The doctor told Sam he must
   a. eat more food.
   b. work harder.
   c. exercise less.
   d. change his life.

4. When Sam heard the bad news, he
   a. told Susan.
   b. didn't tell anyone.
   c. told his patients.
   d. told the doctor.

5. Sam told Susan that he
   a. wanted to exercise.
   b. didn't believe the doctor.
   c. couldn't take a vacation.
   d. didn't know what to do.

6. When she heard the bad news, Susan was
   a. sad.
   b. happy.
   c. sick.
   d. worried.

7. Susan told Sam she
   a. didn't want to exercise.
   b. didn't want to go to Alaska.
   c. wanted to lose weight.
   d. wanted to help him.

8. Susan thought it was a good time to
   a. visit friends.
   b. go to the doctor.
   c. take a vacation.
   d. eat good food.

Sam began to make changes in his life. He went on a diet. No more cookies at lunch, no more ice cream after dinner. It was hard. All day his stomach made funny noises. At night he dreamed about big pieces of hot pizza.

He also began to exercise with Susan. They jogged every morning before work. This was even harder than the diet.

"We're crazy," Sam told his wife one morning. It was a cold, rainy spring day. "My legs hurt and I'm freezing."

"Think about our vacation," Susan said.

Sam really just wanted a warm bath and breakfast. But he thought about hot, sunny beaches. He thought about tropical fruits and strong coffee.

"Let's go to Brazil," he said to Susan. "Everyone says the food is great and the people are friendly."

"Jane says you can see lots of animals in Alaska," said Susan. "And the mountains are beautiful."

They decided to get more information from a travel agent. She gave them some articles from a travel magazine. She told them that Alaska and Brazil were very different, but they were both wonderful. "You have to decide what you want for your trip," she explained. "They're both beautiful places."

Finishing time _________   Reading time _________

Answer the questions on the following page.

Circle the best answer. Do not look back!

1. This passage is about
    a. how Susan and Sam change their lives.
    b. how Susan and Sam jog every morning.
    c. different places to go on vacation.
    d. Susan and Sam at the travel agency.

2. Sam had dreams about
    a. jogging.
    b. food.
    c. Brazil.
    d. work.

3. Sam did not enjoy
    a. jogging.
    b. reading.
    c. traveling.
    d. dreaming.

4. Susan told Sam to think about a vacation because she
    a. was tired.
    b. didn't want one.
    c. was jogging.
    d. wanted to help him.

5. Sam said the food in Brazil was
    a. terrible.
    b. Italian.
    c. very good.
    d. unhealthy.

6. Jane said Alaska had
    a. wonderful food and friendly people.
    b. poor hotels and not very good food.
    c. lots of animals and beautiful mountains.
    d. many dangerous animals in the mountains.

7. Susan and Sam went to a travel agent to
    a. find out about Alaska and Brazil.
    b. buy cheap plane tickets.
    c. make changes in their lives.
    d. find out about other places.

8. The travel agent told them that
    a. Alaska was the best place for a vacation.
    b. Alaska and Brazil were both beautiful.
    c. Alaska and Brazil were both expensive.
    d. Brazil was farther away than Alaska.

This was the beginning of an unhappy time for Susan and Sam. They could not agree on their travel plans. Susan preferred to go to Alaska, but Sam preferred to go to Brazil.

"We want to change our lives, don't we?" he asked Susan. "Then we should go somewhere really different!"

"Yes, but Brazil is very hot, isn't it?" said Susan. "I don't enjoy very hot weather."

"It may not be so hot in June or July. That's wintertime down there."

"You just want to go to Brazil because of the food," said Susan.

"That's not true!"

"You'll eat too much of that rich food," said Susan. "I know you. You'll never be able to diet in Brazil."

And so, they began to argue. They argued while they were jogging. They argued at breakfast. They argued at dinner. And all the time they were in a terrible mood. They didn't enjoy the things they used to enjoy. They stopped going to parties, and they didn't invite friends over for dinner. Sam didn't talk much to his patients. Susan didn't want to work in her vegetable garden. Even the pets were unhappy. The cat ran away, and the dog hid under the bed.

Finishing time _________   Reading time _________

Answer the questions on the following page.

Circle the best answer. Do not look back!

1. This passage is about
    a. how Sam wants to go to Brazil.
    b. why Susan doesn't want to go to Brazil.
    c. an unhappy time for Susan and Sam.
    d. why arguing is a terrible thing.

2. Sam wanted to go to Brazil because
    a. it was very different.
    b. it wasn't very different.
    c. it wasn't expensive.
    d. it was closer than Alaska.

3. Susan didn't want to go to Brazil because it was
    a. winter.
    b. different.
    c. too hot.
    d. too far.

4. Susan was worried about
    a. the food in Brazil.
    b. the people in Brazil.
    c. Sam's diet in Brazil.
    d. the prices in Brazil.

5. Susan and Sam were arguing about
    a. where to take their vacation.
    b. how to pay for their vacation.
    c. what to do with their pets.
    d. where to go out to dinner.

6. They were in a terrible mood because they
    a. wanted to see their friends.
    b. had stopped arguing.
    c. were always arguing.
    d. couldn't find their pets.

7. Because of their arguing, they stopped
    a. going jogging.
    b. eating breakfast.
    c. going to work.
    d. going to parties.

8. The dog hid under the bed because it
    a. liked all the arguing.
    b. was afraid of the cat.
    c. didn't like Susan.
    d. didn't like all the arguing.

One evening, in the middle of an argument, the telephone rang. Susan answered it. Jane was calling from Alaska, and she was very excited.

"Guess what?" she said. "I have a new job! With Delta Airlines! I'll be living in New York, and I'll be flying all over the United States and to Europe!"

"That's wonderful!" said Susan. "When are you coming?"

"I'm starting with Delta next month," said Jane. "So, I'll be in New York at the end of this month."

"How did this happen?" Susan asked.

"I wanted to work for a bigger airline," said Jane. "I wanted to fly to new places and see more of the world. So I applied to several airlines and I got this job. Alaska is a nice place to live, but I didn't want to stay here all my life!"

"Are there any other women pilots with Delta Airlines?" asked Susan.

"I don't know," said Jane. "I hope so. It's hard to be the only one. The men pilots say such stupid things to me sometimes."

"Here comes your Dad. He'll want to hear about this, too! He's picking up the other phone. Now tell us all about this new job!"

Finishing time _________   Reading time _________

Answer the questions on the following page.

1. This passage is about
    a. a phone call from Susan.
    b. Jane's job in Alaska.
    c. living in Alaska.
    d. a phone call from Jane.

2. Jane was very
    a. angry.
    b. sad.
    c. excited.
    d. upset.

3. Jane is going to work for
    a. several airlines.
    b. Alaska Airlines.
    c. a European airline.
    d. Delta Airlines.

4. She said she was going to move to
    a. Europe.
    b. New York.
    c. Alaska.
    d. New Jersey.

5. She wanted a new job so she could
    a. go to new places.
    b. stay in Alaska.
    c. work at home.
    d. meet other pilots.

6. She liked Alaska,
    a. and she wanted to stay there.
    b. but she didn't want to stay there.
    c. but she preferred California.
    d. and she was looking for a job there.

7. Jane
    a. liked being the only woman pilot.
    b. wanted to work with men pilots.
    c. didn't like being the only woman pilot.
    d. didn't like being a pilot.

8. Men pilots
    a. were always nice to Jane.
    b. weren't always nice to Jane.
    c. didn't talk to women pilots.
    d. didn't fly to Europe.

Starting time _________

"Well, isn't this exciting!" said Sam after their phone conversation with Jane. The telephone rang again. This time it was Ted.

"Ted!" said Sam. "Jane just called, too."

"Yes, I know," said Ted. "She sent me an e-mail last week, and we decided to call you tonight. I've got some big news, too."

"Wait! Your mother's picking up the other phone. Susan? Are you there?"

"Hello? Ted!"

"Yes, it's me. Are you ready for this? You're going to be grandparents!"

"Oh, how exciting!" "When?" "How's Maria?" "A boy or a girl?"

Susan and Sam were both talking at once.

Ted laughed. "Slow down! One at a time!"

Ted said Maria was fine, just a little tired. Luckily, she was an artist, so she could work when she wanted.

"I have more news for you," he said. "Starting next month, I have a job at the *New York Times*."

"Does that mean you're moving back up here?" asked Susan.

"Yes, we're leaving Brazil. We'd like to live near New York, but not in the city," said Ted.

"You can stay with us until you find a place of your own," said Susan. "We'll be so happy to have you here!"

Finishing time _________   Reading time _________

Answer the questions on the following page.

1. This passage is about
    a. a phone call from Ted.
    b. family phone calls.
    c. Ted and his wife, Maria.
    d. Ted and his sister, Jane.

2. Ted was calling from
    a. New York.
    b. Alaska.
    c. Brazil.
    d. his office.

3. Ted and Jane
    a. write lots of letters.
    b. talk every day on the phone.
    c. never talk.
    d. use e-mail to "talk."

4. Ted's wife, Maria, is going to
    a. become an artist.
    b. have a baby.
    c. talk on the phone.
    d. stop painting.

5. When they heard the news, Susan and Sam
    a. were excited.
    b. didn't say anything.
    c. weren't interested.
    d. were upset.

6. Ted said that Maria
    a. didn't want to talk.
    b. was not well at all.
    c. was tired, but fine.
    d. didn't want to work.

7. Ted and Maria are going to
    a. work for a newspaper.
    b. work as artists.
    c. stay in Brazil.
    d. move to New York.

8. Susan says Ted and Maria
    a. should live in New York.
    b. can stay with them.
    c. can't live in Rosebud.
    d. should stay with Jane.

That night, Susan and Sam couldn't sleep. They talked and talked about the news from Jane and Ted.

The next day, Susan laughed and said, "I guess we won't be going to Alaska or Brazil."

"We'll go somewhere else, next summer," said Sam. "We've got more important things to think about now."

Susan and Sam stopped arguing, and the time passed quickly. They cleaned out Ted and Jane's old bedrooms. They called many of their old friends and their aunts, uncles, and cousins. They wanted everyone to know all the good news.

Jane was the first to arrive. Susan and Sam went to the airport to meet her. They were surprised when they saw her. She had long hair before, but now it was very short.

"It's my new hairstyle, for my new lifestyle!" she said. She was full of ideas for her new life in New York. She wanted to find an apartment in the city. She wanted to go to concerts and to the theater, and she wanted to eat at different restaurants. "I couldn't do those things in Alaska," she said. "I'll be away a lot for work, but when I'm home, I want to enjoy the city."

Finishing time ________   Reading time ________

Answer the questions on the following page.

1. This passage is about
   a. a trip to the airport.
   b. Susan and Sam's children.
   c. news from Jane and Ted.
   d. Jane's arrival in New York.

2. Susan and Sam decided
   a. to go on a vacation to Alaska.
   b. to take a vacation later.
   c. not to take a vacation.
   d. not to talk about their news.

3. Susan and Sam were busy
   a. working in the garden.
   b. arguing about their vacation.
   c. getting ready for their vacation.
   d. getting ready for Ted and Jane.

4. They wanted to tell everyone about
   a. Jane's new lifestyle.
   b. their exciting news.
   c. their new jobs.
   d. their vacation plans.

5. They were surprised to see Jane's new
   a. hairstyle.
   b. clothes.
   c. apartment.
   d. bedroom.

6. Jane was excited about
   a. starting a new job.
   b. her new life in New York.
   c. seeing her relatives.
   d. living in an apartment.

7. She wanted to live
   a. in Rosebud.
   b. near the airport.
   c. with her parents.
   d. in New York City.

8. In Alaska, she couldn't
   a. go to concerts or the theater.
   b. have a new hairstyle.
   c. travel very much.
   d. talk to Susan and Sam.

One evening, Susan, Sam, and Jane were watching the news on TV. They heard about a terrible airlplane accident in Oklahoma. A DC-9 jet was flying from Dallas to Kansas City. Suddenly, it began to burn and then it fell. All the people on it were dead. The pilot was a woman, Carmen Kreeger.

Susan turned off the television. "Did you know her?" she asked Jane.

"No," said Jane. They were all quiet for a while. Then Jane said, "But I know that airline company. It's like a lot of other small companies. They buy old airplanes and they don't take care of them. They just want to make a lot of money fast. And look what happens!"

Jane was very upset. "Now they'll say it was the woman pilot. They'll say she made a mistake or didn't have enough experience. But did you hear what they said? That plane was twenty-seven years old! It was the company that made a mistake!"

"Was your company in Alaska like that company?" asked Susan.

"Yes, it was. I didn't tell you because I didn't want you to worry," said Jane. "But I'm glad to be with a better company now."

"I'm glad, too," said Susan.

Finishing time _________   Reading time _________

Answer the questions on the following page.

1. This passage is about
   a. an airline company.
   b. a woman pilot.
   c. an airlplane accident.
   d. the news on TV.

2. An airplane
   a. burned and then fell.
   b. landed in Kansas City.
   c. burned in the airport.
   d. was on television.

3. The pilot of the plane was
   a. twenty-seven years old.
   b. Jane's friend.
   c. a woman.
   d. a man.

4. Jane said that the airline company
   a. burned the airplane.
   b. used old planes.
   c. had new planes.
   d. didn't use old planes.

5. When she heard the news, Jane was
   a. sad.
   b. glad.
   c. happy.
   d. angry.

6. Jane thought the accident was caused by the
   a. airline company.
   b. pilot.
   c. airport.
   d. weather.

7. The airplane in the accident was
   a. almost new.
   b. twenty-seven years old.
   c. five years old.
   d. very large.

8. The airline company in Alaska
   a. also used old planes.
   b. never used old planes.
   c. never had accidents.
   d. was a good, safe company.

Before long, it was time for Susan and Sam to go to the airport again. Jane went, too. At the airport, they learned that the flight from Rio was late.

"Oh, no!" said Susan. "Poor Maria."

They had to wait over two hours, but at last the flight arrived. Then they had to wait some more in the arrivals hall. There were a lot of people on the flight, and there were a lot of people waiting. Susan and Sam couldn't find Ted and Maria.

"Maybe they missed the flight," said Jane.

"Here we are!" said a voice from behind them. And there was Maria with Ted beside her. They all hugged and kissed and talked at once. Susan was even crying a little.

"You look wonderful," she said to Maria. She gave her another hug. "How was your flight? Was it very long?"

"It was terribly long," said Ted, "but at least it was smooth."

"I'm sure you both need a rest," said Sam. "Let's go home. You two can rest while I cook up a nice dinner. Then we can talk and celebrate! How about spaghetti with Bolognese sauce? I can forget about my diet for once, can't I?" he asked Susan.

Finishing time ___________   Reading time ___________

Answer the questions on the following page.

Circle the best answer. Do not look back!

1. This passage is about
   a. Ted and Maria's arrival in New York.
   b. Jane's arrival in New York.
   c. Susan and Sam's trip to Brazil.
   d. Ted and Maria's new baby.

2. Ted and Maria's flight
   a. was early.
   b. was canceled.
   c. was two hours late.
   d. never left Rio.

3. The arrivals hall was
   a. crowded.
   b. empty.
   c. quiet.
   d. dark.

4. When the flight arrived, Susan and Sam
   a. were at home.
   b. couldn't find Jane.
   c. didn't know where to go.
   d. couldn't find Ted and Maria.

5. Susan was crying because she was
   a. upset.
   b. angry.
   c. happy.
   d. sad.

6. Susan thought that Maria
   a. looked terrible.
   b. missed the flight.
   c. didn't look well.
   d. looked well.

7. Ted said the flight was
   a. short and smooth.
   b. long but smooth.
   c. long and crowded.
   d. short but bumpy.

8. Sam wanted to
   a. go to a restaurant.
   b. eat dinner at the airport.
   c. go home and rest.
   d. cook a nice dinner.

Starting time __________

Soon Jane found an apartment in New York. It was small but comfortable, and it had a nice view of Riverside Park. One Friday evening she called Susan and Sam.

"What are you and Dad doing tomorrow?" she asked. "Would you like to come see my apartment and have a day in the city?"

"Why not?" said Susan. "We don't go in to New York together very often."

Ted and Maria decided to go, too. They all met at Jane's apartment. From there they went to the Metropolitan Museum of Art. They looked at many pictures, and Maria talked about the painters that she liked.

They had lunch at the museum coffee shop. Then they took the subway to Macy's department store. Susan, Jane, and Maria found some pretty, but comfortable, dresses for Maria. Ted helped Sam buy some new running shoes.

Next, they went down to SoHo and walked around. Jane and Maria were interested in the new shops and galleries. Sam was more interested in the restaurants. On every street, there were wonderful smells. Finally, he said, "How about dinner? I'm hungry!"

Everyone else was hungry, too. They stopped at a Japanese restaurant and had a delicious meal.

Finishing time __________   Reading time __________

Answer the questions on the following page.

1. This passage is about
   a. shopping in New York.
   b. apartments in New York.
   c. Jane's apartment in New York.
   d. the Diamonds in New York.

2. Susan and Sam
   a. never go to New York
   b. don't often go to New York together.
   c. don't ever go to New York together.
   d. often go to New York together.

3. They met Jane at
   a. the train station.
   b. her apartment.
   c. the museum.
   d. Macy's.

4. At the museum, Maria talked about the
   a. building.
   b. city.
   c. views.
   d. painters.

5. They had lunch in
   a. the museum.
   b. a fancy restaurant.
   c. Rosebud.
   d. Jane's apartment.

6. At Macy's, Maria bought some
   a. shoes.
   b. dresses.
   c. pictures.
   d. coffee.

7. In SoHo, they saw many
   a. new shops and galleries.
   b. new coffee shops.
   c. department stores.
   d. interesting people.

8. Sam thought it was time to
   a. take the train.
   b. shop at Macy's.
   c. go home.
   d. eat dinner.

At the Japanese restaurant, Jane and Maria talked about their jobs. They agreed that there are a few similarities. For both pilots and artists, there is a lot of competition and there are few famous women. In both jobs, you have to be very strong and sure of yourself.

Of course, there are also many differences between the two jobs. Pilots and artists have to be strong in different ways. Pilots have to stay awake for long hours, and sometimes they have to make important decisions quickly. Artists, however, have to be strong in their ideas about art and life.

People in the two jobs also work in different ways. Pilots usually work with other people, but artists usually work alone. Pilots must understand other people. Artists must understand themselves.

Finally, there is an important difference in lifestyle. Pilots travel for their job and are often away from home. Artists, however, work at home or in a studio near home. Also, unlike pilots, artists can start and stop working when they want.

"I could never be a pilot," Maria said to Jane. "I hate airplanes."

"And I could never be an artist," said Jane. "I hate working alone!"

Finishing time __________   Reading time __________

Answer the questions on the following page.

1. This passage is about
   a. some famous women.
   b. difficulties at work.
   c. Jane and Maria's jobs.
   d. many different jobs.

2. There are
   a. many famous women pilots and artists.
   b. few famous women pilots and artists.
   c. no famous women pilots and artists.
   d. no famous pilots and artists.

3. Women pilots and artists both have to be
   a. strong.
   b. young.
   c. famous.
   d. nice.

4. Pilots sometimes have to
   a. work by themselves.
   b. have good ideas about life.
   c. think about things carefully.
   d. make quick decisions.

5. Artists have to
   a. stay awake long hours.
   b. have strong ideas about art.
   c. think about people a lot.
   d. make quick decisions.

6. Pilots
   a. usually work with other people.
   b. often work alone.
   c. sometimes work with artists.
   d. never work with other people.

7. Artists
   a. don't have to travel for work.
   b. have to travel for work.
   c. usually don't like to travel.
   d. are often away from home.

8. Jane and Maria
   a. don't like their jobs.
   b. both like their jobs.
   c. wish they had other jobs.
   d. both hate working alone.

Ted and Maria were still living with Susan and Sam. But one Saturday, they found a house for sale in Rosebud. It was just what they wanted. The house was not big, but it was big enough for them. Now they could make a home for their family.

"We can't move there until next month," Ted told Susan and Sam. "This might be a good time for you to go away. We could take care of your house and pets."

"What about Maria?" said Susan.

"There's still lots of time," said Ted. "Dad, the doctor said you need a vacation."

"But where should we go?" said Sam.

"How about England?" said Ted.

"That's a good idea," said Sam. "I hear they have great breakfasts."

"Well, language is not a problem in England," said Susan.

"And we can visit the famous English gardens," said Sam.

"True," said Susan. "There's Kew Gardens and all those country houses. It's the perfect time of year for flowers."

"So it's England?" asked Sam.

"If you don't eat too much at those big breakfasts!" said Susan.

"I won't eat anything until teatime," said Sam.

"Okay, okay," said Susan, laughing. "England, here we come."

Finishing time _________   Reading time _________

Answer the questions on the following page.

1. This passage is about
   a. how Susan and Sam go to England.
   b. how Susan and Sam decide to go to England.
   c. how Sam wants to visit famous English gardens.
   d. how to take a vacation in England.

2. Ted and Maria
   a. sold their house in Rosebud.
   b. had a vacation in England.
   c. needed a vacation.
   d. found a house in Rosebud.

3. Ted and Maria
   a. are moving right away.
   b. can't move until next month.
   c. can't move until next year.
   d. don't want to move.

4. When Susan and Sam are away,
   a. Ted and Maria will stay in their house.
   b. the neighbors will stay in their house.
   c. Jane will stay in their house.
   d. no one will stay in their house.

5. Ted says that Maria's baby
   a. isn't coming soon.
   b. is coming next year.
   c. is coming very soon.
   d. will be coming late.

6. According to Sam, England has good
   a. doctors.
   b. tea.
   c. houses.
   d. breakfasts.

7. Susan and Sam want to
   a. visit English museums.
   b. visit English gardens.
   c. drink English coffee.
   d. speak another language.

8. Susan is afraid
   a. Sam will eat too much.
   b. she will eat too much.
   c. Sam won't like English breakfasts.
   d. she won't like English breakfasts.

Two weeks later, the big day came for Susan and Sam. They were ready to leave on their trip to England. Ted drove them to the airport.

"I'm sure we've forgotten something," Susan said to Sam. "Do you have the plane tickets?"

"Oh yes. They're in my pocket."

"What about our passports?" Susan asked.

"They're in my pocket, too," Sam said, and he looked to make sure. There were the tickets, but not the passports!

"I was sure I put them in this pocket," he said. "Maybe they're in my jacket pocket."

He looked in his jacket pocket, in his travel bag, and in his suitcase. "They must be on my desk at home!" he said.

"Oh no!" said Susan.

"But they were with the travel information. I thought you had all that."

"Wait a minute. Maybe I do," said Susan. She looked in her bag. There were the passports.

"Well, that's a good thing," said Ted. Susan, Sam, and Ted all laughed.

"Look at those lines!" said Susan.

"I think you'd better get in line for the check-in counter," said Ted. "Sometimes there are long lines for security, too."

So Susan and Sam got in line and said good-bye to Ted.

Finishing time __________   Reading time __________

Answer the questions on the following page.

1. This passage is about
    a. Susan and Sam's passports.
    b. Susan and Sam's trip to England.
    c. how Susan and Sam forgot their tickets.
    d. how Susan and Sam left for their trip.

2. At first, Susan was worried about
    a. the plane tickets.
    b. forgetting something.
    c. taking the plane.
    d. going to the airport.

3. Sam thought the passports were
    a. on the plane.
    b. at the airport.
    c. in his pocket.
    d. in the car.

4. When Sam looked for the passports, he
    a. didn't find them in his pocket.
    b. found them in his pocket.
    c. looked on his desk at home.
    d. found the travel information.

5. Susan and Sam's passports were
    a. in Sam's pocket.
    b. in his suitcase.
    c. on Sam's desk.
    d. in Susan's bag.

6. Before Susan found the passports, she and Sam were feeling
    a. nervous.
    b. happy.
    c. unhappy.
    d. relaxed.

7. At the airport,
    a. there were few people.
    b. the flights were late.
    c. there were no lines.
    d. the lines were long.

8. Ted thought they should
    a. get in line.
    b. buy their tickets.
    c. fly to England.
    d. not leave yet.

In London, Susan and Sam were very lucky with the weather. England is famous for its rainy weather, but they had sunny skies for a week! They couldn't believe it. Londoners couldn't believe it, either. Everyone was smiling all the time. At noon, the parks were full of people sitting in the sun and eating lunch.

Susan and Sam walked all around London and visited many historical places, such as Westminster Abbey and Buckingham Palace. They didn't see the Queen, but they watched the changing of the Queen's guards. They also went to a part of London called "The City." There they saw lots of men wearing similar gray business suits. Many of them even wore old-style hats! Susan and Sam thought the hats looked very funny—and uncomfortable!

They went to some of London's famous museums: the British Museum, the National Gallery, and the Victoria and Albert Museum. They enjoyed looking at all the beautiful and interesting things, but they both agreed that the museums were very tiring. For a change, they took some boat rides on the Thames River. First they went down the river to Greenwich. There they visited the old town and the famous Royal Observatory. On another day, they took the boat up the river to Kew Gardens. They had a picnic lunch in the gardens and looked at all the flowers. They especially liked the roses and the huge glass building full of tropical plants.

Susan and Sam also took some trips on the train. They went to Salisbury early one morning. In Salisbury they looked at the very old and beautiful church. It was just as beautiful as the pictures they had seen. Then they took a bus into the country to see Stonehenge. They were surprised to see how big the stones really were. But they didn't like the place. Right next to Stonehenge, there was a huge parking lot full of cars and buses. With all those people, Stonehenge didn't seem so special. It seemed more like a shopping center!

After their trip to Stonehenge, Susan and Sam wanted to leave London. They were getting tired of the city. A Scottish man at the hotel talked about the Hebrides Islands. He said they were very beautiful. Susan and Sam studied the map. The Hebrides seemed far, but maybe they could visit another part of Scotland. So they rented a car and drove north from London.

Finishing time ________   Reading time ________

Answer the questions on the following page.

Circle the best answer. Do not look back!

1. This passage is about
    a. how Susan and Sam walk around the parks.
    b. sightseeing in London.
    c. London's museums.
    d. Susan and Sam's visit to London.

2. Londoners were smiling all the time because of the
    a. rainy weather.
    b. good weather.
    c. American tourists.
    d. men in funny hats.

3. Susan and Sam enjoyed
    a. walking around new places.
    b. riding the trains to new places.
    c. taking taxis around new places.
    d. driving around new places.

4. In "The City," they saw
    a. women with hats.
    b. men in business suits.
    c. the Queen's guards.
    d. many old churches.

5. They took some boat rides because they
    a. were tired of museums.
    b. wanted to have a picnic.
    c. enjoyed going to museums.
    d. were afraid of the water.

6. In Salisbury, Susan and Sam went to see the
    a. museum.
    b. old town.
    c. church.
    d. gardens.

7. They didn't enjoy Stonehenge because
    a. it was far from Salisbury.
    b. it seemed very old.
    c. they had to take a bus.
    d. there were too many people.

8. After Stonehenge, Susan and Sam decided to drive north toward
    a. the Hebrides Islands.
    b. Scotland.
    c. a shopping center.
    d. another hotel in London.

When Susan and Sam drove north, they were very nervous. It was strange driving on the left side of the road! Luckily, they had no trouble, and soon they could relax. In the next few days, they visited many old towns and saw many famous churches.

They also took lots of walks in the countryside. Susan and Sam decided that the English countryside was much nicer than the countryside in New Jersey. It was greener and quieter. It also was full of wonderful footpaths. In New Jersey, there weren't many paths, except in the parks. But in England, there were signs everywhere for public footpaths. These paths went across farmers' fields and through woods. You had to be careful about the cows and the sheep, but you could use the paths anytime.

Every evening, Susan and Sam stayed at a different "bed and breakfast." They were all nice places, but their favorite was near Lincoln. It was a large house with a beautiful flower garden on one side and a vegetable garden on the other. Cows and sheep were in the nearby fields. A smiling woman showed them to their room. It was once her daughter's room, she explained. Now her daughter lived in London, so she rented it to guests for the night. The room was large and pretty, with a nice view of fields and hills.

That evening they also had their best meal of the trip. Near their bed and breakfast was a pub called the Golden Horse. A sign said it was built in 1705. Outside the pub was a garden with tables and a small playground. Inside, the pub had beautiful, dark wood all around. Susan and Sam ordered some beer. It was dark and strong and excellent. Their dinner was excellent, too. Sam had steak and kidney pie, a traditional English dish. Susan had chicken curry, a spicy Indian dish.

"People told me that English food was terrible," said Susan. "But it's not true at all. We eat very well every day." She looked at Sam and said, "Too well, I'm afraid. We're not jogging anymore. And now, I think you're gaining weight."

"I'll eat less breakfast in the morning," said Sam.

But the next morning for breakfast there were fresh-baked scones with butter. And there were fresh eggs and sausages from the farm next door. It was impossible to eat only a little!

Finishing time ________   Reading time ________

Answer the questions on the following page.

1. This passage is about
    a. eating dinner at the Golden Horse.
    b. how English food is terrible.
    c. churches in English towns.
    d. traveling north from London.

2. Susan and Sam liked walking
    a. in the New Jersey countryside.
    b. in the English countryside.
    c. around the English towns.
    d. on the left side of the road.

3. At night they stayed at
    a. a bed and breakfast.
    b. a friend's house.
    c. an old pub.
    d. a fancy hotel.

4. A bed and breakfast is
    a. a kind of room.
    b. a kind of restaurant.
    c. in an English church.
    d. a place to sleep.

5. Susan and Sam had their best meal
    a. at their bed and breakfast.
    b. at the hotel in London.
    c. at an old pub.
    d. at a restaurant.

6. Susan and Sam
    a. didn't like the beer in England.
    b. liked the beer in England.
    c. never drank any beer in England.
    d. usually drank wine in England.

7. Susan was worried about
    a. the old buildings.
    b. English food.
    c. her weight.
    d. Sam's weight.

8. In the morning, Sam ate
    a. only a little.
    b. a lot.
    c. nothing.
    d. only cereal.

For another week, Susan and Sam visited northern England and southern Scotland. They decided not to go to the Hebrides. It was just too far. But they liked Scotland very much. They agreed to go to the Hebrides on their next vacation.

They arrived in Edinburgh on a cool and rainy afternoon. It was their last stop. They found a bed and breakfast on a quiet street. Edinburgh seemed large and noisy after the small towns and the countryside. They had dinner in a pub, and it was crowded and noisy, too. There was also a lot of cigarette smoke. They finished their dinner quickly and started to walk home.

Suddenly, Sam stopped.

"What's the matter?" asked Susan.

"I don't feel very well," said Sam. He sat down on a doorstep. "I feel like I can't breathe."

"Oh, no!" said Susan. "Let's go back to the bed and breakfast. I'll help you."

But when Sam tried to get up, he fell down. He lay on the sidewalk with his eyes closed.

Susan shouted for help, and several people came running. They called an ambulance. It came quickly and brought Sam to the hospital. Susan went, too. It was a terrible experience riding in the ambulance with Sam. But soon, Sam was awake again. At the hospital, the doctor said it was a heart attack, but Sam was not in danger anymore. He had to stay in the hospital for at least a week. He needed complete rest, and he needed to have some tests. But he was going to be fine.

Later that evening Susan called Jane and Ted. She told them all about the heart attack, and she told them the doctor was not worried about Sam. She said the people in the hospital were very helpful. And she said that Sam's doctor was very nice. Jane said she could fly to Edinburgh the next day. Ted wanted to come, too, but he didn't want to leave Maria alone.

"Don't even think of coming," Susan said to Ted. "You can't leave Maria now! How's she doing?"

"She gets tired very easily, but she's fine. She's very large. Only one more month!"

In fact, Ted was a little worried about Maria. She was not very well. She had to stay in bed all the time. But he did not tell this to his mother. She had enough to worry about.

Finishing time _______   Reading time _______

Answer the questions on the following page.

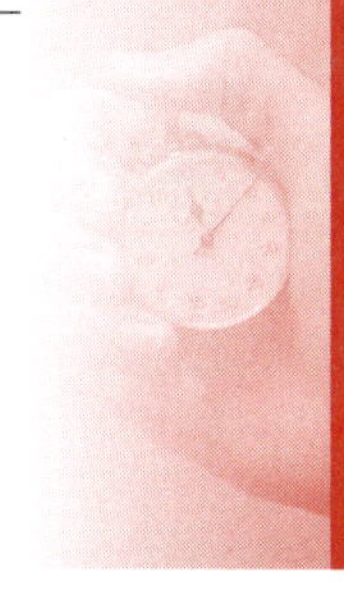

Circle the best answer. Do not look back!

1. This passage is about
    a. Sam's heart attack.
    b. Edinburgh, Scotland.
    c. an ambulance ride.
    d. health problems.

2. Susan and Sam
    a. decided to go to the Hebrides.
    b. never wanted to go to the Hebrides.
    c. decided not to go to the Hebrides.
    d. decided not to go to Edinburg.

3. For dinner, Susan and Sam went to a
    a. Scottish restaurant.
    b. bed and breakfast.
    c. noisy and crowded pub.
    d. large and quiet pub.

4. On the way home from dinner, Sam
    a. didn't feel well.
    b. almost fell asleep.
    c. talked with Susan.
    d. smoked a cigarette.

5. When Sam fell down, Susan
    a. ran to the police.
    b. called for help.
    c. sat down beside him.
    d. couldn't breathe.

6. The doctors said Sam should
    a. have an operation on his heart.
    b. go back to the United States.
    c. go back to the bed and breakfast.
    d. stay in the hospital for a week.

7. Susan told Ted and Jane
    a. to come to Edinburgh.
    b. about the ambulance ride.
    c. the doctor wasn't worried.
    d. Sam's attack was serious.

8. Ted was also worried about
    a. Maria.
    b. his mother.
    c. Jane.
    d. his father.

Starting time ⎯⎯⎯⎯⎯⎯

The next day, Jane arrived in Edinburgh. She went straight to the hospital to see Sam. He was still in bed, but he was laughing and talking. In fact, all the nurses and the other patients liked Sam. There were always people in his room.

Just after Jane came in, Sam's doctor came to check him. His name was Dr. Campbell. He came back several times that day. And every time, he had a longer conversation with Jane. He was very surprised to learn she was a pilot. He had never met a woman pilot before.

After two days of conversations, Dr. Campbell asked Jane to stop for coffee with him. The next day they had lunch together. The day after, it was dinner. Then, on Sunday, he brought Jane to a festival of Scottish music and dancing. It was colorful and fun to watch. The men in the dance wore kilts, the traditional Scottish outfit that looks like a skirt. Jane tried dancing, too. It was fun, but not easy.

After a week, Sam was still in the hospital, but every day he was a little stronger. One afternoon, the telephone rang by his bed. Susan answered the phone. It was Ted.

"Guess what!" he said. "I have some big news for you. You're a grandmother now!"

"What! Already?! Is everything okay?" Susan asked.

"Yes, the baby's fine and so is Maria. It's a girl and her name is Elena. She came almost a month early, so she's small—only five and a half pounds—but she's healthy."

Ted had to repeat the news to Sam, and then to Jane. Everyone was very happy and excited. Susan got back on the phone.

"I wish I could be there," she said. "Now I can't help Maria."

"That's okay," said Ted. "I'm going to work part-time, so I'll be home a lot. I don't know much about babies, but I guess I'll learn! I can change diapers already!"

"That's something your father never did," said Susan. "Men didn't do those things when you were a baby."

"How's Dad now?" asked Ted.

"Much stronger," said Susan. "He can walk around the room and Dr. Campbell says he'll be able to leave the hospital in a few days. Dr. Campbell is such a nice person. He took Jane out to a concert last night!"

"Oh, a Scottish romance, maybe?"

"Well, it's too early to tell, but it's possible!"

Finishing time ⎯⎯⎯⎯⎯⎯   Reading time ⎯⎯⎯⎯⎯⎯

Answer the questions on the following page.

1. This passage is about
   a. Sam in the hospital in Edinburgh.
   b. new things in Jane and Ted's lives.
   c. a Scottish romance for Jane.
   d. Ted and Maria's baby girl.

2. In the hospital,
   a. Susan had many friends.
   b. Sam didn't know anyone.
   c. people were not friendly.
   d. Sam was very popular.

3. Dr. Campbell talked a lot with
   a. Sam.
   b. Jane.
   c. Susan.
   d. nurses.

4. At the Scottish festival, Jane
   a. wore a Scottish kilt.
   b. played Scottish music.
   c. tried Scottish dancing.
   d. ate Scottish food.

5. Ted called Susan and Sam at
   a. the hospital.
   b. the bed and breakfast.
   c. the airport.
   d. their home.

6. Ted and Maria's baby is
   a. not very well.
   b. small and unhealthy.
   c. big, but unhealthy.
   d. small, but healthy.

7. Ted plans to
   a. work extra hours.
   b. learn to change diapers.
   c. help Maria at home.
   d. go to Edinburgh.

8. Susan
   a. thinks Dr. Campbell is good for Jane.
   b. doesn't like Dr. Campbell very much.
   c. thinks Jane shouldn't see Dr. Campbell.
   d. is worried about Jane and Dr. Campbell.

Passage 20: An Extra Vacation

Starting time ___________

At last, the day came for Sam to leave the hospital. But there was a problem. Where should they go? The doctor said Sam shouldn't take a long plane flight yet. So they couldn't go home. But Susan and Sam didn't want to stay in Edinburgh. It was a nice city, but they preferred the countryside.

"You should go somewhere very quiet," said Dr. Campbell. "You need at least another week of rest."

"We could go to the Hebrides Islands," said Sam.

"Why not?" said Susan. "I can do all the driving."

"You don't even need to drive," said Dr. Campbell. "You can take the train and then a boat to the Isle of Skye. That's the most beautiful of the islands."

And that's just what Susan and Sam decided to do. They said good-bye to Jane, who had to go back to New York. They said good-bye to Dr. Campbell, who was planning to meet Jane in London in a month. And they went to the Isle of Skye.

When they arrived on the island, they knew it was a good place for them. The countryside was very different from the English countryside. But it was just as beautiful. There were no forests, only a few trees and bushes. The fields and the hills were rocky and bare. But the views, the light, and the colors were very special. From the beach you could see all the way to the hills. From the hills, you could see far out to other islands and the open ocean. There was blue everywhere, in the sky and the ocean and in the tiny flowers in the fields. From far away, the hills seemed almost purple. And the air was often soft and gray with clouds and rain.

Susan and Sam fell in love with Skye. They stayed at a small guest house where they had breakfast and dinner. They took walks and admired the view. They had lunch in different pubs and looked at the beautiful woolen clothes in the shops. They bought a little sweater for Elena, and gloves for Jane, Ted, and Maria. And they talked about their life in Rosebud. They both wanted to make some changes. They weren't ready to stop working, but they wanted to have more time for themselves. They also wanted to help Maria and enjoy their new granddaughter.

Finishing time ___________   Reading time ___________

Answer the questions on the following page.

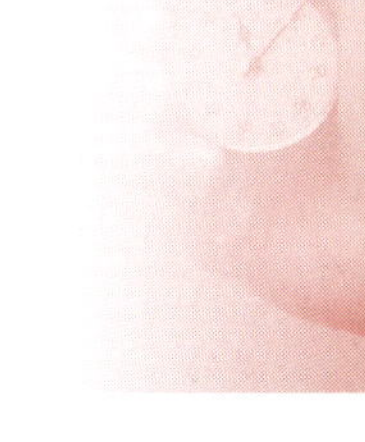

1. This passage is about
    a. how Sam leaves the hospital.
    b. the countryside on Skye.
    c. Susan and Sam's new life.
    d. Susan and Sam's trip to Skye.

2. The doctor said Sam shouldn't
    a. stay in Edinburgh.
    b. fly to New York.
    c. go to the Hebrides.
    d. leave the hospital.

3. Susan and Sam wanted to go to
    a. a quiet place.
    b. New York.
    c. London.
    d. a nice city.

4. Dr. Campbell said they could
    a. drive and take a boat to Skye.
    b. take the plane and a boat to Skye.
    c. take the train and a boat to Skye.
    d. take the bus and a boat to Skye.

5. The countryside on Skye was
    a. just like the English countryside.
    b. not like the English countryside.
    c. just like the countryside in New Jersey.
    d. not as beautiful as the English countryside.

6. The island of Skye had beautiful
    a. views.
    b. trees.
    c. villages.
    d. mountains.

7. Susan and Sam
    a. didn't like islands.
    b. were bored on Skye.
    c. didn't like the weather.
    d. were happy on Skye.

8. When they return to Rosebud, Susan and Sam want to
    a. start new jobs.
    b. buy some new clothes.
    c. make changes in their lives.
    d. stop going to work.

Two Popular Authors

J. K. Rowling

Passage 21: Early Years

Harry Potter and the Philosopher's Stone is a best-selling book in fifty-five languages. So are the other Harry Potter books. The Harry Potter books have also been made into very popular movies. Millions of people around the world know Harry's story. They know about his magical powers, his friends and his enemies, and the school of magic called Hogwarts. But where did the idea of Harry Potter come from? And what led the author, J. K. Rowling, to invent such a popular character?

J. K. Rowling's full name is Joanne Kathleen Rowling. She was born in 1966 in Chipping Sodbury, near Bristol, England. Chipping Sodbury is a strange name for a town. But Rowling likes the name of her birthplace. She likes places with strange names, and she remembers those names when she writes her books.

In fact, books were always important to Rowling and her family. There were lots of books in their house. Her mother loved reading, and so did her father. They often read books aloud to her. Then she learned to read by herself. When she was only six, she even wrote a book. It was called *Rabbit*. She wanted to publish it like a real book. From then on, that was her dream. She wanted to be a writer.

Rowling and her younger sister started school in Bristol. She was very happy at the elementary school there. But when she was nine, Rowling's parents decided to move to the country. They were both from the city, but they had always dreamed of living in the country. So they moved to the village of Tutshill, near Chepstow, in South Wales. The village was in the Forest of Dean, not far from the River Wye. The family's house was next to the church and the cemetery. Rowling's friends were afraid of the cemetery, but she and her sister liked it. She liked reading the names of all the dead people. She says she still likes cemeteries and still goes to them to look for names to use in her books.

There were many interesting and unusual places to visit near Tutshill. For example, near Chepstow there was an old castle on a hill. There was also the river and lots of big rocks to climb on. Rowling and her sister loved to play outdoors. They didn't have computers or video games, and they didn't watch much television. Instead, they invented games and adventures for themselves.

Finishing time __________   Reading time __________

Answer the questions on the following page.

1. This passage is about
   a. the Harry Potter books.
   b. a writer of children's books.
   c. the early life of J. K. Rowling.
   d. J. K. Rowling's birthplace.

2. Rowling was born
   a. in Chipping Sodbury.
   b. in a town near London.
   c. in a town called Hogwarts.
   d. near Chestow, South Wales.

3. In her books, Rowling likes to write about
   a. people in her family.
   b. places with strange names.
   c. places with English names.
   d. people around the world.

4. Her parents
   a. played music often.
   b. never read books.
   c. published many books.
   d. loved to read books.

5. When she was six, she
   a. read a book.
   b. wrote a book.
   c. went to Tutshill.
   d. had a rabbit.

6. Rowling's parents moved to Tutshill because
   a. there was no school in Chipping Sodbury.
   b. they wanted to live near a city.
   c. there was no work near Bristol.
   d. they wanted to live in the country.

7. In Tutshill, the Rowlings lived near a
   a. cemetery.
   b. school.
   c. library.
   d. city.

8. When she was young, Rowling enjoyed
   a. playing outdoors.
   b. watching television.
   c. playing on the computer.
   d. going to church.

When Rowling's family moved to Tutshill, she went to a new school. Her new teacher was not warm and friendly like her teachers in Bristol. This teacher gave math tests every day. If you could answer the questions quickly, you were "smart." If you couldn't, you were "stupid." All the "smart" children sat on one side of the room and all the "stupid" children sat on the other side. On the first day, the teacher put Rowling with the "stupid" children because she couldn't answer a question.

When Rowling started writing the Harry Potter books, she remembered this experience at school. She remembered how she feared and hated this teacher. These memories helped her invent the character of Snape, the teacher that Harry hates the most.

Later, in high school, Rowling liked her teachers and her school better. She had an English teacher who was very important to her. Miss Shepherd was not an easy teacher, but she cared about her students. Rowling learned a lot from her about stories and about writing. When Rowling's first book was published, Miss Shepherd wrote to her to say she liked the book. This letter meant more to Rowling than any newspaper review.

English was Rowling's favorite subject in school, but she was good at other subjects, too. She always wanted to have all the answers in class. She wanted to be the best student. In fact, she was probably a little like Hermione in the Harry Potter books. Hermione is one of Harry's closest friends. But she sometimes makes her friends angry because she is always good in school.

Rowling wasn't good at everything. At her school, all the children had to learn metalworking and woodworking. Rowling hated these subjects. She was no good at making things with her hands. A teaspoon she made was completely flat and useless. A picture frame she made was mostly glue. She was also not good at sports, and she especially hated hockey.

In fact, when she was a teenager, she was not very happy with herself and her body. She thought she was too short and fat, and not as pretty as her sister. She wished she could play sports really well. That may be why she invented the sport of quidditch in her books and she made Harry Potter a champion quidditch player. He does what his author always wished she could do.

Finishing time _________   Reading time _________

Answer the questions on the following page.

Circle the best answer. Do not look back!

1. This passage is about
   a. Rowling's years in school.
   b. Rowling's favorite subjects.
   c. the schools in South Wales.
   d. the teachers Rowling liked best.

2. Rowling's new teacher in Tutshill
   a. thought Rowling was smart.
   b. didn't ask her anything.
   c. was warm and friendly.
   d. thought Rowling was stupid.

3. Miss Shepherd taught Rowling about
   a. math.
   b. writing.
   c. woodworking.
   d. newspapers.

4. Miss Shepherd wrote a letter
   a. to Rowling's parents.
   b. to the editor of the newspaper.
   c. about Rowling's schoolwork.
   d. about Rowling's first book.

5. Rowling was generally
   a. only good at English.
   b. not a good student.
   c. a very good student.
   d. always angry in school.

6. In high school, she didn't like
   a. working with her hands.
   b. answering the teacher.
   c. the other students.
   d. English classes.

7. As a teenager, Rowling
   a. didn't like her body.
   b. liked to play sports.
   c. didn't like her parents.
   d. didn't like school.

8. Rowling wished she could
   a. be an English teacher.
   b. play sports well.
   c. meet Harry Potter.
   d. do metalworking well.

Starting time _________

While Rowling was in high school, her mother became ill with a very serious disease. This had a strong effect on Rowling. As a girl, she was not a relaxed person. She worried about everything. Now she had many new worries and she had to face the thought of losing her mother.

In these years, friends were very important for Rowling. She needed very much to talk to people about her feelings and her problems. Fortunately, she had good friends who could listen to her and help her. In her last year at school, she made a new friend, a boy named Sean Harris. He became her best friend in Tutshill and he remained a friend for life. He was important to her also because he had a car. He would take her on long drives, far from her unhappy home and far from the quiet, boring village of Tutshill.

Much later, when Rowling began to write about Harry Potter, she took some important ideas from this part of her life. She made Harry an orphan, and she wrote with great feeling about the loss of his parents. She also created several close friends for Harry. They give him love and support, and they also help him survive his adventures. In fact, Rowling says that Harry's closest friend, Ron Weasley, is a lot like her friend Sean.

After graduating from high school, Rowling went to Exeter University. She knew she wanted to be a writer, but she didn't study English or writing. She was afraid she might not find a job as an English major. Instead, she studied languages. For one year of her university studies, she lived in Paris. That year, she also taught English to French students.

Her next step after the university was to take a secretarial course in London. In her own opinion, she was a terrible secretary. But she did learn how to type, and this was very useful later. After the course, she got a job with Amnesty International, an international human rights organization.

Rowling's job was very interesting, but the most important thing for her was her writing. She was already working on a book. Every day at lunchtime, she went to a café alone so she could write. She also went out to write in a pub or café on the weekends. She didn't yet want people to know what she was doing.

Finishing time _________   Reading time _________

Answer the questions on the following page.

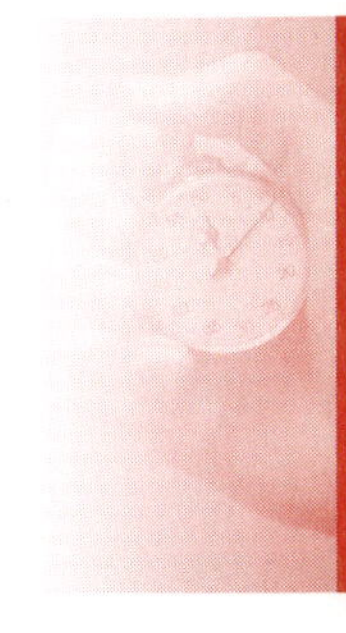

Circle the best answer. Do not look back!

1. This passage is about
    a. the problems Rowling had as a young teenager.
    b. how Rowling's mother became ill.
    c. how Rowling started writing books.
    d. the years from high school until after university.

2. When she was young, Rowling
    a. worried a lot.
    b. was a happy child.
    c. was very relaxed.
    d. never had worries.

3. Rowling's friends
    a. worried about her.
    b. never talked to her.
    c. listened to her.
    d. did homework with her.

4. Sean Harris was an important friend because he
    a. had a car.
    b. was older.
    c. lived nearby.
    d. was ill.

5. When she was a writer, Rowling
    a. wanted to forget this part of her life.
    b. took some ideas from this part of her life.
    c. usually wrote about people in her family.
    d. never wrote about people in her life.

6. When she went to Exeter University, she
    a. didn't know what she wanted to be.
    b. knew she wanted to be a writer.
    c. wanted to be a translator.
    d. didn't like her studies.

7. After the university, she
    a. learned to drive a car.
    b. took a trip to Paris.
    c. met Séan Harris.
    d. took a secretarial course.

8. In the beginning, Rowling did most of her writing
    a. at the library.
    b. in her apartment.
    c. in a café or pub.
    d. in her office.

Passage 24: Harry Potter

Starting time __________

The idea for the Harry Potter books came to Rowling on a train. She was traveling from Manchester to London. Suddenly she thought of a book about a boy named Harry Potter with magic powers. She was immediately very excited. She knew it was a good idea and she knew it was going to be fun to write.

She thought about the book for the rest of the trip. By the time she arrived in London many things were clear to her. She knew the names of Harry's friends and of his school. And she knew what was going to happen to him in the book. She also knew that she was going to write seven books about Harry Potter. At the time, Rowling was working on another novel. But she left that and started writing about Harry Potter.

Soon after that, she moved to Manchester, England, to live with a friend. She only stayed there a short while. That year, after many years of illness, her mother died. Rowling was very unhappy. She decided that she needed to leave England for a while. So she went to Oporto, Portugal, and taught English in a language school. After six months, she met a Portuguese journalist, Jorge Arantes. They got married, and the next year their daughter, Jessica, was born. This was a very happy moment in Rowling's life. However, the happy times didn't last. After only a few months, Rowling realized that the marriage wasn't working. She also needed a better job, so she decided to leave Portugal. She and Jessica went to live near Rowling's sister in Edinburgh, Scotland.

All this time, Rowling was working on the first Harry Potter book. In Edinburgh, it was hard for her to find time for writing. She was taking courses to become a teacher, and she had to take care of little Jessica. Rowling often took Jessica for long walks until the child fell asleep. Then she took her to a café, ordered a cup of coffee, and started writing.

When the book was finally finished, Rowling had to find a publisher. That took over a year. But at last Bloomsbury Publishers accepted the book. According to Rowling, this was the second best moment in her life, after the birth of Jessica. When *Harry Potter and the Philosopher's Stone* was published in July 1997, she walked around all day with a copy under her arm.

Finishing time __________   Reading time __________

Answer the questions on the following page.

Circle the best answer. Do not look back!

1. This passage is about
   a. writing books and publishing them.
   b. the characters in the Harry Potter books.
   c. how Rowling got the idea for Harry Potter.
   d. how Rowling wrote the first Harry Potter book.

2. Rowling first thought of the character of Harry Potter
   a. on a train.
   b. in a car.
   c. on a bus.
   d. in a plane.

3. When she began writing about Harry Potter, she
   a. thought he might be boring.
   b. was very excited about the idea.
   c. was not happy about the character.
   d. wasn't sure it was a good idea.

4. After Rowling's mother died, she
   a. wanted to leave England.
   b. got the idea for Harry Potter.
   c. went to live in Edinburgh.
   d. decided to learn Portuguese.

5. While she was living in Oporto, Rowling worked
   a. at a language school.
   b. in a café.
   c. for a publisher.
   d. as a journalist.

6. After she left Portugal, she went to live in
   a. Oporto.
   b. Edinburgh.
   c. London.
   d. Manchester.

7. In Edinburgh, it was hard for Rowling to find
   a. a good job.
   b. a place to live.
   c. time to write.
   d. good coffee.

8. When Rowling finished the book, she
   a. went to Portugal.
   b. started a teaching job.
   c. never found a publisher.
   d. had to find a publisher.

Passage 25: Success

Starting time __________

When *Harry Potter and the Philosopher's Stone* was published in England, it was not well-known at first. But a surprising number of copies were sold. Children read the book and told their friends about it. Then a big event changed everything. An American publishing company decided to publish the book in the United States and paid Rowling a lot of money. Many people suddenly began talking about the book and about Rowling.

At this time, she was working part-time as a teacher and trying to write the second book, *Harry Potter and the Chamber of Secrets*. She needed more time for writing, but she was afraid to give up her job. Finally, she decided to stop teaching for two years to finish the book.

Rowling never went back to teaching. The second book was quite long for a children's book—341 pages! Some people thought it was too long. But when it was published, it was a best-seller immediately. The same thing happened with *Harry Potter and the Prisoner of Azkaban, Harry Potter and the Goblet of Fire*, and *Harry Potter and the Order of the Phoenix*. Each book was longer than the one before. The fifth book was over 700 pages! But children still lined up to buy them and read them all the way through.

As a famous author, Rowling had to make some changes in her life. She used to enjoy reading aloud from her books at bookstores. However, she had to stop when thousands of people began coming to hear her. Sometimes it is hard for Rowling to have a private life. The publishers and the movie people are always asking her to do things. But her family is very important to her, and she tries very hard to keep her life normal. Fortunately, people usually don't recognize her on the streets in Edinburgh. She doesn't allow journalists to take pictures of her and her family.

After her family, the most important thing for Rowling is her writing. She doesn't write for the money. As one of the richest people in England now, she certainly doesn't need more. She keeps writing partly for herself. After all, writing is what she likes to do best. She also doesn't want to disappoint her readers. Millions of children—and adults—want to know what will happen next to Harry Potter.

Finishing time __________   Reading time __________

Answer the questions on the following page.

1. This passage is about
   a. what Rowling will write next.
   b. why children like Rowling's books.
   c. how Rowling became successful.
   d. J. K. Rowling and her books.

2. At first, children in England heard about Harry Potter from
   a. their friends.
   b. the publisher.
   c. the television.
   d. their parents.

3. Many people started talking about Rowling
   a. when the first Harry Potter book was published.
   b. after an American publisher paid her a lot of money.
   c. when she wrote the second Harry Potter book.
   d. because she enjoyed giving bookstore readings.

4. Rowling stopped working as a teacher because
   a. she needed more time for writing.
   b. the publisher wanted her to stop.
   c. she didn't like teaching children.
   d. her daughter wanted her to stay home.

5. The Harry Potter books are
   a. shorter than most children's books.
   b. easier than most children's books.
   c. harder than most children's books.
   d. longer than most children's books.

6. Rowling had to stop giving bookstore readings because
   a. the publishers wanted her to stop.
   b. no one came to them.
   c. too many people came to them.
   d. children didn't like them.

7. In Edinburgh, Rowling
   a. tries to live a normal life.
   b. is often recognized on the streets.
   c. is always followed by journalists.
   d. almost never goes out on the streets.

8. Rowling continues writing about Harry Potter
   a. to earn more money.
   b. for herself and the readers.
   c. because her daughter wants her to.
   d. for the publishers and the movie people.

Stephen King

Passage 26: First Experiences

People love a good horror, or scary, story. That's why *Frankenstein* and the stories of Edgar Allen Poe are still favorites. And that's why Stephen King has so many readers. He knows how to scare us and tell a good story at the same time. He has done that in more than thirty books, many of them best sellers.

Stephen was born in Portland, Maine, in 1947. When he was only two, his father left the family. After that, Stephen and his older brother, David, lived with their mother. They lived for a while in different parts of the United States, but then they moved back to Maine. Stephen's mother didn't get much help from Stephen's father or from her family. She always had to work to pay for the food and the rent. At different times, she worked in a bakery, in a laundry, and in a home for sick or old people.

Because their mother had to work, the boys spent a lot of time with babysitters. When the boys were very young, there were sometimes problems with the babysitters. One babysitter made Stephen eat seven fried eggs when he was four years old. He got very sick, and that babysitter was sent away. Another babysitter didn't always watch the boys carefully. One day, six-year-old David climbed out the bathroom window and onto the roof. Stephen stood at the bathroom window and watched him. He wondered if his brother was going to fall. Finally, a neighbor called the police. That babysitter lost her job, too.

When he was in first grade, Stephen got sick, and he had problems with his throat and his ears. He missed most of the school year. During those long months at home, he read many books. He especially liked books about adventures. Then he began to write stories. His first stories were taken from comic books. He showed one to his mother, and she told him to write a story by himself. So he did. He wrote a story that was four pages long. It was about magic animals that rode around in an old car and helped little kids. When his mother read it, she said it was good enough to be in a book. That made him extremely happy. He wrote four more stories about the magic animals, and his mother paid him twenty-five cents for each one—his first money from writing.

Finishing time __________   Reading time __________

Answer the questions on the following page.

Circle the best answer. Do not look back!

1. This passage is about
     a. a writer called Stephen King.
     b. the books by Stephen King.
     c. Stephen King's early years.
     d. writers of horror stories.

2. Stephen lived with
     a. his mother.
     b. his father.
     c. a babysitter.
     d. his parents.

3. Stephen's mother
     a. didn't want to work.
     b. worked as a babysitter.
     c. never had to work.
     d. always had to work.

4. Stephen and his brother
     a. always had the same babysitter.
     b. never stayed with a babysitter.
     c. liked their babysitter.
     d. had many babysitters.

5. One babysitter made Stephen
     a. cook eggs for lunch.
     b. eat seven fried eggs.
     c. climb out the window.
     d. stand in the bathroom.

6. When he was in first grade, Stephen
     a. had to stay home a lot.
     b. fell off the roof.
     c. liked his school a lot.
     d. had problems at school.

7. As a young boy, Stephen liked to
     a. have adventures.
     b. watch television.
     c. read about adventures.
     d. stay home from school.

8. Stephen's first stories were about
     a. his mother.
     b. a magic car.
     c. magic animals.
     d. little kids.

While Stephen was young, his family didn't have a television. They got one when he was about eleven years old. He loved television and everything about it, even the advertisements. But he didn't stop reading and writing stories.

When he was eleven, his mother gave him a typewriter for Christmas. In 1960, at the age of thirteen, he sent one of his stories to a magazine. The magazine didn't publish the story, but that didn't stop Stephen. He continued to write short stories and send them to magazines. He also helped his brother Dave with a monthly newsletter, called *Dave's Rag*. They printed the newsletter in their home and sold it to family and friends. Soon they were selling fifty or sixty copies every month. Stephen wrote jokes, news about people in their town, and a continuing story.

But *Dave's Rag* was his brother's idea. Stephen was not really interested in printing or journalism. What he really loved was movies. His family was now living in Durham, Maine. Every weekend, he went to the movies in Lewiston, fourteen miles away. Sometimes he went with a friend. Sometimes he went alone. Many times he couldn't get a ride and he had to walk halfway there. But unless he was sick, he always went. And already the young "King of Horror" knew what he liked. He definitely did not like musicals or children's movies. In his opinion, they were stupid and boring. He liked mysteries, science fiction, crime stories, and especially horror stories.

In junior high school, his favorite horror movies had titles from the stories of Edgar Allan Poe. He called them "Poepictures." They were very, very scary. After seeing one of them, Stephen had an idea. He could write the story from the movie and sell it to his friends! For two days, he worked hard. He wrote eight pages and printed forty copies. He brought them to school and began selling them at twenty-five cents each. By lunch time, he had nine dollars in his pocket. His first best-seller!

But at the end of the day, the school principal stopped him. She was very angry. She told him to give back the money and stop writing horror stories. Stephen gave back all the money, but he refused to stop writing. He wasn't sure if his stories were any good. But he knew that people wanted to read them.

Finishing time __________   Reading time __________

Answer the questions on the following page.

1. This passage is about
    a. what Stephen wrote for *Dave's Rag*.
    b. how Stephen started to write horror stories.
    c. why Stephen loved horror movies.
    d. why people liked Stephen's horror stories.

2. Before he was eleven, Stephen
    a. published many stories.
    b. never saw a television.
    c. didn't read many books.
    d. didn't have a television.

3. *Dave's Rag* was
    a. the junior high school newsletter.
    b. the name of a horror movie.
    c. Stephen's brother's newsletter.
    d. the name of a television show.

4. At this time, Stephen was mainly interested in
    a. sports.
    b. printing.
    c. movies.
    d. jokes.

5. Stephen had a very negative opinion about
    a. children's movies.
    b. horror stories.
    c. junior high school.
    d. his brother's newsletter.

6. "Poepictures" were very
    a. musical.
    b. scary.
    c. long.
    d. expensive.

7. Stephen wrote and printed a
    a. story about Edgar Allen Poe.
    b. story about people in his town.
    c. newsletter about movies.
    d. story from a horror movie.

8. In junior high school, Stephen realized that
    a. people like to read horror stories.
    b. he didn't want to write anymore.
    c. his stories were not any good.
    d. no one reads horror stories.

Stephen continued to write, and he continued to send stories to magazines. Finally, a story called "In a Half-World of Terror" was accepted in a horror magazine. This encouraged him. As a teenager, he already knew that he wanted to be a writer, and he knew just what he wanted to write.

But in high school, he had to do some different writing. His teachers learned about his work on *Dave's Rag*. They made him editor of the school newspaper, *The Drum*. As the editor, he had to write class reports and sports news. He didn't enjoy this kind of writing at all. One night, he was so bored that he decided he had to do something different. He wrote a school newsletter of his own and called it *The Village Vomit*. This newspaper made fun of the school. It gave funny names to all the teachers, and it told about funny things that happened to them. When Stephen brought the newsletter to school, his friends loved it. They laughed and laughed. Then a teacher decided to find out what was so funny. She found the newsletter and saw Stephen's name on it.

Once again, Stephen was in trouble because of his writing. Stephen was afraid he might be sent away from the school. Instead, he had to stay in the detention hall for two weeks. That meant he spent every school day in a special room for bad students. Stephen didn't mind this much. In the detention hall, the students told jokes and made paper airplanes.

But that wasn't the only result of *The Village Vomit*. The high school principal thought Stephen should use his writing skills. He knew that in a nearby town, the *Weekly Enterprise* newspaper needed a sports reporter. So he sent Stephen to talk to the editor. Stephen wasn't happy about this. He didn't like writing for newspapers, and he wasn't interested in sports. But he couldn't say no to the principal.

In the end, Stephen learned a lot about writing from the editor of the *Weekly Enterprise*. In fact, he learned much more at the *Enterprise* than in all the writing courses he took in college. The main thing he learned was how to tell a story, any kind of story. Then, just as important, he learned how to rewrite a story, taking out all the things that were not necessary. This was a lesson he never forgot.

Finishing time __________   Reading time __________

Answer the questions on the following page.

1. This passage is about the
   a. writing Stephen did in high school.
   b. stories Stephen wrote in high school.
   c. jobs Stephen had in high school.
   d. courses Stephen took in high school.

2. When he was a teenager, Stephen knew he wanted to
   a. write for a newspaper.
   b. make horror movies.
   c. be a writer of horror stories.
   d. be an editor of a newspaper.

3. Stephen became editor of the school newspaper because
   a. he wrote good stories in class.
   b. he liked writing for newspapers.
   c. he wanted to be the editor.
   d. his teachers wanted him to be editor.

4. Stephen's newsletter made fun of
   a. his friends.
   b. the school.
   c. his family.
   d. the town.

5. Stephen got into trouble because of his
   a. schoolwork.
   b. newsletter.
   c. stories.
   d. sports.

6. After he got into trouble, Stephen had to
   a. stay in the detention hall for two weeks.
   b. write another newsletter.
   c. stay away from school for two weeks.
   d. take a writing course.

7. When he heard about the job at the *Weekly Enterprise*, Stephen
   a. did not care.
   b. was very happy.
   c. was not happy.
   d. refused to go.

8. At the *Weekly Enterprise* newspaper, Stephen learned a lot about
   a. sports.
   b. college.
   c. the town.
   d. writing.

Passage 29: Becoming a Successful Writer   Starting time _________

In 1966, Stephen became a student at the University of Maine. To pay for his college expenses, he had to work. At different times he worked in the university library, in a factory, and in a high school as a cleaner. He studied English, but he also took education courses so he could become a teacher. This was his mother's idea. She thought he could make a good living as a teacher.

He wasn't making much money as a writer. He continued to write stories, and he continued to send them to magazines. Several stories were published, but he wasn't paid much for them. Finally, in 1969, a magazine paid him $200 for a story. He felt rich, but only for a short while.

1969 was an important year for Stephen in another way. That year, he met a young student named Tabitha Spruce in a poetry course, and soon they fell in love. The next year, Stephen graduated from the university. In January 1971, he and Tabitha got married.

Before long, Stephen and Tabitha had their first child, a baby girl. He couldn't find work as a teacher, so he took a job in a laundry. He sold a few more stories to magazines, but he and Tabitha never had enough money. They had a car, but it often broke down. When their daughter got sick, they didn't have money for medicine.

Then Stephen got a job as a teacher. He earned more money, but sometimes he was too tired to write. At that time, he was working on a novel about a high school girl. One day, he decided he didn't like the story or the girl in his novel. He didn't know enough about high school girls. So he threw all the pages he had written into the wastebasket. But the next day, Tabitha found them and read them. She told him it was a very good story and he had to finish it. She could help him with information about high school girls.

So she did help him, and he finished the book. That novel was *Carrie*, his first real success. Stephen didn't get paid much money at first. But a few months later, the publisher got a lot of money for the paperback edition and Stephen was paid $200,000. He and Tabitha didn't have to worry about money anymore. Stephen was a successful writer.

Finishing time _________   Reading time _________

Answer the questions on the following page.

1. This passage is about
   a. Stephen's first teaching job.
   b. Stephen's life as a college student.
   c. how Stephen got married to Tabitha.
   d. how Stephen became successful.

2. At the university, Stephen took courses so he could become
   a. a teacher.
   b. an editor.
   c. a doctor.
   d. a librarian.

3. While he was a student at the university, he
   a. didn't earn any money at all.
   b. earned a lot of money by writing.
   c. didn't earn much money by writing.
   d. wrote only papers for his classes.

4. Soon after Stephen graduated, he
   a. wrote a story.
   b. bought a car.
   c. started teaching.
   d. got married.

5. At first, Stephen and Tabitha were very
   a. rich.
   b. poor.
   c. unhappy.
   d. sick.

6. Stephen didn't like his job as a teacher because he
   a. was too tired to write.
   b. earned too little money.
   c. wasn't a good teacher.
   d. didn't like the school.

7. Stephen threw out the pages of *Carrie* because
   a. the publisher didn't like them.
   b. Tabitha didn't like them.
   c. he didn't like them.
   d. his mother didn't like them.

8. After *Carrie*, Stephen and Tabitha
   a. still had money troubles.
   b. had plenty of money.
   c. bought a new car.
   d. got married.

After the success of *Carrie*, Stephen stopped teaching so he could write full-time. His next books were *Salem's Lot* and *The Shining*. Both of these were very successful. Meanwhile, the family was growing. He and Tabitha had three children. They bought a house near a lake in western Maine. Later, they also bought a house in the city of Bangor, Maine. They lived in Bangor in the winter and in western Maine in the summer.

Stephen's life seemed perfect. He was famous, he was rich, and he had a happy family. However, he was drinking a lot of beer and other alcoholic drinks. He knew that many famous writers drank a lot. He thought his drinking was normal. But one evening when he took out the garbage, he looked at all the empty bottles. He realized that he was drinking too much.

He wasn't able to do anything about it then. For the next five years, he continued to drink. He also started to use drugs. He hardly remembers the last book he wrote in this period. Then Tabitha decided she had to try to stop him. She told him he had to change or he had to leave her and the children. He was killing himself, and she didn't want to watch him.

Stephen was afraid he couldn't write without alcohol and drugs. But he didn't want to lose his family, so he decided to change his life. He stopped drinking and taking drugs, and he found that he didn't need them to write. His stories were as good as before. In the next twelve years, he wrote many more books, and many of these, too, were best-sellers. When he was working on a book, he wrote every day, sometimes even on special holidays such as Christmas and the Fourth of July.

Then something terrible happened. Every day in the summer, Stephen took a long walk. On June 19, 1999, he was walking by the side of the road near his house. A large van came over a hill. The driver was not paying attention to the road, and he hit Stephen. Stephen was seriously hurt, and he nearly died. Over the next few weeks, he had to have many operations. He was often in terrible pain, and he couldn't walk. But by the end of July, he was back at his desk. He couldn't imagine a life without writing.

Finishing time ________   Reading time ________

Answer the questions on the following page.

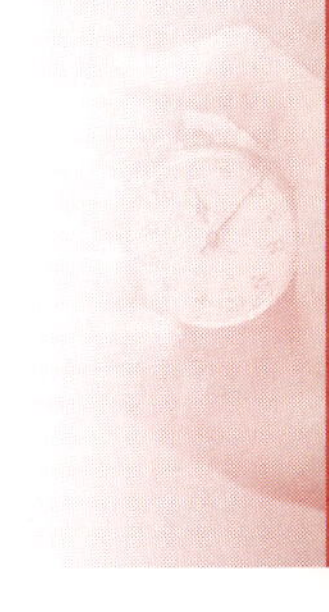

1. This passage is about
    a. why Stephen drank too much.
    b. success and some serious problems.
    c. Stephen's success as a writer.
    d. Stephen's terrible accident.

2. After *Carrie* was published, Stephen
    a. stopped teaching.
    b. continued teaching.
    c. stopped writing.
    d. stopped drinking.

3. One night, Stephen realized he
    a. worked too much.
    b. drank too much.
    c. couldn't write.
    d. was successful.

4. Stephen's wife told him
    a. he should try some drugs.
    b. she wanted to leave him.
    c. he had to change his life.
    d. she was killing herself.

5. At first, Stephen thought that he
    a. couldn't drink alcohol and write.
    b. didn't need to drink alcohol to write.
    c. couldn't write without alcohol.
    d. didn't want to write anymore.

6. When Stephen was writing a book, he
    a. worked in his study.
    b. didn't work on weekends.
    c. worked every day.
    d. didn't use a desk.

7. In 1999, Stephen
    a. drove a van off the road.
    b. was seriously ill.
    c. wrote another book.
    d. was very badly hurt.

8. After his accident, Stephen
    a. started writing again.
    b. couldn't write again.
    c. didn't want to write again.
    d. started drinking again.

Better Living Magazine

Passage 31: Time to Dance
Starting time ___________

Are you the kind of person who likes to move with the music? It's a natural thing to do. Even little children start jumping up and down when they hear music. In fact, people have always danced at important moments in their lives. It's part of the human experience, like music or storytelling.

Scientists say that animals dance, too, but their dancing is different. The "dances" of animals send messages to other animals. These messages are about important physical needs, such as hunger, or danger. But when people dance, they express feelings about life and love, or about death and sadness. From early times, dancing has been a way to show feelings about these very human experiences.

Dances are also an important part of every culture. In the past, each culture had its own dances. In Scotland, for example, everyone learned Scottish dancing. These days, the situation is very different. In the past two hundred years, many people around the world have moved to other countries. When they moved, they brought along their music and their dances. This means that today you can learn many different kinds of dances. You can learn Greek, Scottish, Egyptian, or Indonesian dances. You can learn the Viennese waltz, the Argentine tango, or American swing dancing.

All kinds of dances are good for you in the same ways. For one thing, dancing is good for you physically. It makes your heart work, it makes you breathe fast, and it makes you use your arms and your legs. If you go dancing often, you can keep physically fit. Dancing also is an enjoyable way to try to lose weight.

You may feel very tired after dancing, but you'll probably also feel relaxed and happy. This is the other important point about dancing. It gives you a chance to express your feelings and feel better about yourself. If you are angry or upset about something, dancing helps those feelings go away. If you are afraid or shy, dancing helps you forget your fear. When you're dancing, you can forget yourself completely and feel like another person.

And finally, there is another important point about dancing. It's a social activity. Some dances are for couples and some are for groups. But all kinds of dances give you a chance to meet new people or to do something enjoyable with friends.

Finishing time _________   Reading time ___________

Answer the questions on the following page.

1. This passage is about
   a. different kinds of dances.
   b. reasons for dancing.
   c. how animals dance.
   d. learning to dance.

2. Animals dance
   a. to express feelings to other animals.
   b. because they hear music.
   c. for the same reasons as people.
   d. to send messages to other animals.

3. For people, dancing is a way to
   a. express feelings.
   b. warn other people.
   c. become a child.
   d. become American.

4. In the past, each culture had
   a. Viennese waltzes.
   b. the same dances.
   c. its own dances.
   d. new dances.

5. Now you can learn
   a. many kinds of dances.
   b. how animals dance.
   c. few kinds of dances.
   d. only modern dances.

6. Dancing is
   a. bad for your heart.
   b. not good for your legs.
   c. bad for your body.
   d. good for your body.

7. After dancing, you feel
   a. better about yourself.
   b. angry with everyone.
   c. tired and unhappy.
   d. afraid of other people.

8. One important point about dancing is that you
   a. can become famous.
   b. do it with other people.
   c. can do it only in groups.
   d. don't have to pay much.

Passage 32: How to Improve Your Memory   Starting time __________

Language students often think they have a memory problem. They worry because they can't remember vocabulary. They think something is wrong with their brain. In fact, the problem is not their brain or their memory. The problem is the way they study.

If you want to improve your memory, it's important to understand how it works. There are two kinds of memory: short-term and long-term. All information goes into your short-term memory first. But it can stay there for just a few minutes. In order to remember something for more than a few minutes, it must move into your long-term memory.

Only some things move into your long-term memory. Which things? This is an important question for a student. In fact, your long-term memory keeps things that are interesting or important to you. That's why you remember big events in your life or your favorite sports events. Your long-term memory keeps other things, too. It holds onto things that you have thought about and worked with. So if you want to remember words, you have to work with them in some way.

Many students study vocabulary by repeating the words. This may be enough to remember them for a while. But after a day or a week, you may have lost them. The reason for this is very simple. Long-term memory is like a very big library with many, many books. And like a library, it is organized. When you put away a book—or a memory—you can't just leave it anywhere. If you want to find it again, you have to put it in a certain place.

Repeating a new word doesn't help you remember it for long, because it doesn't give you any way to find it again. You need to make a place for the word in your long-term memory. There are many ways you can do this. You can write sentences with the word. Or you can make a very short story about it. You can also make a picture in your mind with the word. For example, if the word is *height*, you can think of the tallest person you know and try to guess his height.

All of these activities are ways to work with words. They make the meaning of words stronger in your long-term memory. And they give you a way to find a word when you need it.

Finishing time __________   Reading time __________

Answer the questions on the following page.

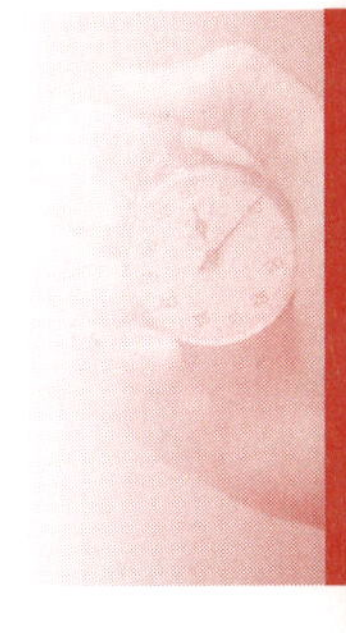

1. This passage is about
   a. how you can improve your memory.
   b. what is wrong with your brain.
   c. why you often forget words.
   d. what your long-term memory does.

2. Language students don't remember vocabulary because they
   a. don't have a good brain.
   b. have a memory problem.
   c. don't study the right way.
   d. worry too much.

3. Information stays in your short-term memory for
   a. a few minutes.
   b. a long time.
   c. your whole life.
   d. a few days.

4. Things that are interesting or important to you
   a. go into your short-term memory.
   b. don't stay in your brain.
   c. stay in short-term memory.
   d. move into long-term memory.

5. If you want to remember words, you should
   a. keep them in your short-term memory.
   b. work with them in some way.
   c. worry about your brain.
   d. go to the library every day.

6. If you repeat words,
   a. they may get lost in the library.
   b. they will always be in your memory.
   c. you are sure to remember them later.
   d. you may not remember them later.

7. Your long-term memory is like a
   a. well-organized library.
   b. very big dictionary.
   c. well-organized school.
   d. very big brain.

8. If you make a little story about a word, you'll
   a. forget the word.
   b. find your library book.
   c. remember it better.
   d. learn to write stories.

Many people have trouble getting to sleep at night. Other people wake up often during the night. Still others wake up very early in the morning and can't get back to sleep again. These people all have *insomnia*. That is, they don't sleep well. People with insomnia are very tired during the day and they are often unhappy, anxious, or just sleepy. This may have a bad effect on their family life or their work. It can also be dangerous to other people. For example, a bus driver with insomnia may fall asleep while driving.

There are two types of insomnia. The first is caused by thoughts and feelings. It happens to almost everyone at some point. You may be worried about a problem, or you may be nervous about an exam. You keep thinking and thinking, and your brain won't go to sleep. But this usually doesn't last long. When the problem is solved or the exam is over, the insomnia usually goes away, too.

The second type of insomnia has physical causes. You may be drinking too much coffee or tea. Even a small amount of coffee can cause insomnia in some people. Your evening meal habits can also affect your sleep. A large meal late in the evening can keep you awake. A lot of alcohol in the evening is also not a good idea. It may help you fall asleep, but later you may not sleep well. Smoking is another habit that can cause insomnia. In fact, the nicotine in cigarettes wakes you up.

In general, you'll sleep better if you lead a healthy life. Exercise is good for your health in general, and it helps you get a good night's sleep. A regular bedtime and waking time are also important. It's easier for your body to fall asleep at about the same time every night.

In addition, think about your bedroom. Is it really a good place to sleep? There are many things to check. First of all, you should check your bed. Is it really comfortable for you? It shouldn't be too hard or too soft. The temperature of the room is also important. A cool room is better for sleeping than a warm room. Finally, there shouldn't be too much light or noise. Some people can sleep in the middle of a brightly lit, noisy room. But most people sleep better in a dark, quiet place.

Finishing time __________   Reading time __________

Answer the questions on the following page.

Circle the best answer. Do not look back!

1. This passage is about
    a. the problem of insomnia.
    b. how to fall asleep quickly.
    c. the causes of insomnia.
    d. why sleep is important.

2. When you have insomnia, you
    a. can't sleep well.
    b. don't eat well.
    c. sleep too much.
    d. need a soft bed.

3. Insomnia can make you
    a. hungry at night.
    b. sleepy during the day.
    c. sleepy at night.
    d. happy during the day.

4. One type of insomnia is caused by
    a. driving during the day.
    b. problems with your brain.
    c. reading and studying.
    d. thoughts and feelings.

5. Late in the evening, you shouldn't
    a. study for an exam.
    b. have a snack.
    c. watch television.
    d. eat a large meal.

6. Cigarettes can cause insomnia because they
    a. have nicotine.
    b. make you hungry.
    c. cause cancer.
    d. aren't healthy.

7. You will sleep better if you usually
    a. go to bed early in the evening.
    b. go to bed at the same time.
    c. drink alcohol before bedtime.
    d. don't exercise too much.

8. You can sleep best in a
    a. large bedroom.
    b. warm bedroom.
    c. cool bedroom.
    d. blue bedroom.

Why do people meditate? The answer is simple: Meditation makes you a happier person. When you meditate, you sit quietly with your eyes closed for ten to forty minutes and you think about only one thing. That one thing can be your own breathing, or it can be a certain word. If it is a word, you repeat it again and again. You don't think about anything else. You don't think about your plans for the day or your problems at work. In this way, you stop thinking about the past or the future. You think more about the present and you become more peaceful.

People have known about the effects of meditation for a long time. In 3000–2000 B.C.E., people in India wrote about meditation. It was an important part of the Hindu and Buddhist religions. People of other religions in other places also practiced meditation. There were Jewish, Christian, and Muslim people who practiced meditation. They all believed that it brought them closer to God.

Then, in more recent times, some people in the United States and Europe became interested in Eastern religions and they began to practice meditation. For them, it was part of a religious experience. For most people, it seemed strange and even scary. But then, in the 1960s, popular music stars like the Beatles became interested in meditation. Other people followed them. Soon there were many courses and books about meditation.

Today, meditation no longer seems strange, and it is no longer just for religious people. Ten million Americans practice it. That's twice the number who practiced it ten years ago. Among those ten million people are students, football players, lawyers, doctors, businesspeople, and actors.

Doctors now know that meditation actually causes changes in your brain. If you meditate often, your way of thinking changes. You think less about your problems. You think more about the good things in your life.

Meditation helps people in many ways. It makes them feel happier about themselves and their lives. It helps them keep away the unpleasant effects of stress. It can also help some people who have medical problems. For example, meditation can help people with heart trouble to lower their blood pressure. Some doctors encourage their patients to meditate. Unlike medicines, meditation is free, and it has no bad side effects.

Finishing time _________   Reading time _________

Answer the questions on the following page.

1. This passage is about
   a. religion and meditation.
   b. how you can meditate.
   c. why people meditate.
   d. the history of meditation.

2. When you meditate, you think about
   a. only one thing.
   b. lots of things.
   c. your problems.
   d. the past.

3. Meditation makes you more
   a. successful.
   b. religious.
   c. intelligent.
   d. peaceful.

4. In the past, meditation was for
   a. religious people.
   b. doctors.
   c. students.
   d. sick people.

5. People became more interested in meditation
   a. ten years ago.
   b. in the past.
   c. in 3000–2000 B.C.E.
   d. after the 1960s.

6. Today,
   a. only religious people meditate.
   b. popular music stars meditate.
   c. many doctors meditate.
   d. many different people meditate.

7. Meditation is good for you because it
   a. makes you feel strange.
   b. changes the way your brain works.
   c. makes you more religious.
   d. changes the way your heart works.

8. People who are ill use meditation to
   a. study for exams.
   b. make them stronger.
   c. lower blood pressure.
   d. breathe better.

Are you afraid of flying on a plane? If you are, you're not alone. About one in four people is afraid of flying. That number increases every time there is a terrible plane crash or a war. But for many people, the fear is always there.

Some of these people fly anyway. They have a few drinks, or they take some medicine. During the flight, they try to forget they are on a plane. For others, the problem is worse. Even the thought of sitting on a plane makes them anxious. If they get on a plane, they can become ill from fear. They may become so ill that they have to get off the plane before it leaves.

In fact, there are really very few accidents with planes. Airline companies check their planes carefully before every flight. If the pilot thinks there is any problem with the plane, it doesn't take off. This means that accidents are very unlikely. The United States National Safety Council says that flying in a plane is much less dangerous than riding in a car. But these facts don't matter to the people who are afraid.

Scientists say that there are two different types of fear of flying. The first is the fear of falling out of the sky. Since the terrorist attacks of September 11, 2001, more people suffer from this fear. They think about all the bad things that could possibly happen. And they can think of lots of bad things that can happen to a plane high in the sky. The second type is a fear of being in a closed place. People with this fear never want to be in closed places. On a plane, they are afraid they might be trapped. If anything happens, they might not be able to get out.

For some fearful travellers, there may be only one solution. They have to travel on the ground—by car, bus, train, or boat. Other people, however, need to travel by air. In this case, they'll have to find some way to get over their fear. Doctors and scientists say it's not easy, but it's possible. They say that the important thing is not to give up flying. There are several ways to do this. Some airline companies offer one-day courses for people who are afraid of flying. In many cities, hospitals or doctors also offer special courses for these people.

Finishing time __________   Reading time __________

Answer the questions on the following page.

1. This passage is about
   a. courses for people with a fear of flying.
   b. what happens to people on a plane.
   c. why people don't like traveling.
   d. how some people are afraid of flying.

2. Fear of flying is a problem for
   a. many people.
   b. only a few people.
   c. people in Europe.
   d. doctors and scientists.

3. Some people are so afraid on a plane that they
   a. call a doctor.
   b. watch a movie.
   c. become ill.
   d. talk to themselves.

4. Flying in a plane is
   a. safer than riding in a car.
   b. not as safe as riding in a car.
   c. not as safe as riding a bicycle.
   d. safer than flying in a balloon.

5. According to scientists, some people are afraid the plane
   a. won't take off.
   b. won't be on time.
   c. will fall down.
   d. will land badly.

6. Other people are afraid they
   a. won't have good food on the plane.
   b. will be trapped in the plane.
   c. may get sick on the plane.
   d. might take the wrong plane.

7. If you're afraid of flying, you
   a. shouldn't watch the news.
   b. can travel on the ground.
   c. can't ever travel anywhere.
   d. should probably stay home.

8. Doctors say it's important not to
   a. give up flying.
   b. fly on small planes.
   c. travel by car and train.
   d. take lots of medicine.

Language Learning Magazine

Passage 36: Successful Language Learning   Starting time ___________

What does it take to be a successful language learner? Gilberto is a good example. He learned Spanish from his family, and he learned English when he started school. He had some classes in Spanish and some in English, so he learned to read and write in both languages. He found that he liked learning languages and he was good at it. What made Gilberto a successful language learner?

First of all, Gilberto learned a second language when he was a child. Children who learn a second language learn important facts about languages. For example, they learn that they can say the same thing in two ways. They also find out that every language has different sounds. In addition, they know how to switch from one language to another. With family, they speak their home language, and at school, the second language.

Second, Gilberto found out that knowing two languages could help him. When he went to the store, he could use English to buy things. And because he knew English, he could succeed at school. On the other hand, when Gilberto visited his grandparents, he could use Spanish. He could also use Spanish with other friends and relatives from Central and South America.

Third, Gilberto was always a very friendly type of person. He liked meeting new people and talking with them. He was also not afraid of trying to speak a new language. He didn't feel bad if he made a few mistakes. He really just wanted to communicate. He wanted to learn about different places around the world and the way people live in other places.

Fourth, Gilberto was a good student. He studied hard and he loved to figure out the rules of a language. In class, he took part in all the activities. At home, he listened to music and watched videos in the new language. When he spoke, he tried to sound like a native speaker of the language.

Being a successful language learner helped Gilberto a lot. In college, he studied Russian and Serbo-Croatian. After college, he was able to find a good job. He went to Russia to teach English in a Russian university. After a few years, he moved back to the United States and worked for the U.S. government at the Language Institute. He taught the Serbo-Croatian language to government workers. Today, Gilberto is a professor of Russian and Serbo-Croatian at Dean University in California.

Finishing time ___________   Reading time ___________

Answer the questions on the following page.

Circle the best answer. Do not look back!

1. This passage is about
    a. how Gilberto got a good job in the United States.
    b. how Gilberto learned English at school.
    c. why Gilberto traveled to Russia to teach English.
    d. why Gilberto became a successful language learner.

2. At school, Gilberto used
    a. English in all of his classes.
    b. Spanish in all of his classes.
    c. both English and Spanish.
    d. English only for speaking.

3. Children who learn two languages
    a. speak English at school.
    b. can't learn English easily.
    c. can't speak Spanish anymore.
    d. learn a lot about languages.

4. It's important to know that
    a. different languages have different sounds.
    b. some languages are too difficult to learn.
    c. all languages have the same sounds.
    d. some languages are taught in school.

5. Children who speak two languages can
    a. learn to read at a young age.
    b. switch between languages.
    c. speak English only in school.
    d. never speak any language well.

6. Gilberto could succeed in school because he
    a. had good teachers.
    b. was good at math.
    c. knew Spanish.
    d. knew English.

7. When Gilberto made mistakes, he
    a. felt very bad.
    b. asked his teacher.
    c. didn't feel bad.
    d. stopped speaking.

8. Gilberto got a good job after college because he
    a. could read and write in Spanish.
    b. was a good language learner.
    c. wanted to live in Russia.
    d. was interested in other places.

All human beings can learn a language. And all babies learn language the same way. It doesn't matter what language they are learning. Babies can learn any language, but in fact, they learn the language that is around them.

At first, babies make only one kind of sound: crying. Parents pay attention when a baby cries. That's how parents and babies begin to communicate with each other. Soon, babies begin to make other sounds. They can laugh and make happy sounds called "cooing." These sounds encourage parents to talk to them, and the babies learn more about language.

By the time they are two months old, babies hear and understand things better. For example, they can tell the difference between human voices and other sounds. They can recognize their mother's voice. In the next few months, their listening skills improve quickly. They can recognize different spoken sounds. For example, babies can hear the difference between "pa" and "ba."

When they are about six months old, babies begin "babbling." This means they make sounds like "mamama" or "bababa." The babies make the sounds to learn how to use their mouths. They usually aren't trying to communicate anything to anyone. In fact, babies often babble when they are alone. At first, the babbling sounds are the same for all babies everywhere. But soon each baby begins to practice just the sounds they hear in the language around them.

Children start using words when they are about one year old. At first, they use just one word at a time. Often they do something at the same time to explain their meaning better. For example, a child says "Up," and she holds out her hands. The parent understands that she wants to be picked up.

When they are about eighteen to twenty-four months old, children begin using two-word sentences. A child might say "Train come." He means "The train is coming." By the time they are two or three years old, children can say longer sentences. For example, they might say "No sit there" or "Car make noise." These are not complete sentences, but they already follow the rules of grammar.

By the time they are six, children know a lot about language. They may still make mistakes, but they usually make good sentences and questions. And if they know two languages, they almost never speak the wrong language with someone.

Finishing time _________   Reading time _________

Answer the questions on the following page.

Circle the best answer. Do not look back!

1. This passage is about
    a. ways to learn language.
    b. how parents speak with children.
    c. why children learn to speak.
    d. how children learn language.

2. At first, babies can
    a. make many different sounds.
    b. only make the sound of crying.
    c. learn to say only "mama."
    d. make many sounds.

3. After two months, babies
    a. speak the English language.
    b. recognize their mother's voice.
    c. cry a lot more than before.
    d. can make conversations.

4. Babies first learn about language from
    a. their teachers.
    b. their toys.
    c. their parents.
    d. books and music.

5. Babies babble so they can
    a. practice sounds.
    b. learn new words.
    c. say things to their parents.
    d. get something to eat.

6. The first babbling sounds are
    a. different in different places.
    b. the same for all babies.
    c. usually in English.
    d. difficult to understand.

7. One-year-old children often use
    a. music to practice language.
    b. nouns and verbs correctly.
    c. cooing sounds and crying.
    d. a single word like a sentence.

8. By the time children are six, they
    a. usually make good sentences.
    b. can speak their language perfectly.
    c. can speak many different languages.
    d. usually still make many mistakes.

Passage 38: Sign Language

Starting time __________

For some people, learning a spoken language is impossible. This is true for deaf people (people who can't hear). Instead of a spoken language, deaf people can learn sign language. In this language, people communicate by moving their hands in specific ways. Deaf people can use sign language with other deaf people or with hearing people who learn sign language.

Sign language is like spoken language in most ways. Both sign language and spoken language have vocabulary, grammar, and sentences. In spoken language, you make different sounds with your mouth. In sign language, you move your hands. Different ways of holding your hand have different meanings. First, you can have your hand open or closed. Second, you can have your hand in front of your head or in front of your chest. Third, you can move your hand up or down. And fourth, you can have your hand facing up or down.

People use sign language all around the world, but every country has its own sign language. There may be differences inside a country as well. In Switzerland, for example, there are five different ways of using Swiss German Sign Language. In the United States, the 500,000 people who use American Sign Language don't all use it the same way. People in different parts of the country have different signs for things.

For children, learning sign language is no different from learning any other language. They can begin learning the signs when they are still small babies. If the parents are deaf, their children will learn sign language from them. If the children are able to hear, they can also learn spoken language from other people. Deaf children sometimes have parents who can hear. These parents often learn sign language when their deaf children are born. That way, they can communicate with their children.

In many countries, people called *signers* help deaf people. The signers are not deaf, but they know sign language, and they can translate spoken language to sign language. Signers sometimes work for television channels. Some television programs will show a signer in one corner of the screen. The signer translates everything during the program. Some meetings at universities or churches have a signer at the front of the room. This way, deaf people can follow what is happening. Sign language has made a big difference in the lives of deaf people.

Finishing time ___________   Reading time ____________

Answer the questions on the following page.

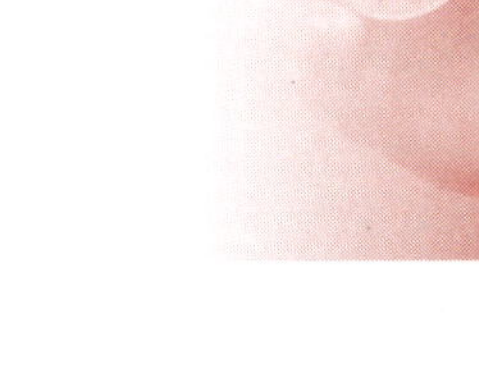

1. This passage is about
   a. sign language for deaf people.
   b. American Sign Language.
   c. how signers help deaf people.
   d. the problems of deaf people.

2. When you "speak" sign language, you use your
   a. face.
   b. mouth.
   c. hands.
   d. pen.

3. In sign language, you
   a. shouldn't move your hand.
   b. can move your hand four ways.
   c. can only open or close your hand.
   d. don't use grammar.

4. Sign language and spoken language
   a. both use the voice.
   b. are exactly the same.
   c. have the same vocabulary.
   d. have many similarities.

5. People in the same country
   a. never use sign language with each other.
   b. always have the same kind of sign language.
   c. may have different ways of using sign language.
   d. learn sign language in different schools.

6. Children learn sign language
   a. differently from other languages.
   b. the same way they learn other languages.
   c. from teachers in the schools for the deaf.
   d. from signers on television channels.

7. Parents of deaf children
   a. can't learn sign language.
   b. never learn sign language.
   c. don't know how to speak.
   d. often learn sign language.

8. Signers help deaf people by
   a. watching television with them.
   b. teaching them sign language.
   c. speaking to them in English.
   d. translating things for them.

People have always wanted to speak with animals. There are many books about this, especially children's books. Now there are also movies, such as *Dr. Doolittle*. When you watch animals, it seems clear that they can communicate with each other. Many people wonder why people can't also communicate with them.

Scientists know how some animals communicate. Bees, for example, use their bodies. They do a kind of dance to give information about food. Birds, on the other hand, share information with sounds. They use certain sounds to protect their nests and to stay together when they fly. Some male birds use lovely songs to attract a female. Other animals communicate with both body movements and sounds. For example, dogs wag their tail when they are happy, and they bark when they are excited.

People used to think it was possible to teach human language to animals. Parrots and other birds, for example, can learn to say words. But the birds just repeat the words. They don't understand them. Some American scientists tried to teach English to chimpanzees, close relatives of human beings. However, this was impossible. Chimpanzees can't move their mouths and throats the right way. They could never learn to speak like people.

Then scientists tried to teach human language to chimpanzees in other ways. Some tried with American Sign Language (ASL). Others tried with a simple computer. But chimpanzees could only learn to use a few words. They could never learn to use grammar. Their brains are very different from the brains of human beings.

Now some scientists are studying the similarities between human and animal language. In fact, some animals use sounds like people do. Dogs, for example, use an unpleasant, low sound to tell other dogs to stay away. People, too, use that kind of voice to say the same thing. A dog's sharp bark communicates that something is happening. People use a similar sharp tone when they shout, "Watch out!"

Scientists want to understand the language of other animals, such as whales and bears. To do this, they go out to the animals' natural homes. They watch the animals for days or even years. They take pictures and make tape recordings and share the information with other scientists. In this way, they hope to learn more about the way animals communicate, and maybe someday we'll be able to communicate better with them.

Finishing time __________   Reading time __________

Answer the questions on the following page.

1. This passage is about
    a. how animals communicate with each other.
    b. how scientists work with chimpanzees.
    c. how people might communicate with animals.
    d. how scientists are studying animals.

2. Bees communicate by
    a. making a noise.
    b. doing a dance.
    c. flying places.
    d. wagging their tails.

3. Birds use sounds to
    a. stay together.
    b. find food.
    c. say words.
    d. speak to people.

4. Some birds can learn to say words,
    a. but they forget them quickly.
    b. and they make up new words, too.
    c. and they use grammar, too.
    d. but they don't understand them.

5. Chimpanzees can't speak because they
    a. are close relatives to humans.
    b. can't make human sounds.
    c. don't want to communicate.
    d. don't like to use computers.

6. Scientists tried to teach chimpanzees to
    a. do some dances.
    b. eat certain foods.
    c. use ASL.
    d. say "hello."

7. Dogs and people use
    a. words when they communicate.
    b. different sounds to mean the same thing.
    c. a low sound to keep others away.
    d. a high sound to keep others away.

8. In the future, people may learn to
    a. communicate with animals.
    b. share their information.
    c. communicate with each other.
    d. speak with scientists.

American and British people both speak English, of course, but sometimes it doesn't seem like the same language. In fact, there are some important differences between British and American English.

First of all, they sound very different. Often, Americans don't say all the letters in each word, especially consonants like "t" and "d." For example, Americans may say I "dunno" instead of "I don't know," or they may say "Whaddya say?" instead of "What do you say?" However, the British usually pronounce their consonants more carefully.

Also, some letters have different sounds. For example, Americans say the "a" in "half" like the "a" in "cat," but the British say the "a" in "half" like the "a" in "aah." The "r" is sometimes said differently, too. Most Americans say both the "r"s in "farmer," but most British people don't. The British say "fahmah."

Sound is not the only difference between British English and American English. The two languages have different words for some things. For example, the words for clothing are different. Americans use the word "sweater," but the British say "jumper." Americans wear "vests" over their shirts, but in England they wear "vests" under their shirts. Americans wear "pants" over their "underpants," but the British wear "pants" under their "trousers."

Many other words and expressions are different in the two countries. In England, if you are going to telephone a friend, you "ring her up." In America, you "give her a call." The British use the word "lovely" to describe something they like. Americans use the word "cool" or "great." If an American says someone is "mad" they mean "angry." If a Englishman says someone is "mad" they mean "crazy."

There are also some differences in grammar. For example, Americans almost always use the helping verb "do" with the verb "have." They might say "Do you have an extra pen?" The British often ask the question a different way. They might say "Have you got an extra pen?"

These differences can be confusing if you are learning English. But there is a reason for the differences. Languages change over time. When the same language is used in different places, it changes differently in each place. This is what happened to English. It also happened to other languages, such as French. Many people in Canada speak French, but their French is different from the French spoken in France.

Finishing time __________ Reading time __________

Answer the questions on the following page.

1. This passage is about
   a. some of the words American people use.
   b. the way British people say certain words.
   c. how American sounds are different from British sounds.
   d. how American English is different from British English.

2. When Americans speak, you often don't hear
   a. any consonant sounds.
   b. some consonant sounds.
   c. any vowel sounds.
   d. any words at all.

3. In the United States and England, some letters
   a. always sound the same.
   b. have different sounds.
   c. sound like French.
   d. have an unusual sound.

4. The words for clothing are
   a. an example of British English.
   b. an example of modern technology.
   c. different in the United States and England.
   d. very difficult to learn in English.

5. People in the United States and in England
   a. always use the same expressions.
   b. often say good-bye to each other.
   c. don't use expressions often.
   d. sometimes use different expressions.

6. When Americans ask questions, they usually
   a. use the helping verb *do*.
   b. don't use a helping verb.
   c. don't use any grammar.
   d. cause some confusion.

7. English learners can get confused because
   a. English never changes.
   b. it is different in different places.
   c. people often ask them questions.
   d. the French language is different.

8. Languages
   a. change over time.
   b. are difficult.
   c. don't change much.
   d. are the same in all places.

Teacher's Guide

Reading Power, Third Edition, is intended for students who need to develop their reading skills in English in a variety of settings: junior high and high school developmental reading classes; adult literacy programs for native speakers of English and ESL/EFL learners; and ESL/EFL classes for students who have studied for about 100 hours and have acquired a vocabulary of about 600 words.

In appearance and approach, this book is different from other reading skills books. First, the focus is different. This book directs students' attention to their own reading processes, whereas most other books call attention to the content of the material.

In addition, *Reading Power* is organized in a different way from most textbooks. It contains four sections that correspond to four important aspects of the development of proficient reading, and whereas most books are meant to be used in a linear fashion from beginning to end, the four parts of this book are designed to be used concurrently. This means that each reading class should include activities and exercises from several different parts of the book. Using all the parts together in this way is a crucial aspect of a successful reading program.

Introduction

In this Teacher's Guide, general guidelines and specific suggestions are provided for making the most effective use of *Reading Power*. For a more complete explanation of the theory and methodology used in this book, see *A Short Course in Teaching Reading Skills*, by Beatrice S. Mikulecky (Addison-Wesley Longman, 1990).

The goal of *Reading Power* is to develop students' awareness of the reading process so that they will be able to read in ways that are expected in school, college, or business. In order to allow the students to focus on the process of reading, the vocabulary and grammatical structures used in these materials have been kept to a minimum (high-beginner to low-intermediate level).

Many students have a concept of reading that is based on prior experiences with reading in another language. This concept can interfere with their ability to read well in English. *Reading Power* aims to help students acquire an accurate understanding of what it means to read in English. To accomplish this, the book addresses the reading process in a direct manner, and the various reading skills involved are presented as part of that process.

Students' awareness of reading and thinking processes is further encouraged in many parts of the book by exercises that require them to work in pairs or small groups. In discussions with others, students need to formulate and articulate their ideas more precisely, and so they also acquire new ways of talking and thinking about a text. Exercises that require a student to write will help enhance their awareness of the connections between reading and writing.

A note about the Answer Key: In this third edition of *Reading Power*, the Answer Key is provided as a separate booklet. It is not included at the back of the student textbook. While some teachers prefer to have the Answer Key separate from the text, others believe that students learn more effectively if they have access to the Answer Key to check their own work. We encourage teachers to make the Answer Key available to students. Suggestions regarding the use of the Answer Key are found throughout this Teacher's Guide. Teachers who do not want their students to use the Answer Key can disregard these suggestions.

Using *Reading Power* in Your Class

The teacher's role in the reading class

The teacher is the most important element in a successful reading class. A good teacher can provide

- an anxiety-free environment in which students feel comfortable taking risks and trying new ways of reading.
- enough practice for the students to master new strategies.
- friendly pressure in the form of persuasion and timing.
- positive examples of how to approach a text.
- a model for the kind of thinking that good reading requires.
- an inspiring example of an enthusiastic reader.

Planning your reading classes

The materials in this book were designed to take approximately 35 hours of class time. This will vary according to the level of the students in your class and the amount of homework you assign. Keep in mind that the Comprehension Skills exercises in Part 2 should be introduced in class and practiced before any of the exercises are assigned for homework.

Classes and individual students also vary in the amount of time they need to complete different kinds of exercises in the book.

A complete, semester-long **sample syllabus** is included at the end of the Teacher's Guide (pages 288–293). Here are some additional suggestions for using *Reading Power* in several different types of classes:

- **In an integrated skills class that meets for two to three hours per day, five days a week, for one semester:** Use *Reading Power* 30–40 minutes, three times a week.

Monday	Reading Faster, 15 minutes Comprehension Skills, 20 minutes
Wednesday	Thinking Skills, 15 minutes Reading for Pleasure and Book Conferences, 20 minutes
Friday	Reading Faster, 15 minutes Comprehension Skills, 20 minutes

Homework assignments can include Reading for Pleasure exercises, Thinking Skills exercises, and selected Comprehension Skills exercises (further practice on skills introduced in class).

- **In an integrated skills class that meets for three hours per week for one semester:** Use *Reading Power* for about one-third of the class time, for a total of one hour per week, divided approximately as follows:
  - Reading Faster, 20 minutes
  - Thinking Skills exercises, 15 minutes
  - Comprehension Skills exercises, 20 minutes.

Homework assignments would be the same as above.

- **In a reading class that meets two hours per week for one semester:** Use the four parts of *Reading Power*, as well as the students' pleasure reading books, in every class. Work for about 20 to 30 minutes on each part of the book. Homework assignments can focus on reading for pleasure.

- **In a reading lab:** As in the classroom, students should work regularly on all four parts of the book, dividing their time about equally among the four parts. It is essential that the lab instructor give students initial instruction on how to use each part of *Reading Power* before they begin to work independently.

Homework assignments for all types of classes can include:

- Reading for Pleasure
- Selected Comprehension Skills exercises. Keep in mind that the Comprehension Skills in Part 2 should be assigned for homework only after the students have practiced them in class.
- Thinking Skills
- Reading Faster passages. These are best done in class under the supervision of the teacher or lab instructor.

Making the Reading Class Exciting and Effective

- Make reading **enjoyable for the students**. Activities in the reading class must always involve them fully and never be allowed to turn into "busy work."
- Make the students aware of the **purpose of their work**. This will increase their sense of involvement and allow them to become more active learners (increasing their metacognitive awareness).
- Always **focus on the thinking process** and not on the "right answers." The answer in any particular exercise matters far less than how the student arrives at it. Encourage students to take this same approach by frequently asking "Why?" or "How can you tell?" or "How do you know?" As the students are required repeatedly to articulate answers to these questions, they become more conscious of their own thinking processes.
- Ask the students to **work in pairs** whenever possible, especially on the Comprehension Skills exercises in Part 2. **Talking about the exercises** and

explaining their reasoning can reinforce the students' awareness of process and purpose. It also facilitates language acquisition (when the conversation is in English).

- Emphasize the importance of trying to **guess the meaning of words** from the context. Students should be discouraged from depending on dictionaries during the reading class or while doing their reading homework.
- The Answer Key is intended to serve as more than just the repository of the "right answers." Students should **check their own answers** so they can work independently when appropriate. When their answers differ from the Answer Key, they should try to figure out how and why they may have made a mistake. However, they should also be encouraged to question the Answer Key and to defend their answers and their reasoning. Some of the exercises, in fact, have alternative answers.
- When students work individually (especially on Part 3), allow them to **work at their own pace**. Speed should be encouraged, but each student must determine what that speed will be. Faster students should not have to wait for slower classmates, and slower readers should not be pressed too hard or they may become anxious and incapable of comprehending.
- **Testing Students' Reading Skills:** Please see the *Reading Power Test Booklet* for further exercises that can be used to test students on the skills presented in this book.

Specific suggestions for using *Reading Power*

Introducing the book to the students

To encourage students to think about reading, start the first reading class with a questionnaire like this one:

Reading Questionnaire

	Yes	No

1. It is important to read every word if you want to understand.

2. You will learn more if you look up every new word in the dictionary.

3. Reading stories and novels is not important.

4. If you read fast, you will not understand.

5. You should be able to say every word you read.

6. Reading class is the same as vocabulary class.

7. Books for ESL students must be simple. ESL students cannot read books for English speakers.

8. You should write the words in your own language above the English words in a book.

A good reader would answer "no" to all these statements. Students may answer "yes" to some questions, and it may be difficult to convince them otherwise. Do not press the point too much at this time, since students will come to understand the reasons as they use the book. However, discussion of these questions and students' answers will help raise students' awareness of the reading process in English and the differences between the reading process in English and the reading processes in other languages, as well as the different values cultures place on reading. This questionnaire will also help clarify for students their objectives in the reading class.

Later in the course, refer to these questions and students' answers as a way for students to note changes in their thinking about reading.

Part 1: Reading for Pleasure

Many students have never realized that reading can be enjoyable and so they have never tried reading for pleasure (extensive reading) in English. Yet we know that to be a good reader, it is necessary to read a lot. To get students reading extensively, it is not enough to say, "Read a book." Students must first come to understand the importance of reading extensively, and then they need to have the opportunity to discover how enjoyable it can be. At the same time, they should be encouraged to make reading for pleasure a regular habit. *Reading Power* provides several motivating features: a rationale for pleasure reading, guidelines for success, goal setting, record keeping, a list of carefully selected books, and suggestions for how teachers can evaluate the students' reading.

The difference between Extensive Reading and Intensive Reading

Intensive reading is an activity in which students (usually in a class group, led by the teacher) carefully read and examine together a reading passage assigned by the teacher. Many traditional reading classes use this approach almost exclusively. Some teachers refer to this activity as "explication of the text."

Extensive Reading, on the other hand, is an activity in which students read a lot, in books that they choose themselves. What matters is that they are encouraged to read as much as possible.

While **intensive reading** plays an important role in developing an appreciation of the

English language and selected English literature, it is by **reading extensively** that students can develop their ability to read with fluency and understanding. Furthermore, extensive reading is essential for practicing and applying reading skills and for developing all areas of language skills. Research shows that vocabulary acquisition and writing ability, for example, are directly related to the **quantity of reading** that students engage in.

Student Selection of Books for Extensive Reading

For pleasure reading (extensive reading) students must be allowed to select their own books on an individual basis. Teachers may help students select books at an appropriate level, neither too easy nor too difficult. The books should not be required reading in another course or in past courses, since that would probably limit their enjoyment. Students also might be bored with a story that they are already familiar with from a film version or from their reading in another language. **The key to the success of extensive reading is that students must be free to choose any book they want—**fiction or nonfiction, literature or popular culture. What matters most is that the book is of interest to the individual student and that the student actually wants to read it.

For pleasure reading, students should read complete books, not newspapers, magazines, or reading textbooks that are collections of short pieces by a variety of authors. They should also avoid books that are made up of extracts of other books (such as *Reader's Digest Selections*) or collections of short stories by many different authors. There are several reasons for this. First of all, many students may never before have read a book in English that they chose for themselves. Thus the selection process will be a new experience for them, one that will help form a new literate identity.

Second, while magazines, newspapers, and book selections may provide reading practice,

the goal of pleasure reading is for students to develop the habit of **sustained silent reading**, which is only possible with whole books. In addition, reading a whole book by a single author allows students to become comfortable with a writer's style and lexicon. This comfort is experienced as success, and actually allows students to read faster and faster as they proceed through their books.

Helping Students Select Books

You can help students select their books by bringing some of your own favorite books to the reading class and tell the students about them. After hearing you talk about your books, students may want to read them, too, so the books should be at an appropriate level for the class.

These "book talks" serve two purposes. First, students find out about books that they might like to read. Second, students are provided with a model for how to talk about books, so that they will be able to talk about their own books and discuss them with others.

When presenting a book to the class, give a brief summary of the book's content, without too many details about the plot, and give your general reaction (Why did you like it or dislike it? Does it relate to your own experience?). Talk about various aspects of the book: the characters, the setting, the mood, the author's intention, and so on. Discussion about books can be an effective motivating tool.

Students can also find books by participating in a class trip to a bookstore or library where they can browse and ask questions about books. Or, if the classroom has a library of suitable books, students can be guided to ones they might enjoy. They can also be encouraged to exchange books with classmates or with other students. Since students do not need to and, in fact, should not write notes or vocabulary in their pleasure reading books, there is no reason for them to buy the books (unless they want to be able to keep them afterward).

Motivating Students to Read for Pleasure

Students often tend to regard reading for pleasure as a less important element of the reading class. Be sure to encourage students to take it seriously. Reading for pleasure is, in fact, essential for successful reading development.

- Require students to bring their pleasure reading books to every class and regularly devote some class time to pleasure reading.
- Assign reading for pleasure as homework and require your students to keep a record of how many pages they have read. Establish a requirement for the number of pages to be read per week or per semester.

Check up on the students' pleasure reading by asking about the books they are reading. This can take various forms:

- Students can keep a reading journal in which they write regularly about their reactions to their book. They can write about characters they like or dislike, parts of the book that are particularly interesting or challenging, aspects of the setting or the style that have struck them, or larger issues that the book deals with (such as racism, war, the generation gap). To set an example, teachers can keep a reading journal of their own and read it aloud to students to give them a model for that kind of writing.
- Students can meet in small groups and tell one another about the books they are currently reading.
- After they have finished a book, students can meet with the teacher one by one for a brief **book conference.**

Book conferences are the surest way to evaluate student progress and promote pleasure reading. Book conferences are essential to a successful extensive reading program. Not only do they provide feedback on the students' reading, but they also serve several other important purposes.

In a book conference, the teacher's questions serve as a model for the kinds of questions that a literate reader habitually asks herself. In fact, there may be a true "knowledge gap" between the teacher and the student, since the student may have read a book that the teacher is not familiar with. Thus, the teacher's questions are authentic, not the kind of "school questions" that usually have no relation to real reading experiences.

The book conference can also help the student acquire fluency in evaluative and elaborative language that will become the basis for good writing.

Some teachers hold book conferences during office hours or just before class. Other teachers meet with one student while the rest of the class is engaged in another activity.

- Students can fill out a Pleasure Reading Report (page 16). Full written book reports are less useful, since they tend to diminish the student's enjoyment of the book.
- Students can give an oral report to their classmates, with a brief description of the book and their opinion of it.
- Encourage students to read faster when they read for pleasure. Students who read slowly often get bored or frustrated and may give up reading for pleasure. If they can read faster, however, they will enjoy their reading more. This will lead them to read more, which in turn will lead to better and faster reading, and so on.

For students to learn to read faster in their pleasure reading books, they first need to find out their reading rates. Then they can try to improve their reading rates by reading against the clock. They can further increase their reading rates with reading sprints.

In following the directions for calculating their reading rates and for doing reading sprints, students also get meaningful practice in the important skill of following printed directions.

Slower readers need to be encouraged to break their slow, word-by-word reading habits and to move their eyes more quickly down the page. They also may need to be reassured about comprehension. They do not need to understand every word or sentence. It is enough to be able to follow the story in a pleasure reading book.

Improving Reading Rate in Pleasure Reading Books

Included in Part 1 (pages 17–19) are instructions for how students can find their reading rates in their self-selected pleasure reading books. Before leading the students through this process, it is important for the teacher to read the procedure carefully. Once students know how to calculate their reading rates, they should keep a record of their progress on the Pleasure Reading Progress Charts (page 20).

Reading Sprints

The teacher can also help students break slow reading habits by having them do reading sprints in their books. The following are some guidelines for using reading sprints in the classroom.

1. Be sure to study the procedure for reading sprints before using them with students. Explain the procedure thoroughly to avoid confusion in the middle of the exercises. Students should use their pleasure reading books for the sprints.

2. After the first session of sprints, students should repeat the sprints at regular intervals in class (once a week, once a month, etc., according to the frequency of class meetings) and at home.

3. Given the concentration required for doing sprints, they should be followed by some relatively relaxing activity.

As students do reading sprints at ever faster speeds, they may object that they can't understand what they're reading. Reassure them that this is not important for the purpose of this exercise. Sprints are intended to show students how it feels to move their eyes quickly across the page and to demonstrate that they can, in fact, do so.

Also, though students may say they don't understand what they're reading, often, if they are questioned, they realize that they have in fact been able to follow the basic story line. In this way, sprints help students become aware of how much text they can skip when they read for the story or general ideas.

Part 2: Comprehension Skills

Many students have trouble comprehending what they read in English. Since they can read in their own language, they sometimes blame their comprehension difficulties on the English language or on their own lack of ability. In fact, the problem usually lies in their approach to a text.

In order to comprehend a text in English, the reader must grasp the writer's intended meaning. This is possible only if the reader can follow the thinking processes of the writer, which means that the reader must learn to think the way writers of English think. With a better understanding of how information is presented in English texts and a greater awareness of the cognitive processes involved in reading, comprehension will almost certainly improve.

In Part 2 of *Reading Power,* students focus on eight essential reading comprehension skills. The skills include both "top-down" (concept-driven) and "bottom-up" (text-driven) ways of reasoning and comprehending. Each skill is introduced with a rationale, which is followed by practice in the skill in a series of exercises sequenced from simple to more difficult.

This approach builds the students' mastery of the skill.

When introducing students to this part of the book, teachers should also start with a rationale, to explain the approach. The following comparison may be helpful for students:

Work on reading comprehension skills can be compared to weight-lifting. The coach explains to the weight-lifter how and why he or she must exercise certain muscle groups. Once the muscle group is targeted, the exercises proceed with gradually increasing weights.

This is the same process that students should follow in reading comprehension lessons. As the "coach," you must be sure that the students understand how and why to do the exercises, and then stand by to provide advice, support, and increased challenges.

Before beginning to work on the reading skills, ask the students to read and discuss the Introduction to Comprehension Skills at the beginning of Part 2 in the student text. As with any new instructional materials, you will have the most success with these exercises if you do them yourself before introducing them to students.

How to Use the Comprehension Skills Units in the Classroom

1. Focus on one reading/thinking skill at a time.

2. With each skill, go through the introduction to the skill with the students. Explain the purpose for doing the exercises and how the skill is important for effective reading.

3. Do an example or a sample exercise with the whole class. Think aloud to let the students know what you are thinking as you do the exercise. (This is called "modeling.")

4. Put the students into pairs (whenever possible and appropriate) and assign one exercise for practice.

5. When the pairs have completed the exercise, discuss it with the whole class. Ask the students how they arrived at their answers. Encourage friendly disagreement in the pairs and in the class as a whole. Ask, "What was your thinking as you decided on that answer?" Students are not necessarily "wrong" if they come up with an answer that is different from the Answer Key, as long as they can give a rationale for their choice.

6. In the same class and in the next few class meetings, assign additional exercises that focus on the same skill, increasing the complexity of the tasks. Make sure the students work in pairs whenever it is feasible.

7. Next, assign an exercise to be done by individual students, either in class or as homework, so they can check their own ability and confidence in using the skill.

8. Assign further exercises as needed, based on your sense of the students' mastery of the skill.

Principles to keep in mind while working on the comprehension exercises:

- **Don't simply judge answers as right or wrong.** Instead, respond to students' answers with questions such as "Why?" or "How can you tell?" to encourage them to examine their reasoning processes.

- Whenever possible, **direct the students to work in pairs or small groups** because talking about the exercises helps develop awareness of thinking processes.

Unit 1: Previewing and Making Predictions

1. Students should be encouraged to preview and make predictions about everything they read. Students will benefit from this unit because by previewing and making predictions before they read,

- They will be able to place the text in context or within a mental framework.
- They will learn to judge the level of difficulty of a text and the extent of their background knowledge of the subject before they read.
- They can learn that it's possible to extract information from a text without reading every word.
- They'll be prepared for working on reading rate improvement and for learning how to skim.

2. Before you begin work on the exercises, it is important to discuss the introduction to this unit and work on the examples.

3. Encourage students to guess as they work on the exercises. Often, they can remember more than they realize from their brief preview.

4. Predictions should be done in a "brainstorming" fashion. That is, students should feel free to make any prediction that they believe is based on the text.

Unit 2: Scanning

1. Note the **differences between scanning and skimming**. Although scanning and skimming are often taught as the same thing, they are really two very different skills. Scanning is a fairly simple skill that involves only a visual search for information on a page. Skimming, on the other hand, involves processing a text for ideas, and that requires far more complex thinking skills. (Skimming is introduced in Unit 8.)

2. Remember to discuss with your students the introduction to scanning and do the example.

3. Speed is essential in these exercises. To encourage speed, students may be timed, or they may do the exercises (in pairs) as a kind of race to see which pair can find all the answers first.

4. Don't spend time correcting or having students correct their answers, which are of very little importance to the exercise. Take a few minutes to discuss the cultural content of some of the scanning materials because it may be unfamiliar to your students.

5. In all of the scanning exercises, students have an opportunity to practice writing questions. Formulating questions for another student will help students learn to ask themselves questions as they read.

6. Continue to require the students to practice scanning after they have completed this unit by asking them to scan other materials. Continued practice is necessary for students to retain the skill.

Unit 3: Making Inferences

1. All reading is, of course, inferential. The goal of this unit is to make students aware of what it means to make infererences and how it is an essential part of reading. In these exercises, there is often no single "correct" answer. Any answer that a student can support with evidence may be considered acceptable.

2. Be sure to work through the introduction to this unit with the students.

3. **The dialogs in Exercises 1 through 8 are NOT intended to be read aloud** by students to the class. Oral reading requires a different set of skills, which can interfere with comprehension because students tend to concentrate on trying to pronounce correctly what they are reading. The class should work together on the example exercise on page 53, so that the teacher can emphasize using clues to guess the topic and location of each conversation. The students should work in pairs on the rest of the dialogs.

4. Writing practice: Some of the inference exercises have questions requiring short

answers. Stress the importance of clear and complete sentences in answering those questions.

In exercises 9–12, students are asked to tell what they think will happen next in the story or play. These questions can be the basis of additional writing assignments.

Unit 4: Building a Powerful Vocabulary

In this unit, students will learn strategies that they can use whenever they encounter unknown vocabulary. These strategies are using the context to guess unknown words and using pronouns and synonyms to connect ideas.

1. The importance of trying to guess word meaning cannot be stressed too much. Students are often bound to their dictionaries. They need to learn that materials written in English often give multiple clues to meaning. They also need to realize that there are many advantages to guessing meaning, as pointed out in the introduction to this section (page 63).

2. Exercises 1–3 are designed to help students understand what context is and how it influences the choice of a word. Students should always read the entire passage first and then go back and try to write in the missing word.

3. Notice that in these exercises the students are asked to work in pairs or to compare their work with another student. This is important, because working with another student makes the exercises less intimidating and increases their value as language acquisition activities.

4. The exercises using pronouns and synonyms will make students more aware of the way writers commonly use these words in English and how important they are for understanding a text. In fact, ESL/EFL students often run into comprehension problems because they cannot identify the referent for a pronoun, or they fail to notice the way they can connect ideas.

In these exercises, the emphasis is not on content words, but on **function words**, the small words (such as pronouns and synonyms) that connect ideas in a passage. Be sure to work on the introduction to these exercises.

Research has shown that function words play a fundamental role in reading comprehension because these are the words that tie ideas together in a text. Thus, it is far more important for readers to understand how function words work in sentences than to know the meaning of all the content words in a sentence. Point this out to your students as a further argument for skipping over unknown content words.

Pronouns: The whole class should work together on the introduction and examples on page 76. Exercises 10–13 give students practice in identifying pronouns and their referents. Exercise 13 includes some pronouns that summarize earlier facts or ideas.

Synonyms: The whole class should work together on the example on page 82. The exercises on synonyms are designed to alert students to their function in connecting ideas and to the way the related words usually are used progressively: A specific noun is used first, then a less specific one, and then a more general term.

5. Writing practice: Students can gain further awareness of how function words operate in a text and they can learn to control their use of function words by analyzing the function words in their own writing.

Use writing done for previous assignments or give a new writing assignment. Then ask the students, in pairs, to exchange papers and analyze the function words as they did in Exercises 10–13. If some of the referents are unclear, students should work in pairs to figure out how they might correct the problem.

Sometimes it is also helpful to take samples from several student papers for a class discussion of how referents can help or, if missing, confuse the reader.

Unit 5: Learning to Look for the Topic

1. Since **discourse in English is usually topic-centered**, finding the topic is an important key to understanding a text. Thus, work on comprehension must begin by teaching your students what a topic is.

2. Encourage your students to work quickly in order to develop efficiency.

3. Working in pairs on these exercises, students will begin to internalize the key questions: What is this about? How do I know that?

4. Writing practice: Understanding and being able to work with topics is a fundamental skill in writing as well.

   Exercises 6–8 require students to write out the details for given topics. This is an important first step toward writing coherent paragraphs.

Unit 6: Understanding Paragraphs

1. This unit introduces the concept of a well-formed paragraph in English. Work through the unit introduction on page 94 together to make sure that students are prepared to work in pairs on Exercise 1.

2. Choosing the Best Topic: In these exercises, three possible topics are given. Students must select the topic that best fits the paragraph and is neither too specific nor too general. Help students understand the meaning of the terms

"general" and "specific" by using a visual representation. You can draw this diagram on the board:

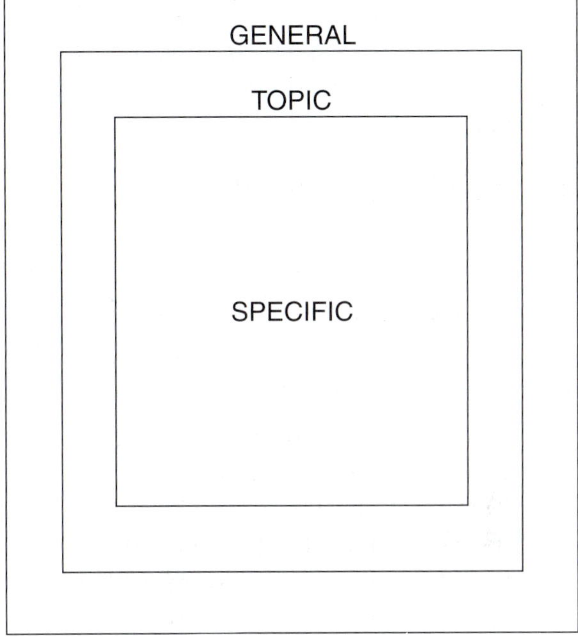

2. Alert students to the fact that the topic sentence of a paragraph is often the first sentence. In both oral and written English, people expect to find out right away what something is about. With English-language texts, readers expect to find the topic at the beginning so they can orient their thinking. Thus, writers almost always provide the topic early on.

3. Point out to your students that the topic of a paragraph is usually mentioned more than once in the paragraph. This is the writer's way of ensuring that the reader remembers it.

4. In a class that combines work on reading and writing, Unit 5 can also be used to discuss the concept of unity, or the idea that a paragraph has a single topic and all the sentences in the paragraph relate to it.

5. On page 103, students are introduced to the concept of the main idea. In exercises 8–12, students learn how to go beyond the topic to find the main idea of a

passage by asking, "What is the author saying about that topic?" Go through the examples on page 103 with the whole class. **Remind the students that the main idea of any passage should be stated in a complete sentence to ensure that it is really an idea and not just a topic.** All the exercises in this unit require students to identify the main idea. In Exercises 8–10, students simply choose the best main-idea sentence. Exercises 11 and 12 require students to write out the main-idea sentence themselves.

6. Writing practice:

   • Give students a list of five or six topics and ask them to write main-idea statements about each topic.

   • From those statements, students should choose one and write a paragraph. They use their main-idea statement as the first sentence of the paragraph.

   • When students have finished writing the paragraphs, they should exchange them with a classmate and discuss the main idea. Are all the sentences in the paragraph about the main idea?

Unit 7: Finding the Pattern of Organization

1. Research has shown that readers comprehend and remember best those materials that are organizationally clear to them. However, many students are not familiar with the patterns of textual organization used in English and so have a more difficult time comprehending and remembering.

   The explanation given here for why recognizing patterns can help comprehension is similar to the explanation given for the advantages to reading faster in the introduction to Part 4. In both cases, the same basic factors are at work: The brain does not work well with random pieces of information that must be stored in the memory as so many separate items. It works more efficiently with information that has a recognizable order. Thus, to allow the brain to work well while reading, the reader must constantly look for order in the text, by grouping words according to meaning and by following the patterns of discourse that writers normally use to express certain kinds of ideas in English.

2. The activity on the first page of this unit is meant to be a whole-class activity. After the students try to draw the pictures from memory, have the class discuss the results and immediately introduce them to four common patterns in English, as given on page 110.

3. In many of the exercises, students are asked not just to identify a pattern, but also to write out the signal words and the details that are signalled. Although this may seem time-consuming and repetitious, it gives the students important practice that will help them gain confidence in their ability to recognize patterns and read for important points.

   The patterns exercises also require students to write the topic and the main idea of each paragraph. This is an excellent review of previous units.

4. In an appropriate class context, you may want to point out to students (and do additional work on) the connection between the patterns present here and the patterns used in outlining for note-taking or preparing for writing.

5. In a writing/reading class, point out that the "signal words" for patterns can also be referred to as "transitional words." They are the signposts that writers use to mark the shifts and turns in their thinking and that readers should use to follow the writer from one idea to the next.

6. Writing practice: A writing exercise is included with each pattern so that students can have practice using the pattern and signal words in their own writing.

   To give students further practice with the pattern and signal words, assign topics that fit clearly into the pattern and ask students to write paragraphs, using at least three signal words per paragraph.

7. The last three exercises in the unit require the student to identify the patterns of individual paragraphs in a longer piece.

Unit 8: Skimming

1. Skimming is not, as is sometimes thought, a simple matter of reading very fast. **Skimming is selective reading, in which only certain parts of the text are actually read.** To know what to select, students must call on all the reading skills previously practiced in this book. Thus skimming practice involves a review of all the skills and concepts in previous units.

2. Skimming exercises must be timed in order to force students to work quickly through a text. Without the pressure of time, they will be tempted to read unnecessary parts and may be distracted from the purpose of the exercises.

3. As in the previous units, students should work in pairs to compare and explain their answers. This also helps students realize that there is no absolute right way to skim a text. What readers actually read while skimming depends on what they already know about the topic and on their interpretation of the text. In other words, it depends on what they are thinking; and, of course, no two people ever think exactly alike. Point this out to students and allow for different responses to the exercises.

4. Students can be given additional skimming practice in the classroom with multiple copies of a newspaper or magazine (preferably publications for students with easier text, such as *Student Update*). You may then divide the class into small groups and give each group a newspaper or magazine. The groups should skim the newspaper or magazine for articles of interest and discuss them.

Part 3: Thinking Skills

Learning to read well in English involves learning to think in English. This means students need to know how to follow the logic of ideas in English and how to think critically about them. In fact, many students are not thinking about the ideas when they are reading. Instead, they are thinking about the single words. ESL students, in particular, often translate as they read, focusing on one word at a time. The exercises in Part 3 are designed to help students make a transition from focusing on single words to following ideas and thinking in English. To complete the Thinking Skills exercises successfully, students will need follow the ideas, which will involve understanding a variety of syntactic, semantic, or logical connections.

Since the exercises gradually increase in length and complexity, it is important for students to work on the exercises in the order in which they are presented in the book.

1. For students to get the most out of Part 3, be sure to go through the introduction carefully with the whole class. In fact, teachers will come to a better understanding of the thinking process involved in these exercises if they work on at least ten exercises themselves before introducing this part of the book to students.

2. Some students may have trouble at first in following the logic of these exercises. If so, assign several exercises in class to pairs or small groups of students. They should discuss and decide on the answers and on the thinking processes involved.

Afterward, those logical processes can be further clarified in a whole-class discussion.

3. Keeping track of progress is an important aspect of this part of the book. As described in "Guidelines for Thinking Skills Exercises" on page 152, students should keep a record of their progress in the Thinking Skills Progress Chart that precedes Exercise 1. This also makes it possible for teachers to monitor students' work.

4. Students should work individually on these exercises at their own speed. However, they should be encouraged to work as quickly as possible. If they work slowly, they may continue to translate as they read and will not develop efficient reading habits.

5. Students may look back at a paragraph if they wish, but they should not study it for long. Their first response is often the correct one.

6. Students should not use dictionaries or ask anyone about word meanings while they are working on these exercises. They should be encouraged to use the context of the paragraph to guess word meanings on their own.

7. Once students are confident about doing the Thinking Skills exercises, teachers can assign them for homework. In the next lesson, students can read aloud the items they have done and the whole class can discuss the answers. In fact, students enjoy reading aloud short passages that they are familiar with, and the discussion can be useful and involving.

Part 4: Reading Faster

Teaching students to read faster must be a key part of any reading improvement program. There are two basic reasons for this. First, students in most academic settings need to complete an enormous quantity of assigned reading. Many ESL/EFL students take three to four times longer than native-language students to complete reading assignments. This means that they have little time left to assimilate what they have read.

The other main reason for training students to read faster is that it leads to better comprehension. When reading faster, the eyes cannot focus on every word; they must focus on groups of words together. This makes it easier for the brain to reconstruct meaning. Furthermore, since reading faster forces the reader to skip unknown or nonessential words, the brain can concentrate better on the general meaning of the text.

(This aspect of reading is explained in the introduction to Part 4, "Why Read Faster?" For a more complete explanation of the rationale and methodology for teaching faster reading, see *A Short Course in Teaching Reading Skills*.)

Be prepared to meet some resistance on the part of students! Breaking them of the habit of word-by-word reading is not always easy. The habit may be of long standing and may be connected with the student's insecurity about his or her ability to understand English. If this is the case, don't push too hard for immediate change, but try to build up the student's confidence and willingness to take risks. Some students may be reluctant to read faster because of different attitudes toward reading in their native culture that lead them to feel that reading word by word is the only "real" way to read. With these students, teachers may need to spend extra time discussing the nature and variety of purposes of reading in English.

Why Read Faster?

1. It is important for teachers to have a thorough grasp of the rationale behind

reading rate improvement so they can explain it in terms the students will understand. For this reason, teachers should go through the students' introduction carefully first and, if necessary, consult other reference books for clarification.

2. Notice that the reasons given here for improved comprehension with faster reading are similar to those given in the rationale to Part 2, Unit 7: Finding the Pattern of Organization. Both explanations are based on a fundamental understanding of how the brain works in receiving and storing information, and that it works most efficiently when the pieces of information can be grouped into some kind of order. This is the basic reason for reading faster. When reading faster, the eyes sweep over larger pieces of text, so the brain receives more data. It is thus possible for the brain to make connections and find meaning in what it receives, which allows the reader to build up comprehension and retain information.

3. Along with discussing the rationale for reading faster, it is important to discuss with students the diverse ways of reading. Students may need to be reassured at this point that not all reading must be fast. There are times when slow reading is appropriate, as in reading poetry, complex technical material, instructions, or other material dense with essential information. More often than not, students read slowly when they don't need to. They need to understand that learning to read faster will give them more flexibility and allow them to vary their reading speed based on what they are reading and why they are reading it.

How to Read Faster

1. *Check your reading habits.*

Some students may have a habit of moving their lips or following the text with their fingers while they are reading. These students should be alerted to this habit, of which they are often unaware, and led to understand that it slows them down as they read.

While reading the passages in Part 4, students should not write the meanings of words in the text. This would only reinforce the habit of translation and drastically slow down reading. Students may need to be reassured that it is useful to write down new vocabulary, but not during faster reading sessions. They can always go back to the passage later and make a list of words that they'd like to learn.

2. *Skip over unknown words.*

1. Teachers may be familiar with the use of cloze passages to determine reading ability or to teach grammar and vocabulary. The cloze passages here, however, serve a very different purpose: to convince students that they can understand the main points of a passage without reading every word. This kind of work with cloze passages encourages students to infer general meaning from partial information—a fundamental skill.

2. As always, students should know the rationale for these exercises before they begin. Do not ask students to fill in the blank spaces, because this would completely alter the purpose of the exercise in the students' eyes.

3. Stress the idea that unknown words can usually be ignored. Occasionally, it may be necessary to understand some words in order to comprehend the general meaning. When this is the case, the

reader should continue reading and try to guess word meanings from the context. This skill is developed in Part 2, Unit 4: Building a Powerful Vocabulary.

4. Teachers who wish to provide students with additional practice with cloze passages can choose a suitable text and blank out every seven or five words (the more frequent the blanks, the more difficult the exercise). The text should not contain difficult vocabulary or complex ideas that will be hard to grasp.

3. Do timed readings.

1. Examples c and d, pages 181–184, introduce students to the timing procedures for all the Reading Faster passages. Students will have more success with the passages if they learn to time themselves. This allows them to work independently at their own pace.

2. Students should be instructed to preview all the passages for timed reading, starting with Examples c and d. If they have not yet done Part 2, Unit 1: Previewing and Making Predictions, teachers will need to introduce the concept of previewing to them.

3. Note that students should <u>time themselves only while reading the passage</u>, not while answering the questions! In answering the questions, students may need to be reminded that they should look for the best answer according to the text. After completing each passage, students should correct their own work using the Answer Key.

Timing Procedure

1. When the class is ready to begin Example c, the students should write the starting time on the line at the top of the passage. They then start reading and read as quickly as possible with understanding.

If there is a large clock visible in the classroom, the students can use it to read the time. If not, write the starting time on the chalkboard. (Many students prefer to use their own watches, which often have timing devices on them.)

2. As soon as they have finished reading the passage, students should write their finishing time on the line at the end of the passage. If there is no clock, students should signal when they finish and the teacher can write the time on the board.

3. Students then turn the page and circle the best answers to the questions (according to the text) *without referring to the passage.*

4. After they have finished answering the questions, students should check their answers in the Answer Key and write down the number of correct answers. This is their comprehension score.

5. Students then calculate their reading time by subtracting the starting time from the finishing time. Using this reading time, they find their reading rate in the table on page 186.

    When they work on Example c, students often come up with questions about the timing procedures. Be sure to review the timing procedures before the students work on Example d. Make sure that the procedures are clearly understood before students start on the first unit of Reading Faster. The reading rate for Example d is the student's initial (baseline) reading rate.

Passages for Reading Faster

1. After students have gone through the introduction and before they start the Reading Faster passages, re-examine with them their answers to the questionnaire they did about reading (from page 274 of the Teacher's Guide). By now, students

will have gained some insight into the reading process and changed some of their views about what makes for good reading habits. In reviewing the questionnaire, students will, in effect, be reviewing some of the important aspects of reading covered so far.

2. Students are more likely to improve their reading rates if they set goals for themselves after they have established their initial rates. Many students find that they can double their rates by the end of a semester. A class discussion may help each student decide on a realistic goal. He or she should then be reminded of that goal and pushed to try to achieve it.

3. Remind students regularly about previewing. They need to know that previewing will not slow down their reading. The few seconds they spend on previewing (it should only take a few seconds) will save them reading time afterward.

4. In this edition of *Reading Power*, three sets of passages are provided for practice in Part 4: Reading Faster.

   Unit 1—fiction—contains 20 passages. Passages 1-10 are only 200 words long, and the remaining passages are 400 words long.

   Unit 2—biography—contains five 400-word passages on each of two famous contemporary authors.

   Unit 3—non-fiction—contains five 400-word passage on each of two general topics.

5. The timed reading passages should be used first for practice in reading faster, not for purposes of discussion, comprehension skills, or grammar. The sole purpose of reading a passage should be to give students the freedom to take risks and experiment with rate-building strategies. However, after all the students have completed a passage, it may be used in another context of the reading class. Many of the passages provide interesting material for intensive reading lessons and general class discussion.

6. Make sure that students record their reading rate and comprehension score on the Faster Reading Progress Chart on pages 187–189. This visual record helps students evaluate their progress.

7. As they chart their progress in reading rate improvement, students may notice that their rate varies with the type of passage. They may have a slower rate on the passages of expository prose than on the narrative passages. They should be reassured that readers naturally react differently to different kinds of writing, especially when the content is also new. In fact, the more familiar the subject, the easier it is to read—and so reading rate and comprehension are higher.

8. For additional practice materials for timed reading, consult the bibliography in *A Short Course in Teaching Reading Skills*.

	Part 1 **Reading for Pleasure**	**Part 2** **Comprehension Skills**	**Part 3** **Thinking Skills**	**Part 4** **Reading Faster**
Week 1	• Read Teacher's Guide, pp. 271–277. • Read and discuss Introduction, pp. v–vi • Read and discuss p. 2 about the importance of reading for pleasure in learning English. • "Talking about Your Reading." Do Ex. a, pp. 3–5. and Ex. b, pp. 6–8. • Use the Book list on pp. 10–14 to help each student choose a book for pleasure reading.	• Read Teacher's Guide, pp. 277–283. • Introduce Part 2. Discuss the Introduction, p. 24. • Introduce Unit 1, Previewing and Making Predictions, p. 25. • Discuss the examples on pp. 25–27. • Do Ex. 1, p. 28. Have students explain their predictions by referring to the picture. • Do Ex. 3, p. 30 & Ex. 6, p. 32.		
HOMEWORK	Pleasure Reading, 30 min./day	Unit 1, Ex. 2, p. 29. Exs. 4 & 5, p. 31. Ex. 7, p. 33.		
Week 2	• Check students' progress in their pleasure reading books. Ask each student to tell the class the title of the book and how many pages they have read.	• Check homework. • Introduce "Guidelines for Previewing Passages," p. 34. Make sure the students understand that previewing means very, very fast reading. • Do Ex. 8, pp. 34–36. Ask students to explain their predictions by referring to the story. • Introduce Unit 2, Scanning, p. 39. • Do Exs. 1 & 2, pp. 40–43.	• Read Teacher's Guide, pp. 283–284. • Introduce Part 3. p. 152, "How to Think in English." Go over Guidelines, p. 152. • Do Ex.1, p. 153. **Students should work alone without a dictionary.** Ask volunteers to give their answers and explain their choices. Encourage discussion when answers vary. Students should record the number of correct answers in the progress chart on p. 152.	
HOMEWORK	Pleasure reading, 30 min./day	Unit 1, Ex. 9, pp. 36–37. Do not assign scanning for homework.	Thinking Skills, Ex. 2, p. 154.	

	Part 1 **Reading for Pleasure**	**Part 2** **Comprehension Skills**	**Part 3** **Thinking Skills**	**Part 4** **Reading Faster**
Week 3	• Check students' progress in their pleasure reading books. • Explain book conferences and how students should sign up for a conference when they finish their books. Teacher's Guide (See p. 276.) • Introduce "Using Your Pleasure Reading Book to Practice Reading Faster," pp. 17–21. Show students how to figure out their reading rates in their own books and use the Pleasure Reading Progress Charts, p. 20.	• Check Unit 1 homework. • Do Unit 1, Ex. 10, p. 38. • Do Unit 2, Exs. 3–8, pp. 44–52. • Introduce Unit 3, Making Inferences, p. 53. **Students must not read the conversations aloud!** • Do Unit 3, Exs. 1, 2, 3, & 4, pp. 54–55. Require students to explain their inferences by referring to specific information in the conversations.	• Check homework on Ex. 2. Ask volunteers to read the items aloud for oral reading practice. Encourage discussion when answers vary.	• Read Teacher's Guide, pp. 284–287. • Introduce "Why Read Faster?," p. 179. Go over the three steps to reading faster. • Use Examples a & b to teach students to time their reading, p. 180, and use the Reading Rate Tables, pp. 186–189. • Show students how to record their reading rate and comprehension scores on Progress Chart 1, p. 187. • Discuss the Guidelines, p. 185. • Begin work on Unit 1. • Time the class while they do passages 1 & 2, pp. 191–194. • Students record their progress on the charts.
HOMEWORK	Pleasure Reading, 30 min./day	Unit 3, Exs. 5, 6, 7, 8, pp. 56–57.	Thinking Skills, Exs. 3 & 4, pp. 154–156.	Do not assign Reading Faster for homework.
Week 4	• Check students' progress in pleasure reading books. • Begin to schedule book conferences. • Do "Reading Sprints" p. 21. • Introduce "Writing about Your Pleasure Reading Book, pp. 15–16.	• Check homework, Unit 3. Require students to explain their inferences. • Introduce "Making Inferences from Stories," p. 58. • Do Ex. 9, p. 58. Discuss.	• Check homework, Exs. 3 & 4. Ask volunteers to read the items aloud. Encourage discussion.	• Time students on two passages, three times this week. • Do passages 3, 4, 5, 6, 7, & 8, pp. 195–206. • Check students' progress charts, p. 187. • Give positive and encouraging feedback.
HOMEWORK	Pleasure Reading, 30 min./day	Unit 3, Ex. 10, p. 59 & Ex. 11, p. 60.	Thinking Skills, Exs. 5 & 6, pp. 156–158.	Do not assign Reading Faster for homework.
Week 5	• Check students' progress in pleasure reading books.	• Check homework. • Do Ex. 12, pp. 61–62	• Check homework. Ask volunteers to read the items	• Time the class on passages 9, 10, 11,

	Part 1 **Reading for Pleasure**	**Part 2** **Comprehension Skills**	**Part 3** **Thinking Skills**	**Part 4** **Reading Faster**
	• Schedule more book conferences. • Assign a letter or a report about their books. (pp. 15–16)	• Introduce Unit 4, "Building a Powerful Vocabulary," p. 63. • Make sure students understand the meaning of *context*. • **Students should not use dictionaries while working on this unit.** • Do Exs. 1 & 2, pp. 64–65. • Discuss "Guessing word meanings from the context" p. 67. • Do Ex. 4, p. 68.	aloud. Encourage discussion.	12, 13, & 14, pp. 207–218. • Check the students' progress charts, p. 187. Give positive and encouraging feedback.
HOMEWORK	Pleasure Reading, 30 min./day	Unit 4, Ex. 3, p. 66. Exs. 5, 6, & 7, pp. 69–71.	Thinking Skills, Exs. 7 & 8, pp. 158–159.	No Reading Faster for homework.
Week 6	• Check students' progress in pleasure reading books. • Hold book conferences. • Check students' Pleasure Reading Progress Charts, p. 20. • Do more reading sprints.	• Check homework. • Do Unit 4, Ex. 8, pp. 72–73. • Introduce "Using Pronouns and Synonyms," p. 76. • Do the examples, p. 76. • Do Ex. 10, p. 77. • Discuss "More about pronouns," p. 80. • Do Ex. 13. • Discuss "Synonyms: General and specific" and the terms *general* and *specific*, p. 82. • Do Ex. 14, p. 82.	• Check homework. Ask volunteers to read the items aloud. Encourage discussion.	• Time the class on passage 15, pp. 219–220. • Mention that from now on the passages will be 400 words long. Show new progress chart, p. 188. • Time the class on passages 16, 17, & 18, pp. 221–226. • Check the students' progress charts (p. 188). Give positive and encouraging feedback.
HOMEWORK	Pleasure Reading, 30 min./day	Unit 4, Ex. 9 pp. 74–75. Exs. 11 & 12, pp. 78–79. Ex. 15, p. 83.	Thinking Skills, Exs. 9 & 10, pp. 160–161.	
Week 7	• Check students' progress in pleasure reading books.	• Check Unit 4 homework.	• Check homework. Ask volunteers to read the items	• Time the class on passages 19 & 20, pp. 227–230.

	Part 1 Reading for Pleasure	Part 2 Comprehension Skills	Part 3 Thinking Skills	Part 4 Reading Faster
	• Hold book conferences.	• Introduce Unit 5, "Learning to Look for the Topic," p. 84. **Students should not use dictionaries with these exercises.** • Do Ex. 1, p. 85 • Introduce "Thinking of the Topic," p. 86. • Do Ex. 3, pp. 86–87. • Do Exs. 5 & 6, pp. 88–89. Notice the directions are different here.	aloud. Encourage discussion.	• Introduce Unit 2. Time the students on passages 21 & 22, pp. 231–234. • Do two passages, two times per week, from now on.
HOMEWORK	Pleasure Reading, 30 min./day	Unit 5, Ex. 2, pp. 85–86; Ex. 4, p. 87; Exs. 7 & 8, pp. 91–93.	Thinking Skills, Exs. 11 & 12, pp. 162–163.	No Reading Faster for homework.
Week 8	• Check students' progress in pleasure reading books. • Hold book conferences.	• Check Unit 5 homework. • Introduce Unit 6, "Understanding Paragraphs," p. 94. Discuss concept of the paragraph. • Do Ex. 1, p. 95. • Discuss "Choosing the Best Topic," p. 96. • Do Ex. 2, pp. 96–97. • Introduce "Thinking of the Topic," p. 99. • Discuss the terms *general* and *specific*. • Do Ex. 4, pp. 99–100. • Do Ex. 6, p. 101.	• Check homework. Ask volunteers to read the items aloud. Encourage discussion.	• Time the class on Unit 2, passages 23, 24, 25 & 26. pp. 235–242. • Check the students' progress charts, p. 188. Give positive and encouraging feedback.
HOMEWORK	Pleasure Reading, 30 min./day	Unit 6, Ex. 3, p. 98; Ex. 5, p. 100 & Ex. 7, p. 102.	Thinking Skills, Exs. 13 & 14, pp. 164–165.	
Week 9	• Check students' progress in pleasure reading books.	• Check Unit 6 homework. • Introduce "Main Ideas	• Check homework. Ask volunteers to read the items	• Time the class on passages 27, 28, 29 & 30, pp. 243–250.

	Part 1 Reading for Pleasure	Part 2 Comprehension Skills	Part 3 Thinking Skills	Part 4 Reading Faster
	• Hold book conferences.	of Paragraphs," p. 103. Work through examples a, b, & c and discuss fully. • Do Ex. 8, p. 104. • Do Ex. 11, p. 107. • **Remind students that the main idea must be a complete sentence.**	aloud. Encourage discussion.	• Same as in previous weeks.
HOMEWORK	Pleasure Reading, 30 min./day	Unit 6, Exs. 9 & 10, pp. 105–106.	Thinking Skills, Exs. 15 & 16, pp. 166–167.	
Week 10	• Check students' progress in pleasure reading books. • Hold book conferences.	• Check Unit 6 homework. • Do Ex. 12, p. 108. • Introduce Unit 7, "Finding the Pattern of Organization," p. 109. • Discuss with students the drawing activity, pp. 109–110. • Introduce the Listing Pattern, pp. 110–111. Work on Examples a and b. • Review Topic and Main Idea. • Do Exs. 1 & 2, pp. 112–113.	• Check homework. Ask volunteers to read the items aloud. Encourage discussion.	• Introduce Unit 3. • Time the class on passages 31, 32, 33, & 34, pp. 251–258. • Same as in previous weeks.
HOMEWORK	Pleasure Reading, 30 min./day	Unit 7, Ex. 3, p. 114 & Ex. 4, p. 115.	Thinking Skills, Exs. 17 & 18, pp. 168–169.	
Week 11	• Check students' progress in pleasure reading books. Hold book conferences.	• Check homework. • Introduce Time Order Pattern, pp. 115–116. • Explain examples fully. • Do Ex. 5, p. 117 & Ex. 7, pp. 119–120. • Introduce Comparison Pattern, pp. 122–124.	• Check homework. Ask volunteers to read the items aloud. Encourage discussion.	• Time the class on passages 35, 36, 37, & 38, pp. 259–266. • Same as in previous weeks.

	Part 1 Reading for Pleasure	Part 2 Comprehension Skills	Part 3 Thinking Skills	Part 4 Reading Faster
		• Work on Examples a, b & c, pp. 122–124. • Do Ex. 10, pp. 124–125.		
HOMEWORK	Pleasure Reading, 30 min./day	Ex. 6, p. 118 & Ex. 8, pp. 120–121; Ex. 9, p. 122; Ex. 12, p. 126.	Thinking Skills, Exs. 19 & 20, pp. 170–171.	No Reading Faster for homework
Week 12	• Check students' progress in pleasure reading books. • Hold book conferences.	• Check homework. • Do Ex. 11, pp. 125–126. • Introduce Cause/Effect Pattern, p. 127. • Explain Example, p. 127. • Do Ex. 13, p. 128. • Explain Examples a, & b, p. 130. • Do Ex. 15, p. 131.	• Check homework. Ask volunteers to read the items aloud. Encourage discussion.	• Time the class on passages 39 & 40, pp. 267–270. • Discuss students' rate improvement, with praise!
HOMEWORK	Pleasure Reading, 30 min./day	Ex. 14, p. 129. Ex. 16, p. 132. Ex. 17, p. 133.	Thinking Skills, Exs. 21 & 22, pp. 172–173.	
Week 13	• Check students' progress in pleasure reading books. • Hold book conferences.	• Check homework. • Introduce Using All Four Patterns, p. 133. • Do Ex. 18, p. 134. • Introduce Unit 8, "Skimming," p. 137. • Introduce Skimming for Point of View, p. 137. Do Examples a & b. • Do Ex. 1, p. 138. • Introduce Skimming for Pattern of Organization, p. 140. • Do Examples a & b. • Do Ex. 3, pp. 140–141.	• Check homework. Ask volunteers to read the items aloud. Encourage discussion.	• Discuss the way Reading Faster can help with comprehension and with learning English.
HOMEWORK	Pleasure Reading, 30 min./day	Unit 7, Exs. 19 & 20, pp. 135–136. Unit 8, Ex. 2, p. 139 & Ex. 4, p. 141.	Thinking Skills, Exs. 23 & 24, pp. 174–175.	
Week 14	• Check students' overall progress. • Discuss with the class the number of books they have read. • Give praise!	• Introduce Skimming for Ideas, p. 142. Do Examples a and b, pp. 143–144 • Do Exs. 5–9, pp. 145–149.	• Check homework. • Do Ex. 25 in class, p. 176. • Discuss as in previous weeks.	

Credits

SCC
Seminole Community College
English Language Studies Dept.